Endorsements

A few years ago, I was privileged to attend the graduation ceremony for a class of Navy SEALs. One statement made by the Commanding Officer in his address to the class was: "Ninety percent of the situations you face, you will not have trained for." The CO's statement implied, "We train you in such a way that, whatever you face, you will be ready to handle it." This is what comes to mind as I interact with the principles and process found in *Soul Tending*. They provide a framework for thriving amid pain and chaos—both as an individual and in community. Though I wish these principles had been taught when we were beginning our cross-cultural ministry, it is because of those experiences of life and ministry that this book carries much greater weight for me now. I highly recommend this book!

Steve Coffey
Global Ministries Pastor

Virgil Tanner's *Soul Tending* is more than a how-to guide to live well and lead wisely. He stresses that a well-rounded personal development plan helps global workers thrive. But what makes this book different is it also considers the value of community at the same time. Tanner's emphasis on "whole-souled" service does not stand alone. That, along with a growing self-awareness, develops more proactive and less reactive leaders. Tanner encourages readers to lead with a towel over their shoulder. He challenges us to truly see one another which promotes a flourishing community. After one read-through, I wanted to go through it again with others. By using the practices in this book, we can become healthier individuals and a more robust community.

Sue Eenigenburg
Author, mentor, global worker

It's rare you find a book that draws from orthodox theology and sound research and then makes it readily accessible in practical, concrete steps. I've been leading teams for over twenty years, and although I've employed a few of these concepts at different times, this book gives me a comprehensive and easy-to-follow system for shepherding myself and my staff in loving, straightforward ways. Read this book and enjoy a healthier, more anti-fragile you—alongside those you lead and serve.

Alex Galloway, PsyD
SentWell

This book is not just for mission leaders or cross-cultural workers—it's for anyone who seeks to lead as Jesus led, with a heart to cultivate human flourishing and a willingness to walk with others toward God's greater purpose. *Soul Tending* is both a theological gift and a practical manual for leaders in every sphere. I cannot recommend it highly enough for those seeking to lead well for the glory of God.

Rev. Brent McHugh
CEO, Christar International

Multiple books have been written on the how and why of wholistic care and formative growth steps for cross-cultural workers. What sets this book apart is the deeper understanding of how workers can healthfully thrive as they foster glory. This much-needed emphasis is masterfully addressed by someone who has done that himself in the crucible of ministry. As a seasoned member care professional, Virgil Tanner brings practical, hands-on models that can be readily implemented no matter where one serves.

Marvin J. Newell, DMiss
Ambassador at Large, Missio Nexus
Author, *A Third of Us: What It Takes to Reach the Unreached*

Early in this book, the author writes, "Power is used as a channel of blessing and not as a means to protect or accrue more power. Leadership becomes a sacrament, a means of grace, and an accelerant for vibrant, verdant life." This vision of leadership shapes the entire book. Virgil and his family have lived on three continents in the last decade. He has been on mission for over a quarter of a century. This book is a dive into understanding leadership sourced from the unction of the Holy Spirit but also how to live and thrive in ministry in the midst of adversity. Virgil also explores the path to recovery that is possible for leaders who experience Davidic failures.

Francis Patt
Legal Office Director and Board Member, Frontier Ventures

Virgil's vision in this book has the power to ignite transformation in people and in communities around the world. Over the past few years, as our organization has allowed these ideas to shape the DNA of who we are together, we've seen our culture enriched, our members' resilience deepened, and beautiful fruit emerge—even in the face of pressure and adversity. This is a critical read for anyone seeking to make disciples in hard places—where external stress threatens to unravel the very work they've been called to.

Luke Perkins
President, Crossworld

Chaos, relational stress, and the myriad effects of sin too often derail cross-cultural Kingdom workers or make them ineffective or unproductive in the work to which God has called them. In this wonderful book—written especially for missionaries and those who lead and send them, but also for any Christian who wants to be effective in their calling—Virgil Tanner lays out a strong argument for intentionally prioritizing movement in the direction of soul thriving. He offers helpful tools and strategies for regularly assessing how fit our souls are—spiritually, physically, cognitively, emotionally and relationally—and for moving toward flourishing in each of these areas for the glory of God and the good of the church, without becoming self-obsessed. He also provides many real-world examples from his extensive experience as a leader, spiritual director, and mission strategist that help guide us down the path to joyful, integrated service. I will be highly recommending this book to everyone I know who is passionate about the Great Commission.

Steve Stonehouse, MD

Soul Tending

Leadership for Strategic Human Flourishing

Virgil Tanner

visit us at missionbooks.org

Soul Tending: Leadership for Strategic Human Flourishing
© 2025 by Virgil Tanner. All Rights Reserved.

No part of this book may be reproduced, stored in a retrieval system, or transmitted in any form or by any means—electronic, mechanical, photocopy, recording, or otherwise—without prior written permission from the publisher, except brief quotations used in connection with reviews. This manuscript may not be entered into AI, even for AI training. For permission, email permissions@wclbooks.com. For corrections, email editor@wclbooks.com.

William Carey Publishing (WCP) publishes resources to shape and advance the missiological conversation in the world. We publish a broad range of thought-provoking books and do not necessarily endorse all opinions set forth here or in works referenced within this book.

The URLs included in this workbook are provided for personal use only and are current as of the date of publication, but the publisher disclaims any obligation to update them after publication.

All Scripture quotations, unless otherwise indicated, are taken from the ESV® Bible (The Holy Bible, English Standard Version®), Copyright © 2001 by Crossway, a publishing ministry of Good News Publishers. Used by permission. All rights reserved.

Scripture quotations marked NIV are taken from the Holy Bible, New International Version®, NIV®. Copyright © 1973, 1978, 1984, 2011 by Biblica, Inc.™ Used by permission of Zondervan. All rights reserved worldwide. www.zondervan.com. The "NIV" and "New International Version" are trademarks registered in the United States Patent and Trademark Office by Biblica, Inc.™

Scripture quotations marked NKJV are taken from the New King James Version®. Copyright © 1982 by Thomas Nelson. Used by permission. All rights reserved.

Published by William Carey Publishing
10 W. Dry Creek Cir
Littleton, CO 80120 | www.missionbooks.org

William Carey Publishing is a ministry of Frontier Ventures
Pasadena, CA | www.frontierventures.org

Cover and Interior Designer: Mike Riester

ISBNs: 978-1-64508-661-1 (paperback)
      978-1-64508-663-5 (epub)

Printed Worldwide

29 28 27 26 25   1 2 3 4 5   IN

Library of Congress Control Number: 2025935899

To my lovely wife, my *arbolita*.
Many find home in your branches.

Contents

Foreword	xi

Part I: Thrive | Roots

Introduction to Part I		3
1.	Thriving in Uncertainty	5
2.	Spiritual: Withdraw, Gather, Obey	15
3.	Physical: Eat, Move, Recover	27
4.	Cognitive: Learn, Focus, Play	41
5.	Emotional: Notice, Interview, Manage	49
6.	Relational: Discern, Invest, Grow	59
7.	Thriving in Real Life	65
8.	Leading Toward Thrive	79

Part II: Work | Trunk

Introduction to Part II		97
9.	Integrating Your Work and God's Work	103
10.	Integrating Your Vocation and Your Ministry	117
11.	Integrating Your Oikos and Your Mission	127
12.	Integrating Yourself and Your Communities	145
13.	Leading Toward Integration	167

Part III: Develop | Crown

Introduction to Part III		179
14.	Poiesis by (Reflective) Experience	181
15.	Poiesis by Christification	191
16.	Poiesis by Self-Discovery	201
17.	Leading Toward Development	219
Afterword: On Leading and Following		229
Appendix		243
Bibliography		249

List of Figures

Figure 1	5 Dimensions Circle	10
Figure 2	Vector lines	16
Figure 3	Vector lines with labels	16
Figure 4	5DVector check	18
Figure 5	5DThrive Practices	21
Figure 6	After-Experience Reflection	186
Figure 7	YouBoat	203
Figure 8	Who am I?	206
Figure 9	The false self emerges as a strategy to protect me	206
Figure 10	The world is perceived as a story in which the false self makes sense	207
Figure 11	If I am made in the image of God, God must look like me	207
Figure 12	Thrive-Work-Develop	233

Foreword

Now these are the last words of David:
>The oracle of David, the son of Jesse,
>>the oracle of the man who was raised on high,
>
>the anointed of the God of Jacob,
>>the sweet psalmist of Israel.
>
>"The Spirit of the LORD speaks by me;
>>his word is on my tongue.
>
>The God of Israel has spoken;
>>the Rock of Israel has said to me:
>
>When one rules justly over men,
>>ruling in the fear of God,
>
>he dawns on them like the morning light,
>>like the sun shining forth on a cloudless morning,
>>
>>like rain that makes grass to sprout from the earth."
>
>(2 Sam 23:1–4)

King David knew something of leadership. The story of his life is learning to lead. He led sheep, and he led armies. He led from the throne and from exile. He led with integrity and learned to lead after that integrity was fractured. He was a flawed man, a beautiful man, a strong man. Yes, David knew something of leadership, and he came by that knowledge hard.

About five years ago as I was reading 2 Samuel, I came to the last words of David. This passage is remarkable. The last words of God's first chosen king for his people, and at the same time an oracle—the words of God himself on the matter of leadership. God gives us the image of righteous leadership as nourishing—like the sun and rain to plants. The idea of leadership feeling like a source of life took my breath away.

The power in the word *rule* cannot be mistaken. As an American by birth and upbringing, I have an innate bias toward flat social structures, but authority inhabited and exercised like this would be better news to a community than weak or hesitant leadership ever could be. There is an over/under structure: the leader rules over people, but rules under God. Power is used as a channel of blessing and not as a means to protect or accrue more power. Leadership becomes a sacrament, a means of grace, and an accelerant for vibrant, verdant life.

I want to rule like the rain. I want to lead like the sun leads trees ever heavenward, supplying their needs for the journey. I want this leadership to become ubiquitous among Christian communities all over the world. I want us to lead well, to know how to lead well, and to teach those we lead how to lead well with us and after us.

> Power is used as a channel of blessing and not as a means to protect or accrue more power.

Such leadership is described as *developmental*. Developmental leaders try to cultivate connections with and among those they lead. These connections cultivate each person's internal strengths in order to create an external change in the world. Developmental leaders are extremely effective disciple-makers. They nurture their followers as they follow Jesus, resulting in meaningful, lasting change both internally and externally.

But developmental leadership in the way of Jesus is after something more than just competencies or outcomes. When we lead well in the fear of the Lord, and when our leadership is given and received like the rain and sun, we are fostering glory.

Glory

Twenty years ago, I had the opportunity to hear Dallas Willard speak about what the future held in store for those who love God. He remarked, "Jesus said the righteous will shine forth like the sun in the kingdom of their father. This means you! Just hold that thought in your mind for a moment." I did. I'm still holding it, in fact.

As children of God, glory is our destiny. Paul says to the Colossians, "When Christ who is your life, appears, then you also will appear with him in glory" (Col 3:4). *In glory* here is best understood, not as immersed in glory, but rather *glorious*. Willard defines glory as the effulgence of power, suggesting that God's glory is the magnificent outpouring of brightness that results from the overabundance of his power. One day, as children of God, we will be so superabundantly powerful that we will glow—like superheated metal that gives off light, we will shine like the sun. There will be so much reality to us that we will be luminous.

This is very good news, and not just for us, but for the whole cosmos. In Romans 8, Paul says,

> For the creation waits with eager longing for the revealing of the sons of God. For the creation was subjected to futility, not willingly, but because of him who subjected it, in hope that the creation itself will be set free from its bondage to corruption and obtain the freedom of the glory of the children of God. (Rom 8:19–21)

Did you catch that? The cosmos is broken and subject to entropy. It waits to be set free by the revealing, not of God's glory, but of ours. The world is waiting for the freedom of the glory of the children of God. Our glory—derivative of God's and dependent totally on the work of Christ, but still ours—is good news to the world. It is God's answer for the entropy that is unmaking everything he has made.

So, Paul can say, "I consider that our present sufferings are not worth comparing with the glory that will be revealed in us" (Rom 8:18, NIV).

Glory is not just the random glow of overflowing power but is rather the effulgence of power *and* beauty. "Strength and beauty are in his sanctuary," declares the psalmist (Ps 96:6). It is not enough that we are made to be strong. We are made to be wonderous as well—a spectacle to draw eyes and hearts to the maker of the vessel and the wellspring of the glory within. As the pinnacle of God's creative self-expression, we are made to provoke worship.

Ten years ago, I was in a secret meeting of cross-cultural workers hiding in a living room in Central Asia and plotting together how to best serve the resistant people we had come to love. I overheard a woman say to the fellow leading the conversation, "I could never do what you did here tonight, bringing all these people together, helping them hear one another across culture and denomination, and guiding them to hear the voice of Jesus together. What I saw here tonight was beautiful, and it makes me want to worship God for making you like that." She saw power and beauty displayed in the unique and vibrant creation of a child of God, and it provoked in her a desire to worship the source of strength and beauty. God is glorified in his children's glory.

Once a month I have a call with each of my direct reports who are scattered all over the world. The people I lead are remarkable. Sometimes I am moved to tears; sometimes I laugh out loud, and sometimes I just sit back and smile. I can see the glory effervescing from every pore of their beautiful, bedraggled souls. They are wonders to behold. One such call was with a woman working with refugees in the Middle East, and as she sat on the other side of the call wiping away tears of frustration and disappointment at dysfunctional team dynamics, I said to her, "Sometimes, when I look at you, I almost have to squint. I can see the glory of Jesus in your beautiful broken heart. You are remarkable, lovely, and a credit to your maker." That sentence was the best I could do, but it didn't touch the edge of what I was seeing even through a choppy Zoom connection.

This woman (let's call her Lisa) is made in the image of God himself. Though this image is bent and tarnished through sin—original and her own—it remains, and when it catches the light right, it can blind you with its beauty. This is even without considering the effect of the indwelling Christ, the express and utterly unwarped image of the Divine Godhead. As the uncreated glory of Jesus living in her passes through and suffuses the created glory of Lisa's flawed and slowly healing soul, a marvel burns in real time, and those who see it take off their shoes. The ground she walks with Jesus is holy.

The same is true of you, and of me. But how, as we lead ourselves and others, are we to steward this marvel? What is the role of leadership in God's endeavor to flush life-giving glory through his children into an entropic world, bringing light into darkness and order into chaos?

Fostering Glory

We used to live in Spain, and I loved it. I had an orange tree in my front yard. It wasn't mine, as we rented, but I really enjoyed the fruit, the perfume the blossoms give, and the way the leaves shimmer green in the sun. I loved that little tree. I loved the glory in its juice, in its fragrance, and in the lovely role it played in the view off my porch.

I watered it every other day or so, because I know how photosynthesis works, so I know that more water plus more sun equals more orange tree and more oranges. Should bugs or birds do it harm, I would deploy appropriate strategies. We had a rabbit too, which makes for lots of compost, so I'd occasionally manure around the little tree to make sure it had what it needed to not just get by, but to thrive, and to come to its full stature and fruitfulness.

To be clear, and at the risk of being a little pedantic, I myself make no oranges. I exude no orange blossom perfume, and I don't dance in the wind. I can't actually force nutrients from the soil into the tree, and should I foolishly choose to hack into its bark looking for oranges, I'd extract no fruit. I have almost no direct power over the internal processes of that tree. I didn't plant it, and it will likely outlive me. I stand at neither end of its story. I am incapable of photosynthesis and couldn't do that for my little tree no matter how many books on botany I read or how committed I was to its survival.

> When we lead well,
> we foster glory in those we lead.

All I can do is foster the processes already inherent in the tree's design. I can cultivate; I can nurture; I can promote an environment friendly to orange trees. I can increase the likelihood that the tree will thrive and come to its full magnificence—especially if I understand how it works and if I do my small part faithfully over the long haul.

When we lead well, we foster glory in those we lead. They do not belong to us, but we steward their lovely souls with them for a while. This book is designed to increase our competence in this endeavor. This process has three parts: Thrive, Work, and Develop. Think of the structure like my tree. Thriving is the roots, the part of the tree that secures nutrients and gives the organism a base and stability. At the other end is development where the tree stretches toward the sun. The crown of the tree gives it its unique profile—its branches growing out in a signature all its own, carrying the organism's reproductive potential. Between the two, holding them together, is work—the real time clocked in real places where the vast majority of life happens. We were made for work, and it is at work—in the context of our day jobs—that we are apprenticed by Jesus. Roots, trunk, and crown—thrive, work, develop.

How to Read This Book

In part one, Thrive, we will consider five dimensions of human life, explore how to regularly increase self-awareness in each dimension, and learn how to plan intelligently and intentionally to thrive in each of those five dimensions. Part two, Work, will unpack four key points at which integration is necessary if we are not to become unraveled. It's easy in an entropic universe to lose the strength and vibrancy we gain by thriving if we aren't wise and purposeful about how we approach our work in the world. In part three, Develop, we'll examine the concept of poiesis and learn three ways to develop intentionally: Christification, reflective experience, and self-discovery.

Each chapter will open with a few key ideas, and each part will conclude with a chapter discussing how to lead people toward thriving, integrated work, and purposeful development, respectively. I'll offer two coaching cues for each part to guide your praxis. These cues will be oriented both toward what we can do for the individual, and what we can do in the individual's context to foster glory.

Finally, in the afterword I offer some considerations for leaders and followers beyond the two cues offered in each part. You may have observed a pattern: five dimensions to thrive, four integrations for work, three avenues for development, and two cues each, all make one tree. It's almost too much structure, I know, but there's a reason for it. A final metaphor will help me make that clear.

There Are No Naturals, but We Can Be Complete

I'm not good at most sports, but fight sports are my strong suit. A fight has three levels—three almost distinct games that a fighter needs to know how to play. First, there's the stand-up game, where the boxing and kickboxing matters. Second, the ground game, where chokes and submission holds apply. In between is the transition game—how a standing fighter throws his opponent to the ground or successfully takes a grappling match back to a standing fight.

There are no untalented professional fighters. Most fighters are naturals at one of the three games. Most successful fighters' careers take a predictable arc. They appear on the scene and dominate the stand-up game by winning several fights in a row by knock-out. Or they're dominant on the ground and win consistently in the second round with a wizardly submission.

But this good fortune runs out eventually, and their deficiencies in the other two levels of engagement lead to a disappointing series of losses. What happens next is critical. The fighters that go on to become great usually step back and address their weaknesses. They don't become phenomenal there, but they gain adequate skill and composure to hold their own at all three levels. The striker learns some jiujitsu, the grappler learns to box and move her head, and everyone learns some wrestling or judo.

The fighter comes back and works through the ranks again maybe even to a title shot. She started out a gifted natural at one aspect of fighting, but eventually she became what we call a complete fighter—a threat on the ground, standing up, and in between.

Likewise, I've met a lot of people who are gifted leaders, even developmentally oriented leaders, who are naturals at one level of our glory tree. They're great counselors or coaches or maybe excellent problem solvers. Rarely, they're uncanny leader developers. Almost none of us start out as complete fighters, but that's what we must become if our leadership is to become like the sun and rain.

The people we lead are worth being stewarded well. They're worth being called to greatness and supplied with what they need to get there. I'm a teacher at heart, so I've done all I can to make what comes naturally to some reproducible for everyone. I hope you find it useful as you foster the glory God has placed in you and in those you lead.

Part I
Thrive | Roots

Introduction to Part I

Over decades of working in demanding, cross-cultural contexts, my team and I have had to figure out how to thrive in some pretty challenging contexts. The journey hasn't been easy, but it's been fruitful. And understanding where our approach to thriving comes from may offer you a deeper foundation as you seek to bear lasting fruit in your own life and calling.

Rich is known throughout the Northwest of the US as the guy who knows how to make things grow. In a recent year, the crop conditions were *perfect*. Perfect rainfall predicted, perfect soil composition, perfect everything. When asked if he thought it was going to be a good year for the local crops, Rich said, "Yeah, probably not."

"But the conditions are perfect!" his friend objected.

"That's the problem. Crops do better when the conditions are mostly right, but with some meaningful stress somewhere. In perfect conditions, the plants grow great. But to produce fruit, you need stress."

> An organism thrives when it metabolizes its environment—both nutrients and stressors—and turns it into growth and fruit.

That insight captures the tension we'll explore in this book. We all long for good conditions—supportive relationships, healthy systems, enough resources. And we should work toward them. But if our goal is to bear fruit that lasts, we must also embrace the stressors that shape us, stretch us, and teach us to lean into something deeper than comfort.

Part one of this book will explore how to maximize opportunities to create good conditions without insulating ourselves from the stress we need to bear lasting fruit. Moving forward, we will use the following definition of thriving: An organism thrives when it metabolizes its environment—both nutrients and stressors—and turns it into growth and fruit. In part one, Thrive, we will consider five dimensions of human life, explore how to regularly increase self-awareness in each dimension, and learn how to plan intelligently and intentionally to thrive in each of those five dimensions.

1

Thriving in Uncertainty

In this chapter we'll:

- Unpack how the 5DThrive Approach was hammered out over a decade across three continents
- Introduce the five dimensions of the human soul (spiritual, physical, cognitive, emotional, and relational) and how they work together
- Posit that it's possible to thrive in chaos and uncertainty

Central Asia, 2009–2017

I walked into the kitchen to find my wife, Joy, staring at her hands. The water in the city we lived in caused a strong inflammatory response in her skin, and because of the way life worked there, her hands were always in the water. When it got bad, the skin would crack and split.

Hands bleeding, she looked up at me and said, "I thought these were supposed to be the best years of our lives."

Before moving to the capital of a post-Soviet Central Asian republic a few years prior, we helped lead a wonderful church in Nashville, TN. I had studied biology in my undergraduate program and completed a Master's of Religion with a concentration in cross cultural studies while I waited for Joy to finish her degree in education. We moved to Nashville where I completed a Master's of Education, because we knew my seminary degree would be objectionable in a country unfriendly to the gospel.

We moved to Central Asia with friends from the church full of the certainty that only the young and naïve can muster. In our first year, we joined another team, helped start a business, worked hard on language and culture acquisition, and tried to put down roots in our new home, all while managing a growing family. It was a lot to take on. In less than five years, I'd held four different jobs, moved four times, and had an almost complete turnover of teammates. This kind of instability is incredibly hard.

But there are different kinds of hard, and some places seem harder than others. The city we lived in seemed to chew expatriates up. I think it chewed up its citizens, too, but it was harder to see. By our fifth year, we had grown accustomed to near constant change and instability—it was almost comical. In one apartment, in order to get hot water, you needed the water, gas, and electricity to all be functioning. Most days, we were missing one or another of those utilities, and you never knew which one or for how long. When you're cooking for six and running four kids' laundry in a developing country, these kinds of things wear you out.

Everything was three times harder. In year one, we'd begin each day with ten things to do, and become frustrated when none of them would happen. By year four, we'd laugh when we started the day with three simple tasks and considered ourselves heroic for accomplishing one.

Some uncertainties were more serious. One day in 2015, I got a phone call from the kid who managed the visa applications at the university where I taught. The day before, he told me our visas were approved, and I should be ready to meet him at the immigration office the next morning with all of our passports and money for the processing fees. We were good to go.

When the call came that morning, things went a little differently.

"Hello, Virgil-teacher. How are you?" Anar asked.

"I'm well, Anar," I replied. "How are you? Are we to meet this morning?"

"I am afraid I think there may be a small problem." Given how indirect the culture was, I knew we were in trouble when he opened this way.

"Tell me," I said.

"The not-so-good news is that I have here an official letter from the immigration office stating your visas are all denied, and you have ten days to leave the country or you'll be arrested and deported."

"Wow, that is bad news," I answered.

"No, that is the not-so-good news."

"Okay," I sighed. "Let's have the bad news."

"Yes. Well, I'm very sorry."

"Just tell me, Anar. It's okay."

"The letter is back-dated nine days. You have twenty-four hours to pack your children and your wife, and to get out of the country, or you'll be arrested, deported, and denied any chance of coming back. I'm sorry."

This set off a twenty-three-hour scramble to get tickets, pack, and fly out. Our departure kicked off a fantastic seven-month voyage around the eastern US for our family of six, living in basements and bonus rooms. We never spent more than two weeks in one city, and were never clear if or when we could get back home, which is how we had come to see Central Asia. Eventually we did get back and spent another fruitful eighteen months there before moving to Spain.

This kind of uncertainty, with the very real threat of the hammer dropping any minute, was normal there. It ground you down. One year, a colleague did an informal survey of the people who had moved to our city thinking they'd stay for decades. The average stay was 2.7 years. As much as we loved it, life there was like running blindfolded in the dark over uneven ground littered with glass. If you fell, you'd bleed, and even if you could get your eyes open, it wouldn't help. After a while, those of us who stayed resigned ourselves to never knowing when a trusted friend or confidante would have to leave.

A few years before our expulsion, we had begun to reconsider how best to make an impact in the city and among the people we had come to love. It occurred to us that some of the locals wanted only their own gain, while others wanted to make their city beautiful and filled with the image of Jesus. We noticed the expats in the city fell into those two groups as well. So, we wondered if the most strategic contribution we could make would be to give a portion of our energy to strengthening the hands of the people—local and expat—whose hearts held the desire and determination to see Christ formed in our city. This question, and the adventure that followed, was the beginning of our exploration of strategic human flourishing in Jesus.

Spain, 2017

While we were bouncing around the eastern US waiting to get back to Central Asia, the organization we worked with approached us about stepping into a broader leadership role. With considerable prayer and discernment, we agreed to join a team that would oversee and look after cross-cultural workers doing beautiful work all over the world, and particularly, in some rather hostile environments. In the summer of 2017, we moved to southern Spain and began a new chapter.

Despite the grace of our teammates and the beauty and hospitality of Spain, we had a rough start. The trials of the previous decade all seemed to come to a head at once. My strong, compassionate, and gifted wife had a complete breakdown.

We learned that the body keeps the score,[1] and the bill always comes due. We learned how deeply each part of ourselves connects to the others, and we learned a bit about how to take care of each one in tandem with the others. We learned that breakdowns like Joy's were common among workers like us, and perhaps, they could be prevented. It was a trying six months, but Jesus held us through it, and we learned a lot.

The experience of breaking down and coming back stronger reinforced and accelerated the thoughts that had been percolating in us for some time. As our new team considered what our most strategic first step might be, we decided that the most impactful thing we could do for the communities our staff served would be to help our people become as healthy and vibrant as possible. For this to happen, things needed to change.

> This care would have to become proactive,
> not just reactive or palliative.

First, leaders at all levels had to understand that their work includes—and should prioritize—staff care. This care would have to become proactive, not just reactive or palliative. Cross-cultural Christian workers in caustic contexts face many of the same challenges that believers in their home countries face: marriage and family issues, professional development hurdles, emotional disturbances rooted in family-of-origin, leadership and teaming challenges, and the like. However, due to the remoteness of these environments and limited internet security, our workers were facing these challenges with little access to the mental health resources that their counterparts take for granted.

Add in challenges such as political instability, systemic gender inequality, and trauma—challenges which are ubiquitous across these environments—and you have a recipe for diminished capacity and attrition. Working and serving in situations like these is like playing a game where you lose half your pieces every few turns, and the remaining half is impaired. Such a game cannot be won. But this is the game we play when staff-care resources are limited and only employed when needs become critical. Too often, it's too little, too late. To reduce attrition and to keep our people vibrant enough to execute their callings, leaders need to recognize care and development as crucial to our leadership—not something we farm out to experts when things get bad enough.

---

1 van der Kolk, *Body Keeps the Score*.

Leadership isn't all that needs redefining though. Our staff would have to understand that their work *includes* self-care. They have to assume the responsibility of investing in their own vibrancy. The mention of self-care can conjure images of pampering, navel-gazing, and lounging about sipping Mai Tais. That is not what we're talking about. Perhaps a better term is *self-leadership*.

As disciples of Jesus, we are convinced that Jesus is good, that he's brilliant, and that apprenticeship to him is the only real path to change for ourselves and for the world. So, when we stride out into the world to make disciples of Jesus, entering marketplaces as entrepreneurs, teachers, doctors, lawyers, accountants, scientists, clergy, or businesspeople, we are the message. The vividness of our lives and the wisdom with which we lead them says more to the world about our Teacher than most of us will ever say with words. We must understand that our work in leading people to Jesus must include leading ourselves well.

These two adjustments, one to our understanding of leadership and the other to our understanding of good work, formed the basis of what would become 5DThrive: a community approach to intentional self-care and development toward strategic human flourishing in Jesus.

> Our staff would have to understand that their work *includes* self-care.

An organism thrives when it metabolizes its environment, both nutrients and stressors, resulting in growth and fruit. That's what we want for our people. The preposition is important. We aren't expecting that *from* our people. We want it *for* them. An organism doesn't bear fruit or grow by trying. Rather, growth and fruit are consequences of thriving. Thriving is the key.

The human organism in the Bible, and especially the Old Testament, is referred to as a soul. The Hebrew word, *nephesh*, doesn't refer to the immaterial part of you. It's not, as in Greek thought, that you have a soul trapped in a body. Rather, you *are* a soul, and the word refers to a complete, integrated, embodied self. To make caring for your soul simple enough to be achievable, we identified five dimensions—the 5 Ds of 5DThrive—that, if cared for and invested in properly, are likely to result in a vibrant, thriving human being. We want our people to thrive spiritually, physically, cognitively, emotionally, and relationally.

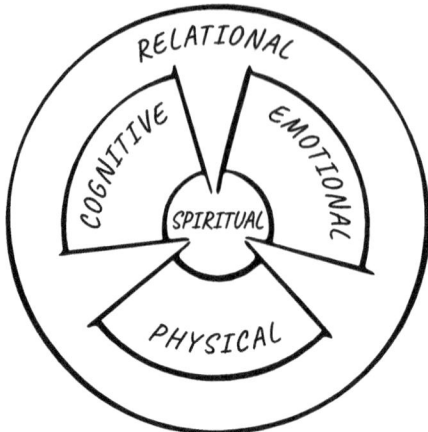

Figure 1 | 5 Dimensions Circle

We put the dimensions on a wheel with the spiritual dimension at the center. For the follower of Jesus, the spiritual dimension is where the power comes from. It's the axle in the wheel, which holds the rest of it together and fuels its processes for life.

The physical, cognitive, and emotional dimensions form a triad. The physical is on the bottom, not because it's least important; on the contrary, it's the base upon which the others are built. You have no lever stronger than your physicality to effect change in your thoughts, feelings, or even your spiritual life.

The cognitive and emotional together comprise much of what the Hebrews would have thought of as your heart, and the Greeks, perhaps, as your mind. We delineate them because we've noticed some people are good at living in their thoughts, and some with their feelings, but few are naturally adept at both. However, adept with both we must become if we are to be fully alive.

Relational is the rim of the wheel, not because it's peripheral, but rather because it's where the rubber meets the road. Your relationships are how the other parts of you are experienced by the world, and you experience the world through your relationships.

We developed some simple tools which helped our staff assess their relative thriving in each dimension, built capacity where our people were weakest, and developed ways to help people plan to actually thrive.

We held a conference for all our international staff in the autumn of 2019. We devoted half of every day to equipping them with this approach, and half of every day to individual professional care from a team of counselors, therapists, spiritual directors, and coaches. The feedback, from our international staff and from the team of care professionals, was overwhelmingly positive. We had struck on something deeply important and had managed to make it simple enough that it would be hard to fail.

As our staff began to understand their work to include their thriving and started to implement what they were learning, they began flourishing in Jesus in ways they'd never known before. Then 2020 happened.

Everywhere, 2020

In 2020 we lived in Spain. So, by the time the Covid-19 quarantines started in the US, we had been locked down for a while. We watched Italy's healthcare system brush against collapse. Spain quickly became the country with the highest infection rate and the worst death toll per capita. Adults were only allowed out of our houses to walk the dog or get groceries, and learning was attempted online. It was difficult, but we felt prepared.

We were prepared, in part, by the particularly difficult lives we had led so far—lives which had demanded the cultivation of preparedness and coping skills that came in handy. But we were also prepared because we had every intention of coming out the other side of the pandemic stronger for having endured it with a plan. While the rest of the world struggled with the crisis and the felt loss of personal agency, we primarily only suffered the former.

In his book *Antifragile*, Nassim Taleb described three kinds of systems. Fragile systems break under stress. Resilient systems are not changed by stress unless it's catastrophic. They may deform a little, but they return to their shape when the stress has passed. Antifragile systems benefit from stress and chaos because the system is designed to respond to stress by becoming stronger. Like the way my bones get denser and my muscles get stronger after I lift weights, antifragile systems metabolize their environments—nutrients and stressors—and become more for it. That's what I want for you in all the dimensions of your soul.

It seemed no coincidence that God led us to develop and deploy 5DThrive on the eve of 2020. Soon everyone was living in protracted uncertainty, not just those of us living in warzones. We are all still feeling a distinct loss of control over key areas of our lives, and none of the other difficulties, diseases, or disasters have subsided. We have never needed to know how to thrive more than we do now.

This book is, in part, my contribution to your thriving. Because right now, I believe the best way I can help the world move toward the beauty and goodness Jesus has secured for it, is to help his people become strong, integrated, and fully alive.

You, Today

Let's start right now. My spiritual director taught me an exercise to help me check in with myself in depth. She calls it the SoulGPS. It's like the "You Are Here" dot on a map. God can only bless us where we are and as we are, so knowing these things can only help us. You will need about twenty minutes to complete this exercise. Don't cheat yourself—you are worth the time it takes.

You'll need a pen and paper. Try to remember, in as much detail as you can, the last week. Whom were you with? What did you do? How did it go? What else happened? What didn't?

Below is a series of questions. Try to spend one minute with each one and write the answers down. There will be another step or two when you're done.

1. What were your three most dominant thoughts in the last week? A thought is dominant if you thought hard about it or if it repeatedly came to mind unbidden.

2. What were your three dominant emotions in the last week? An emotion is dominant if you felt it powerfully, or if you felt it steadily in the background or under the surface, like a mood. (An emotions wheel is a helpful tool here.)

3. What did you notice in your body this week? What felt strong? Weak? Tight? Painful? Off?

4. How happy and supported did you feel in your most important relationships? What interactions or circumstances bring you to that answer?

5. What, if anything, have you discerned God saying to you or showing you this week? Feel free to give an answer or not to.

6. What longings have you noticed in your heart this week? Longings sometimes present with language like "I miss," or "I wish," or "Wouldn't it be great if."

7. What questions do you feel like you're living right now?

Now, take a few minutes and slowly read your answers out loud three times. When you're done, consider what you notice about yourself. Don't try to figure anything out, diagnose dysfunction, or explain yourself. Just notice without judgement or excuse.

What did you notice? Offer that to God in prayer. Ask him to restore the parts of your soul most in need of strengthening, but most importantly, just tell God what you noticed about your soul and give yourself the opportunity to be present with him as he's present with you.

Us, Tomorrow

In the coming chapters, we will explore how to plan to thrive, even in chaos, and we'll consider how communities and leaders can support thriving together. Tomorrow might not be awesome, but it can be more aligned to God's good intentions for you than today. Tomorrow we can assert a little more personal agency, and we can go to bed knowing that God will do for us all that we cannot do for ourselves.

2

Spiritual

Withdraw, Gather, Obey

In this chapter we'll:
- Introduce the 5DVector Check and the 5DThrive Plan
- Explore how to thrive spiritually by withdrawing, gathering, and obeying
- Explore Jesus's practice of solitude for coaching on how we can WITHDRAW to connect with him
- Consider how to connect with him communally as we GATHER
- Contrast reflexive and reflective obedience in order to OBEY Jesus in ways that form us

We moved to Spain with a single woman and another couple from our organization. We came from different places with very different life experiences. We knew that in order to create the kind of environment where souls could be restored and innovations in leadership could flourish, we would need a lot of time together. So, we spent our first year living together in a big Spanish villa. Nine people from three units. It was quite the experiment.

As a result, we had the same landlord and used a lot of water. When discussing the water bill with the landlord, my colleague and housemate, Paul, brought up the fact that a few of the toilets ran continually.

"Well, they didn't when you moved in," countered the landlord.

"Yes," replied Paul. "But entropy means that a system not proactively maintained, will, by itself, without any help from us, tend toward disorder." My landlord wasn't convinced. But it stuck with me.

A few months passed, and my son got sick. Paul, being a doctor, looked him over, gave some advice, and a few days later asked how he was.

I told Paul how things had progressed, and he replied, "Good. Sounds like it's going in the right direction."

It struck me that it was more important to the doctor what direction things were moving in than where exactly they were at the moment. What set him at ease was the vector.

I'm a synthesizer, so once I had entropy and vector, what came next was a matter of course. I was watching a video about CrossFit's Health Continuum.[1] It basically contends that sickness, wellness, and fitness all fall on a single continuum called "health," and that the things that make well people fit can also help sick people become well. It occurred to me that this would also hold true across the other dimensions of our souls that CrossFit doesn't train. When entropy, vector, and continuum met, the 5DVector Check was born.

Checking Your Vectors

Grab a piece of paper and draw five parallel lines, with the right end higher than the left:

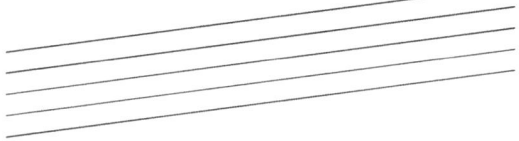

Figure 2 | Vector lines

Label each line *Spiritual*, *Physical*, *Cognitive*, *Emotional*, and *Relational*. Divide the lines into thirds, as below. Label the regions *Sick*, *Well*, and *Fit*.

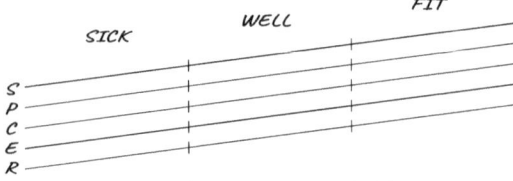

Figure 3 | Vector lines with labels

The area in the middle is Wellness. When one of your dimensions is well, you usually don't notice it. It doesn't hurt. It's not preventing you from functioning normally, but it also isn't giving you anything extra.

The area to the left is Sickness. The line between Wellness and Sickness is *impairment*. When a dimension prevents you from being happy or accomplishing your work, you can consider yourself somewhat impaired, and the dimension impairing you is sick.

---

1 Glassman, "Fitness, Luck, and Health."

On the right is Fitness. A dimension is fit when it's so healthy that it catalyzes thriving in other dimensions. Further, fitness in a given dimension often catalyzes thriving in other people in the same dimension. Like sickness, fitness is contagious.

- Spiritual thriving is a function of the vividness of your companionship with Jesus. How easy or hard is it to connect with him? Do you notice the fruit or effect of the Spirit's inhabiting and empowering, or do you notice the effect of sin or dullness toward God?
- Physical fitness, wellness, and sickness have been fairly well defined, and their definitions are pretty standard.
- To check cognitive thriving, look for obsessive thinking, difficulty concentrating, or fuzziness. These are indicators of some level of impairment. Fitness is often marked by sharpness of focus and steadiness of attention when you're thinking about something, and quietness of mind when you're not.
- Emotional thriving is being able to experience emotions appropriate to the situations you're in without being numb or flooded. Emotional flooding or absence are often indicators of impairment. Likewise, fitness looks a lot like high emotional intelligence—the ability to notice, understand, and manage emotions in yourself and others.
- Relational thriving involves knowing which relationships are the most important to you, knowing how to invest in and receive from those relationships, and being adequately skilled to make and receive those investments. If you're feeling under-supported, or if thinking of your relationships makes you feel sad or exhausted, you might be relationally impaired. Relational fitness is being surrounded by people who make you strong, and whom you strengthen.

One at a time, consider each dimension of your soul. How does it feel or seem to you? For each dimension, place a circle on the continuum, representing your thrive factor in each dimension. Don't overthink it, and don't worry about perfect accuracy. Just try to be honest with yourself. It's purposefully subjective.

Now think back over the last month. Which direction are you moving each dimension? Toward sickness, or toward fitness? Again, don't judge or excuse; just notice. Does it feel like things are getting better or worse? Remember, the continuum is sloped, so if it's not getting better, it is probably getting worse. For each dimension, draw a small arrow over the circle you placed on the continuum, representing which way things are moving in that dimension of your soul this month.

Congratulations! You've completed your first 5DVector Check. This is when I usually lean back and take a slow look at my self-reporting.

It may look something like this:

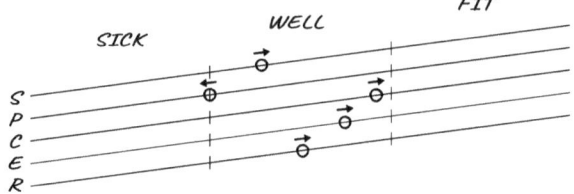

Figure 4 | 5DVector check

At the end of this exercise, I often ask myself the following questions:

- Which dimensions do I need to pay a little more attention to? Usually, the answer is the ones going the wrong way, because I need to turn those around if I can. Sometimes I need to pay attention when I am feeling fit in a dimension because it suggests something's working. I want to celebrate that and see what I can learn.

- Where do I need help? Help from my wife, my household, or my team? Maybe help from a supervisor or colleague? Maybe even help from a professional? There's no shame in needing help. I need help maintaining my car; pro athletes need help maintaining their performance, and we all occasionally need help to thrive. Being too embarrassed or proud to seek help is negligence in the line of duty.

- Where have I noticed Jesus meeting me this month in the different dimensions of my soul? As I lifted weights? In the Scriptures? In pursuing important relationships? In interviewing my emotions? Conversely, where do I most need his touch right now to restore or strengthen my soul? "On the day I called, you answered me; my strength of soul you increased" (Ps 138:3). What kind of strengthening do I want to call out for?

When and How Often?

We encourage people to run a 5DVector Check monthly. The goal is to cultivate and maintain enough self-awareness that we can properly execute self-leadership.

On one hand, we don't want to look under the hood so rarely that serious pathologies or deficiencies crop up and take root before we can mitigate or correct them. That leads to lifestyle comorbidities—physical states that make illnesses more deadly than they would be in a healthier person. Physical comorbidities are fairly well-known, but it's also possible to live with emotional comorbidities that make traumas splash down much harder than they might have if we had been tending our hearts. Relational comorbidities can turn us into time bombs for any team we are part of, and we'd never know without regular self-reflection.

On the other hand, it's possible to look under the hood too often. We want self-awareness, not self-obsession. To that end, checking in monthly is better than daily or weekly. It's too hard to track meaningful trends or patterns more frequently.

I've found that taking a deeper look is most useful when something significant or out of the ordinary has happened—or when I feel like I'm not myself, I'm in a haze or a funk, or when I've been inordinately busy for too long. Anytime I've lost track of myself, the deep-tissue exploration helps me find exactly where I am. Since this deeper look takes longer and invites slower focus than the Vector check, it can break me out of rhythms of inattention, distraction, or avoidance. It moves me toward the kind of awareness and honesty I need to regain traction.

The vector check, however, provides a quick, data-rich snapshot with an accurate sense of where the momentum lies. Two of the teams I'm part of currently use the 5DVector Check monthly as a check-in to start team meetings. This doesn't replace curious questions or deeper investigation. On the contrary, the shared vocabulary gives us access points to follow up with what we're hearing our teammates share. Together we are seeking to cooperate with Jesus in stewarding each other's souls toward the kind of flourishing that positions us to act on strategic objectives. It helps us know what kind of help to ask for without expecting anyone to read our minds or find our way for us.

Toward Planning

A good plan must take into account where you are, where you want to go, and the means you need to cover that distance. The SoulGPS and 5DVector Check provide a thorough picture of where you are at any given moment, but they also help you define where you want to go.

But things happen. The world is broken. Entropy is real as are sin and misfortune. We want to be antifragile, so that we can make steady forward progress without being derailed when we face setbacks. We want to be making enough progress in all five dimensions of our souls, that when something unfortunate happens, we have enough momentum toward thriving and fitness that we don't tumble toward sickness and impairment. We call this Minimum Viable Progress (MVP).

The community I serve most often can't afford to devote huge amounts of time and energy to self-improvement, but that's never been the goal. My colleagues have placed themselves in harm's way in order to bring Christ's love to the world's neediest places. We ask them to invest in themselves enough to assure viable progress: enough upward momentum to overcome temporary, unexpected setbacks. This is how uncertainty is planned for. We want just enough investment in each dimension that the return is worth it.

> We want to be making enough progress
> in all five dimensions of our souls,
> that when something unfortunate happens, we have
> enough momentum toward thriving and fitness that we
> don't tumble toward sickness and impairment.

We aren't looking to arrive. We're looking to progress. We are cultivating vectors of thriving. Vectors have direction and magnitude. For us that means moving up the continuum with enough momentum so that losing a step doesn't mean losing the game.

This only leaves the means. If we know where we are and where we want to go, we have to choose means that can get us there. When we're talking about human change, that means choosing *practices*.

Practice, Practice, Practice

People don't thrive by sheer force of will. We don't thrive by wishing for it or agreeing that it would be a good idea. People thrive by developing practices that align with how God made us and by adding energy to the systems that increase strength and vibrancy. Followers of Jesus thrive even more dynamically by inhabiting practices with him. We want practices that align us with who he is, where he is going, and how he intends to indwell and invigorate all the parts of our souls. We thrive by thoughtful practice.

Practice is how we learn Arabic, guitar, baking, and active listening. It's how we get better at everything we do. So, when you tell me you want to thrive physically, I don't care what you *think* about macronutrients or gluten. I care about what you eat. When you say you want to thrive cognitively, I don't care what your IQ is or where you graduated. I care what practices you're espousing now to steward your attention. When you plan to thrive, you choose the practices that can lead you to thrive—the practices that best position your soul to receive strength and multiply it. Then you build your schedule to include those practices first.

A good plan to thrive will, of course, include practices that support MVP in all five dimensions. But the plans that work the best tend to be a little more nuanced. When we coach people in Thrive Planning, we ask them to think about three verbs for each dimension.

Figure 5 | *5DThrive Practices*

First, Take Stock

Very few people do nothing to secure their wellness. Certainly, you already have practices in your routine to keep you healthy and happy. The first step in creating a profitable Thrive Plan is taking stock of what you're already doing. Do you work out? Do you watch what you eat? Maybe you gather with believers regularly, see a counselor or spiritual director, or manage your screen time. Take a moment and write those things down. This list is your current Thrive Plan.

The two questions you need to ask now are: How well is it working? and What's missing? Measure whether the practices you've chosen are working against the idea of Minimum Viable Progress. Are you becoming more fit because you're prioritizing that practice? If so, it's probably working. If not, you need something else.

To find out what's missing, consider the following sections. Each section will provide some initial guidance to help you choose practices that will work for you in your real life. I'm being careful not to over-describe or prescribe practices that I like, because what works for me may not work for you. What you'll find in the pages that follow, I hope, will be just enough to shore up any holes in your capacity and to catalyze some initial investment in your own vibrancy.

At the end, I'll give you a few tips to help you pull it all together and make a plan of your own. I know life can be overwhelming, and the idea of adding more feels like it will sink your boat. However, I have two encouragements for you. First, sometimes the best thrive practice is a subtraction and not an addition. It's about removing stuff that's dragging you down. Second, after we've outlined how to make a *great* plan, we'll discuss how to make a minimal field-expedient plan that's good enough to get you out of a state of overwhelm and moving toward thriving again.

Thrive Spiritually

Withdraw

Mark's gospel is characterized by constant action. The most repeated word in the story is *immediately*. It's breathless from verse one, and never lets up. But he writes an interesting vignette near the beginning of the narrative, and it lets us know something about Jesus's priorities. Sandwiched between "he healed many who were sick with various diseases, and cast out many demons" (Mark 1:34), and "he went throughout all Galilee, preaching in their synagogues and casting out demons" (Mark 1:39), Mark tucks away an awkwardly constructed, ugly, yet beautiful sentence.

"And rising very early in the morning, while it was still dark, he departed and went out to a desolate place, and there he prayed" (Mark 1:35).

Jesus, it seems, was very intentional about his solitude. He didn't just rise in the morning. He rose early in the morning. Very early. While it was still dark, in fact. And left. He left and went out. He left and went out and kept going until he reached a desolate place with no one in sight.

Mark stacks these phrases intentionally, building a redundancy we can't miss, letting us know that Jesus, in the midst of a life full of vital work helping desperate people, prioritized getting far, far away from those people for a good while. Far away from their voices and their needs, their hopes and expectations. Far enough away and for long enough to pray and to listen.

For Jesus, and for his students, solitude isn't primarily "me time." Solitude allows us to show up to ourselves and to God so we can hear his voice, without the noise of the crowd muddling the encounter.

Surely, if Jesus considered solitude with God to be a non-negotiable, how much more do we, who are not God incarnate, need to do the same. If we are to sustain lives of meaningful service to the people around us, we have to step away from them regularly.

To thrive spiritually, we have to withdraw to engage with Christ alone. For each of us, the disciplines we include in our solitude will be different, and sometimes different by season. I have had long stretches where intense Bible study was where he met me most, and times when I connected best in simple silence. The point is the direct experience of Jesus without the aid or distractions that others bring.

Richard Foster and Dallas Willard have written extensively about the proper use of solitude in Christian discipleship as has Henri Nouwen. For those unaccustomed to this kind of withdrawal, these authors could provide a good place to start. But more importantly, ask Jesus how he'd like to meet you in solitude, and as you explore wise guidance and experiment with disciplines, be listening for his answer.

Gather

Withdrawing isn't enough though. We must gather as well. Jesus told his disciples that when two or three gather in his name, he is also there in their midst. When we gather, Jesus is present with us in a different way than when we are in solitude. Discipleship to Jesus is first a communal endeavor and then an individual one.

When his disciples asked Jesus to teach them to pray, he said, "When you pray, say, 'Our Father in heaven,'" (Luke 11:2, NKJV). *Our* Father. For Jesus, the assumption is they are praying and speaking to God as a community. While the postmodern, Western mind, sees prayer as a personal, private matter with occasional communal implications, Jesus seems to view it as a primarily communal matter that we sometimes do alone.

This reality undergirds the commands in the rest of the New Testament to not forsake the gathering of the saints, to strive to live as one, and to practice that list of verbs some call the "one-anothers"—commands to love one another, forgive one another, encourage one another, consider one another, and so on. Following Jesus is not a solo sport. It's incumbent upon us, then, to discern with Jesus exactly with whom and how he would have us "pursue righteousness, faith, love, and peace along with those who call on the Lord from a pure heart" (2 Tim 2:22). This gathering to follow Jesus with others is the second practice to spiritual thriving, and it's as critical to vivid friendship with Jesus as pursuing him alone.

Obey

But what kind of friendship with Jesus do we enjoy? Well, Jesus says we're his friends if we obey his commands (John 15:14). The notion of obedience being a good thing can be hard to embrace—so hard, in fact, that a few friends have encouraged me to try different words: *act, serve, engage, get involved*. But obedience can be beautiful. Further, if the one we are obeying is better and wiser than we are, and if that one has committed himself to our freedom, obedience is the best possible course for us.

Discipleship in the Ancient Near East more closely resembled an apprenticeship than simply going to study under a teacher. A disciple learns from her master by working alongside him. What's more, she gets to know him in the context of working with him and doing the things that he tells her to do.

This makes sense of something Jesus said to his first disciples not long before he was arrested.

> You are my friends if you do what I command. I no longer call you servants, because a servant does not know his master's business. Instead, I have called you friends, for everything that I learned from my Father I have made known to you. (John 15:14–15, NIV)

We are friends to our *Master* if we do what he says. If you've ever been in leadership, you know how frustrating it can be when a direct report says he wants to be your friend, but he refuses to come through on his responsibilities. He wants your trust and to spend time with you, but he won't comply with instructions or do his job. It's a contradiction. Any leader knows that when you follow someone, the first kind of friendship is coming through on directives.

But Jesus isn't asking his friends for mindless, reflexive obedience. Reflexive obedience—the kind of compliance born of fear, that hurries to obey without ever considering the purpose of the instruction, or the desires of the one who gave it—is the obedience of servants and slaves. Jesus says, I'm not treating you like servants, but as friends, because I'm explaining to you what's in my mind as we go. The obedience of friends is reflective, not reflexive.

The third spiritual thrive practice, then, is to obey reflectively. Consider what practices you can put in place to help you assure that:

1. You're listening for Jesus, and expecting to receive actual instructions,
2. You're executing on what you receive and trusting him with the outcomes, whatever they may be,
3. And you're reflective on the event in which you obeyed; not on your performance, per se, but in how you experience Jesus in action.

This kind of reflective obedience assures that we don't cut our lives in half—the inner world with Jesus, and the outer world on our own. Rather, we pursue him alone, we pursue him with others, and we pursue him in his work in the world.

We withdraw, gather, and obey.

3

Physical

Eat, Move, Recover

In this chapter we'll:
- Consider the centrality of our bodies in our overall flourishing
- Explore simple heuristics to help us EAT and MOVE well
- Uncover the role of rest in a life lived biblically and its implications for how we RECOVER

Your body is the operating platform of your soul—your integrated self. Everything you do for the other four dimensions you do with your body. Spiritual disciplines are practices you inhabit with your body to facilitate spiritual connection. When you fast, you don't put food in your body. When you practice solitude, you bodily remove yourself from the company of others. When you pray, you may prefer particular postures to help you express your Godward inclination. Emotions are experienced as physical sensations you feel in your body. Your brain is part of your body. While the mind is more than the brain, it includes it, and injuries or repairs done to the brain have direct carry over in the cognitive function of the mind. Finally, in the era of social distancing, we have all experienced how rooted human relationships are in touch, gestures, and other physical cues. Our lives are embodied stories, so it shouldn't surprise us that our bodies can be either significant obstacles or our greatest allies toward thriving in the rest of our souls.

The Psalms are replete with poets lamenting physical symptoms as the consequences of their sin or their estrangement from God. But sin isn't the only source of spiritual stress we can feel in our bodies. Anyone who has worked or lived in a spiritually dark place knows first-hand the physical toll spiritual oppression can take. Long periods of intense concentration are physically exhausting, and when something weighs on our minds it is often felt in the shoulders, neck, and head. Relational and emotional stress can be carried all over the body, but who hasn't had that sick feeling in the gut, that sinking feeling, or that pain in the neck we all get from folding ourselves in half in response to protracted emotional stress as we slowly, unconsciously curl into the fetal position, trying to protect ourselves from more?

This phenomenon highlights stress as a bodily thing—it's a physiological response to stressors. But while stress is physical, the stressors can come from any part of the soul. The body keeps the score,[1] and the bill always comes due. It can come due in obvious ways over time in our bodies, in chronic pain, hypertension, and even some forms of cancer. It can come due spiritually as well like habitually seeking satisfaction in bodily sins. The price can land emotionally and cognitively as obsessive thinking, fight-or-flight, or hypervigilant physical configurations like tension in the abdomen or hunched shoulders. These positions send signals to the brain insisting that we still feel the stress, long after the stressor has passed. They lock us into a feedback loop of continual and compounding stress. The bill can also come due relationally, as we carry the physical postures, sensations, and facial cues from one interaction into the next, spreading tension and anxiety wherever we go.

However, because the body is the Grand Central Station for all five dimensions of soul, it is also our longest lever to engender thriving in every corner of who we are.

My friend Ann moved to Europe from Asia some years ago, and this move occasioned an unexpected breakdown. She started having intense general anxiety which eventually culminated in acute, daily panic attacks that would occupy entire mornings and leave her emotionally wrecked for the rest of the day. With some undulation in intensity, this state persisted for months. It was awful.

To be clear, she wasn't having a breakdown because she moved. She had a breakdown because of *everything*. All the stress of life in a caustic context. All the stress of relationships disappointing her or breaking her heart. All the stress of unhealed wounds received in childhood finally insisted on being heard. All of it came due at the same time, as it often does in midlife for strong and highly capable women. Crippling anxiety was her body's signal that it was time to settle up.

Upon arriving in Europe, she found a psychologist who works in member care and made her first appointment. After listening to her for some time, he laid out a plan for recovery and, beyond that, for growth.

---

[1] Van Der Kolk, *Body Keeps the Score*.

He said she would learn how to manage the emotions that were flooding her, and she'd learn what was underneath some of them. She would learn to listen to them compassionately without drowning in them. She would become more and better for this experience.

To do that, she'd first need to cultivate a few cognitive skills—some ways of thinking about emotions and managing her thoughts to keep them out of repetitive or destructive loops. To do that, she'd need a covering of prayer from trusted friends to keep her safe from the enemy of her soul while she did this inner work, and she'd need her body to be on her side. The first order of business to reclaim her emotional health was thirty minutes of vigorous exercise every day. Her psychologist explained that thirty minutes of daily, vigorous exercise has been shown clinically to be more effective than Prozac in managing depression and anxiety.

The psychologist, a trained trauma specialist widely respected around the world, told her that her body would be her first ally in cultivating healing and strength in all the parts of her soul. She could begin paying the bill with her exercise and invest its effects in processing the accumulated damage in her soul. It worked.

The prophet Elijah's story in 1 Kings is similar. After Elijah's confrontation with the prophets of Baal—a spiritually, emotionally, and relationally intense episode—he broke down. He walked off into the desert, sat down under a tree, and politely asked God if he could die (1 Kgs 19:3-4). God's prescription had two parts. The second part was an extremely vivid encounter with God that would alter Elijah's experience of himself, his God, and his world, as well as give him a new direction for his work. The first part, however, was going to sleep and receiving food from an angel (1 Kgs 19:5). God saw to Elijah's physical needs to make it possible to strengthen the rest of him.

Recognizing this connection between body, mind, and spirit, isn't just in the purview of the healing arts. The US Army has known for some time that physical wellness is a necessary component to cognitive and emotional function, decision making, and success in nearly any endeavor. Our physicality supports not only our own healing, but our usefulness in work.

Here are a few selections from a US Army manual for leader development:

4.2. Fitness: having sound health, strength, and endurance, which sustain emotional health and conceptual abilities under prolonged stress.

4.3. The Army recognizes a holistic emphasis on fitness prevents unnecessary harm whether from dangerous missions, routine operations, or a family outing. ... Leaders follow policies and adopt practices to maintain total fitness. Leaders pay special attention to fitness when preparing for demanding deployments and for the restoration, sustainment, and enhancement of total health during redeployments.

4.5. Physically fit people feel more competent and confident, handle stress better, work longer and harder, and recover faster. These attributes provide valuable payoffs in any environment.

4.6. Physical fitness and adequate rest support cognitive functioning and emotional stability, both essential for sound leadership. If not physically fit before deployment, the effects of additional stress compromise mental and emotional fitness as well.

4.8. Since leaders' decisions affect their organizations' effectiveness, health, and safety, it is an ethical and practical imperative for leaders to remain healthy and fit. Staying healthy and physically fit protects Soldiers from disease and strengthens them to cope with the psychological effects of extended operations. Leaders and Soldiers need exercise, sufficient sleep, nutritional food, and water to enable peak performance.[2]

Clearly, there's a case for thriving physically that doesn't bow to gluttony and hedonism or to the worship of health and beauty. We need to be strong to serve well, and we cultivate that strength by being wise with how we eat, move, and recover.

---

2 *FM 6-22 Leader Development*, 4,1–4,2.

Eat

Diet is one of those words that seems to make an emotional splash disproportionate to how mundane the word actually is. It just means what you eat. A diet isn't something you go on. It's something you have, and everyone has one. The most troublesome thing about diets is that most people aren't conscious of what theirs is.

They say you are what you eat, and there's some truth to that. We're not plants, so we don't access nutrients by photosynthesis or by standing in the dirt. We're not goats, so we can't just eat anything and trust our digestive systems to sort it out. The human gut, compared to most other creatures, isn't terribly efficient. What we put in our mouths, by and large, becomes our bodies. So, if we want to thrive, we can't eat by accident.

Diet is difficult to discuss, in part because the last twenty years has seen so many diets touted as the solution to all our problems. No carb, low carb, vegan, carnivore, ketogenic, calorie counting, intermittent fasting, and even WWJE—What Would Jesus Eat? None of these agree with the others, and trying to figure it out can leave us with analysis paralysis, or worse, just eating garbage.

Compounding this cacophony of nutritional noise is the human predisposition to tribalism. I heard the term *food tribe* for the first time this fall. It's natural for people to organize themselves around what they care about, and for groups to form in support of mutual preferences that seem to improve their lives. When people organize themselves around particular diets, food tribes form. This is not necessarily a bad thing, but an unfortunate side effect is that particular foods can get labeled *good* or *bad*. When food is moralized this way, we drift perilously close to the kind of religion that both Jesus and Paul decried as dangerous and foolhardy.[3]

My undergraduate degree is in human biology. I've been a martial arts instructor, a high school strength and conditioning coach, a biology teacher, and a lifelong athlete. I've belonged to a food tribe or two and have lived cross-culturally for more than a decade. Most of that time was in a culture where no meal was complete without bread, and no social event happened without a lot of sugar—which pretty much eliminates all food tribes except Santa's elves.

Unless we are only going to relate deeply with others who share our particular food preferences, I've found that we need fewer rules

---

3 Matthew 15:11–20; Colossians 2:21–23.

and more guidelines. Maybe you have your diet dialed in. If not, here are a few rules of thumb that cover about 80 percent of proven dietary guidance.

First, eat real food. Things that grew out of the ground and creatures that ate those things are a good start. You can eat almost all the fruits, vegetables, meat, poultry, and fish you want. Every step of processing that food goes through decreases its nutritional value, and often introduces chemicals or fillers that aren't actually food. Eat the food; skip the processing.

Second, drink water. Lots and lots of water. Numerous surveys have suggested that 75 percent of Americans are chronically dehydrated. I've found water with a few grains of salt (sea salt if you can get it) and some lemon to be a cheap, easy, and incredibly effective hydration solution. Adding more lemon to your water at meals helps prevent the water from diluting your digestive juices. If you drink coffee or tea, drink it black. Don't drink much else.

Third, avoid sugar. It's inflammatory, and it provokes an endocrine response that over time reduces your body's sensitivity to insulin, leading to a range of metabolic diseases. I say avoid and not eliminate because absolutes with food are rarely sustainable unless you have total control of almost every part of your life. I've never had that. I do, however, have a friend who says, "Never drink alone." He only partakes of alcohol when in good company. This is good guidance for sugar as well (and maybe bread and pasta, too). Never eat dessert alone.

There is, of course, so much more that can be said. However, if you follow those three rules of thumb, take a multivitamin and maybe some magnesium, and pay attention to your own food sensitivities, that'll get you most of the way. These are not moral laws, they're guidelines. So while I don't adhere to them perfectly, I try to do so most of the time because I know how my diet affects how well I can serve my neighbor. Diet is not moral, but it is important.

Move

When I was a boy, my sister took me to a tiny local zoo in a battered roadside attraction off Highway 12 in the middle of nowhere, Michigan. These were the days before animal cruelty laws controlled outfits like this. I remember seeing Bobo the bear. He was in a ten-foot-by-ten-foot enclosure made of hurricane fencing. There was a long metal pipe that led from the observation spot into his cage. Next to the pipe was a gumball machine, and for a quarter, you could send a gumball rolling down the pipe to Bobo. I have an image in my mind of this once-magnificent black bear, sitting on a concrete slab in a puddle of waste, glassy-eyed and waiting to die, staring at the end of the gumball pipe. As a culture, we have become Bobo the bear.

We were made to move, and sitting is killing us. Excessive sitting raises the risk of cardiovascular disease, cancer mortality, depression, and increases all-cause mortality by 25 percent.[4] Our sedentary lifestyles are not only inhibiting our ability to thrive—they are actively making us sick.

But, like diet, exercise has somehow become inaccessible because it's not properly taught in schools and it's improperly taught online. There is so much information out there that the quest to learn how to move well usually ends in hours seated in front of a computer trying to figure out what to do. For the people I serve around the world, this paralysis is compounded by external limits like not having a gym in their town, living in an apartment in a crowded city, restrictive rules about what women are allowed to do, and financial constraints. Efforts to overcome these limits have given rise to another set of guidelines for movement.

The first belongs to Dan John, a Fulbright Scholar, religion professor, throwing champion, and legendary strength and conditioning coach. Of all the voices in the storm of opinions that is the internet, when it comes to movement, more people trust Dan John than anyone else. I think it's because he works with high school athletes, geriatric clients recovering from surgery, and all kinds of people in between. He has found what works for just about everyone. "Little and often over the long haul," says Dan.[5]

You're way better off moving vigorously for forty minutes four or five times a week than you are doing something for three hours on a Saturday. If Saturday is all you can do, do it, but doing something frequently at a sustainable intensity over a period of years is the magic anti-aging hack.

The second guideline is that if you're going to stick with something for the long haul, you need to find something you enjoy. Biking, swimming, dancing, a sport, whatever. When I lived in Central Asia, it was aikido three days a week and weights for another two. My friend Cristina walks. Dan bikes for miles, Tim swims, and Tia plays padel. But there's a caveat: when you can't do what you love, or while you're still trying to find it, do what works. Doing nothing is permanently off the table.

---

4 Bahl, "No, Sitting Isn't."
5 John, "Being Reasonable."

What works? Anything works better than nothing unless it leads to injury—but movement skills do have a hierarchy. This is the third rule of thumb: be strong first. You can develop strength with barbells, bodyweight, bottles of water, or bags of sand. The important thing is to develop strength in all movements through their full range of motion.[6] Nothing will increase your likelihood of survival in chaos like becoming stronger. Strength protects you in falls, increases tissue density, hormonally de-ages you, and decreases the likelihood of significant injury and all-cause mortality.

Of course, strength isn't the only thing to consider. Thus, guideline number four: short lifts, long walks, and occasional fun. The hierarchy of skills suggests developing strength first, conditioning and work capacity second, and then everything else. What that translates to in real life is short strength workouts a few times a week, long easy walks (or maybe jogs or rides) a few times a week, and sports when you can. Walking is magic. It's the most human movement in that no other creature God made walks upright. It resets our brains, our spines, and our moods. For significantly overweight people, starting with just walking for forty minutes 3 or 4 times a week has almost instantaneous results.

> Thus, guideline number four: short lifts, long walks, and occasional fun.

For me, these rules translate to barbell lifts and kickboxing twice a week and weighted calisthenics and rucking twice a week. When the weather gets bad, I'll make a new plan for the winter quarter. For some people, the joy of their chosen sport displaces the hierarchy, and their movement practice is just the sport, and that's okay. But eventually strength and conditioning will need to be addressed for progress in the sport to continue unhindered.

Recover

When I deadlift, I recruit my whole body to safely pull a very heavy weight up off the floor. Every Thursday morning, I do this multiple times, and each Thursday I add weight to the barbell, progressively increasing

---

6 John, "Dan John: 5." Dan John identifies six basic loaded movement patterns. Push, Pull, Squat, Hinge, Loaded Carry, and something he calls Sixth Movement, which encompasses the survival-oriented movements like crawling, climbing, and getting on and off the ground safely. A good strength program usually has all six of these movements appearing twice a week or so.

the load by small increments over time. So, every Thursday I am a little stronger than the Thursday before, but I don't get stronger in my garage with that barbell in my hand. I get stronger after I put the barbell down.

You grow when you rest. *Only* when you rest. After I'm done lifting weights, my body begins the process of rebuilding the tissue I broke down during the training. My system will anticipate being faced with that load again, so it will actually rebuild my tissues just a little bit stronger than it thinks they need to be in preparation for future stress. This is how antifragile systems work. You break them just a little, and they get a lot stronger afterward. The vast majority of this recovery happens not only at rest but during sleep. The processes your body uses to heal—from a lift, from a virus, from trauma—are either sleep dependent or sleep related. You heal, grow, and become strong when you rest.

Recovery is more than rest, though. Recovery includes things like improving mobility, so we are less chair-shaped and more able to do the things human bodies were designed by God to do. Recovery also includes recovering from chronic illnesses and disorders as God gives grace. For me, this means regular check-ups, occasional visits to a local osteopath to correct injuries from my sedentary years, and daily stretching.

While recovery includes those practices, nothing replaces sleep. In *Essentialism: The Disciplined Pursuit of Less*, Greg McKeown notes a Harvard study demonstrating that a week of sleeping four hours per night reliably results in impairment equal to a blood alcohol level of 0.1 percent.[7] That's more impairment than drunk driving. Operating a car, a career, a ministry, or a relationship at that level of impairment might be considered negligent. Most people need seven to eight hours of sleep per night. Sleep hygiene is currently *en vogue*. With glasses to eliminate blue light from screens, and apps to whisper us lullabies, you probably know all you need to know about *how* to get more rest. Here, let's instead consider *why* it's so important to us, in particular, as disciples of Jesus and agents of God's grace.

The Evening and the Morning and the Sabbath Day

I discovered Sabbath keeping and proactive rest in an article by Eugene Peterson.[8] Peterson points out that the rhythm set for human flourishing in Genesis 1, which continued to be the Hebrew view of how we live our days, isn't a day/night cycle, but rather, "and there was evening and there

---

7 McKeown, *Essentialism*, 97.
8 Peterson, "Good-for-Nothing Sabbath."

was morning, the first day" (Gen 1:5). In a life with God, night precedes day—rest comes before work. We begin each day by taking ourselves out of commission and rendering ourselves helpless and inert. Hours later we wake up, as Peterson says, to a world we didn't create and a salvation we didn't earn. We join God in the work he joyfully started while we slept and which he will continue once we punch out. In this way, human work is a matter of discernment, discovery, and participation. It is decidedly not initiation, productivity, or manipulation.

With the daily rhythm, we are given a weekly rhythm, as well, along with a command to keep it and keep it holy. The word *sabbath* means *stop*. Not slow, not downshift. Stop. It's not just a state of mind, but a matter of what we do and what we refuse to do with our bodies. The Scriptures tell us that God gives the people of Israel two reasons to keep the Sabbath. The first is that God rested on the seventh day, and when we do likewise we are identifying as his people (Exod 20:8–11)—a people who receive life from him by his grace—and not a people who have to scramble tooth and nail, terrified that if we stop working our world will grind to a halt. The second is that they were slaves in Egypt, so it's critical that when they rest each week, they allow every member of their household, including servants and guests, to rest as well (Deut 5:12–15). In Egypt, the Israelites were units of productivity, not human beings. Now, each week, they insist on their humanness by collectively refusing to be productive for twenty-four hours. Sabbath keeping is a demonstration staged to relentlessly teach us that we are people, not producers.

To be clear, Peterson insists, this practice is not to make us better workers for the other six days. We do not work like slaves for six days and collapse into rest on the seventh, hoping to recuperate the strength we need to slave at it again. Rather, we begin with rest. We join God in his work, discovering our place in the hierarchy of cosmic power (as creatures and not the Creator), and we remember ourselves, who we are without attachment to what we do. And then, at the end of seven days, we return to rest, knowing that when we rest, God still works. We use the practice to continually teach ourselves that it is God, not us, who is saving the world. Sabbath-keeping is a practice given us by God to help us experience him as our God and to help us experience one another and ourselves as people in his image.

Sabbath keeping became, from the day I read that article, an indispensable spiritual discipline for me. In time, my wife picked it up, and it became a cornerstone of our household. When we moved overseas, it became a central practice for our life together as a team. Now, in international leadership, we do not write a new law and insist on this practice, but we do ask our international staff to observe some kind of Sabbath, and our local team protects a twenty-four-hour Sabbath each week. Without it, I would forget that I am saved by grace and not by my works. I would be overwhelmed by the needs of the world and of those I love because my body would not be often enough teaching me that I am not God.

But how does this long aside into biblical exposition on Sabbath fit into a discussion of recovery and physical thriving? Because of how people learn. Before I moved to Central Asia, I thought the order of engagement for human change was *explain, express, experience*. I went to seminary and studied my Bible and could explain the Jesus way with incredible accuracy and panache. Occasionally, a worship song or an opportunity to share testimony allowed me to express a fraction of what I could explain, but I could connect with it so much more deeply than my Bible knowledge had allowed. Rarely, I'd experience a sliver of what I could express which was a fraction of what I could explain. This, however, is not really how people learn or change.

> Our spiritual and physical thriving are never more entwined than when we use our bodies to rest our whole selves in God.

Instead, it goes *experience, express, explain*. We only really learn and only really believe what we experience. When we experience it often enough, we begin to be able, quite spontaneously, to give it some language—to express it. When we reflect on the experiences, and on the expressions, in time we come to find ourselves able to explain what was happening in the process. For example, after twenty years of experiencing Sabbath weekly, and expressing to those who live in my circle its value and its effect, I can finally explain why I need it, and why I think we all need it to live embodied spiritual lives with God. It's in having this order backwards that believers who preach grace practice workaholism. We talk about rest we have rarely ever entered and certainly don't know how to sustain.

Our spiritual and physical thriving are never more entwined than when we use our bodies to rest our whole selves in God.

Lead Measures and Lag Measures

A word here about what is helpful to measure as we consider whether we are making progress toward physical thriving or in any intentional venture where the outcomes and the inputs are separated by time. There are two kinds of measurements to pay attention to: lead measures and lag measures.

Lead measures predict outcomes. They're behaviors that predict what will likely happen. More safety glasses worn on a worksite predict fewer eye injuries at that site. In this case, wearing safety glasses is the input, the thing you can control. The number of eye injuries is the lag measure, the outcome, the part you can't directly control but which amounts to the bottom line.

Lead measures for physically thriving include what you actually eat and drink, how often and how well you move your body, how much sleep you get, and the rest you protect. These practices are your lead measures. They predict likely outcomes. Lead measures should be noted at least weekly.

The outcomes in your body are the lag measures. These should be noted monthly or less. Why? Because it takes time to change tissue. But what are the changes we're watching for? What, exactly, are the lag measures we should focus on? I suggest lag measures for physical thriving include capacities, composition, and contentment.

The most important lag measure for physical thriving is how your capacities change. What are you able to do now that you couldn't do last month? You want to be able to lift more, run faster, walk farther, bend deeper, play harder, whatever. If you're getting better, your lead measures are working. If not, reconsider them.

The second lag measure is composition—what is your body actually composed of? It's important to note that, with a few exceptions, how much your body weighs is a meaningless measurement. What's more important is how much of your body is adipose tissue or inflammation, and how much is lean muscle, bone, and organs. Think in inches, not pounds. According to the Body Mass Index on the wall in my doctor's office, my weight suggests I'm obese. But I'm not. I strength train a lot, and carry a lot of youth-preserving, disease-fighting, metabolically active muscle on my frame. Losing pounds for me would be going backwards. What matters is where the weight is. Abdominal fat is especially bad for you.

Waist circumference is a reliable clue to your relative risk of Type 2 diabetes, high blood pressure, high cholesterol, and heart disease.[9] The recommended measurement is less than forty inches for men, and less than thirty-five inches for women. An athletic man would aim to keep his waist in inches equal to half his height.

Finally, contentment, or how you feel, is the last lag measure. Notice if you feel vibrant or run down, supple or stiff in the joints, upright or crunched over. How much wellbeing do you feel in your physical frame? Some of us have debilitating diseases, injuries that healed such that we will never regain full function or any function at all. But month to month, is it getting better or worse? And how fast?

Those lag measures are what you consider when you do your monthly 5DVector Check. At the beginning of each week, you plan your lead measures. At the end of each week, you notice if you executed on them. But each month, you're measuring if what you're doing works, and if it's taking you in the direction you want to go.[10]

---

9   Khatri, "Measure Your Waist."

10 Or, in case of advanced age or degenerative disease, how effective are your lead measures proving for slowing decline?

4

Cognitive

Learn, Focus, Play

In this chapter we'll:

- Explore the power of worship, wonder, and wisdom as we LEARN
- Consider the necessity and function of FOCUS and abstention
- Understand the essentialness of PLAY in cognitive wellbeing

Survival and Vibrancy

A month after the Covid-19 lockdowns started in the US, Clark got word that his father's cancer had come back in force. Three months later, Clark and his family were on a plane from Europe back to the US to be with his dad before he died just three weeks later. Three months after that, Clark and his family were finally able to get back into the country where they live.

Clark led a team in the midst of significant transition, in a country reeling from high Covid death counts and economic crisis during a pandemic. Clark was significantly diminished as were the people he leads. One day, we were talking and he said, "Yeah, um. I, uh … I'm shot."

This presentation is always worrisome especially when nothing external is likely to get better any time soon. But what Clark said next alleviated my concern somewhat.

"I get up, and I don't want to do anything. I have, like, no emotional motivation to work. I can't concentrate. Grief brain. But I'm doing two things I know to do. I spend some time with Jesus every day. I can do that. And I exercise. That doesn't take any focus, and I know it has to be a good choice."

Unassisted, that was the extent of Clark's capacity for self-leadership at the time, but that's okay. It is a starting point. All five dimensions of soul are important to cultivate. Later, we'll talk about when the wheels come off of life and you have to adjust for suffering. In those cases, sometimes a trimmed-down, field-expedient Thrive Plan is appropriate. But for now, let's just notice that Clark's instincts, the Spirit of God in him, or both, have led him to the two dimensions we must secure to survive. We need our daily bread (physical), but we do not live on bread alone (spiritual). The other three dimensions—the cognitive, emotional, and relational—are not less important, but they are built upon the first two. If spiritual and physical vitality support *survival*, vitality in the other three produces *vibrancy*.

Thriving Cognitively: Learn, Focus, Play

Recent social trends in the West have demonstrated what happens when people don't maintain and cultivate their ability to think. General inability to consider multiple sides of an issue and an utter dependence on social media to learn our opinions, combined with the echo-chamber of algorithms designed to keep us hooked on canned ideas, have conspired to engender a profoundly uninformed and unthinking population who are drowning in a sea of information. It's a grotesque and catastrophic irony.

> If spiritual and physical vitality support survival, vitality in the other three produces *vibrancy*.

Most of us don't need to be brilliant, but we all need to be clear-headed. Our transformation as believers happens as the tracks of our thoughts are re-laid (Rom 12:2). A sound, disciplined, and well-ordered mind is part of what God makes available to us through the Spirit (2 Tim 1:7). However, if we are to love our God with all our minds, as we are commanded, and if we are to apply ourselves intelligently to the transformation of the world, we must learn to cultivate our minds. An insightful, useful, quiet mind is nurtured as we learn, focus, and play.

Learn

Bill Gates reads fifty books a year, as do numerous other CEOs and global leaders. The TED Talk phenomenon has made complex and fascinating ideas accessible to almost anyone with eighteen minutes to spare. My friend Jillann listens to a book a week; my friend Cris pursues continuing education credits; my wife consumes nature documentaries, and my buddy Pete reads theology and Church history for fun. They are increasing the vitality of their minds by broadening their view of the cosmos and its Creator.

In the information age and beyond, the question isn't where to find things to learn, but how to aim our learning in ways that make us sharper and more awake. This kind of learning consists of worship, wonder, and wisdom.

Worship

Psalm 119 was probably composed by Levites charged with the cultivation of Hebrew young adults. It's an acrostic which suggests order over chaos with each set of eight verses beginning with a letter of the Hebrew alphabet. There are other acrostic psalms, but this one is unique in that the entire Hebrew alphabet appears showing both order and completeness. The subject of the psalm is how life with God is facilitated by life with his written word, the Scriptures. Thus, a whole life, a full life, and a well-ordered life, is a life with God that is scaffolded by a rather intense engagement with the Scriptures.

> In the information age and beyond, the question isn't where to find things to learn, but how to aim our learning in ways that make us sharper and more awake.

The second set, verses 9–16, demonstrates this beautifully. These eight verses form an *inclusio*—a literary device whereby the central idea and interpretive lens for the content in the middle appears at the very beginning and the very end. In this case, the idea is paying steady attention to God's words. In English it is rendered, "By guarding it according to your word," (v. 9) and, "I will not forget your word" (v. 16). In Hebrew it's a little easier to see—essentially, "By paying attention to it and to your word," and, "I will not fail to pay attention to your word." Thus, these eight verses can be expected to develop the notion of what a life is like in which the mind is trained on God's words.

Directing the mind like this leads to purity of life: the whole-hearted, unfractured pursuit of God, and an unwavering path in a chaotic world (vv. 9–10). The psalmist internalizes God's words and protects his relationship with him to such a degree that his lips have begun to spontaneously utter the rules of God's mouth (vv. 11, 13). This poetic structure suggests that by internalizing the words of God, the thoughts and character of God have begun to soak into the psalmist, and this internalization wasn't just duty, but delight. It has become the psalmist's joy to internalize, incarnate, and express God's words and ways (v. 14).

The psalm ends with two "I will" statements set against the "I will not fail to attend" that closes the inclusio. "I will meditate [hold steadily before my attention in unhurried reflection] on your precepts and fix my attention on your ways" (v. 15) and, "I will delight in your statutes" (v. 16). These are acts of will—choices about what the psalmist will do with his limited and precious attention. As with many inclusios, this one has a central assertion, like a tent pole in the middle that the psalm builds toward and resolves from. This idea is found in verse 12: "Blessed are you, O LORD; teach me your statutes!" A statement of unprovoked, explosive worship paired with a desire that the psalmist's investment of attention be met with teaching. For the writer of Psalm 119, a life where obedience is a delight and not just a duty, with God's own thoughts in your mind, is a life of steady, focused attention on God's words. A life of *learning worship*.

This pairing of worship and attention isn't unique to the Psalms. Paul draws similar connections. In Colossians 3 we're told to set our attention and affections on Christ in a passage parallel to his assertion in Ephesians that we "learned Christ" (Eph 4:20). To the Romans he says that we're transformed by the renewing of our minds, and that this cognitive renewal is part of our spiritual worship (Rom 12:1–2). In contrast, Paul says of people who refuse to worship God, that since they did not like to retain God in their knowledge, God gave them up to minds that therefore could not work (Rom 1:28).

As persons formed in the image of our Creator, our minds were made to consider mystery and our finite brains to hold the edges of infinity. Nothing makes us more ourselves than considering God. Worship, and the things we learn to provoke it, is what our minds are for.

Wonder

Two months before we moved to Spain, we lost half our funding in a day. It was a rough day. Once we got to Spain, my wife faced debilitating anxiety. Our kids started a new school in a totally different educational system a continent away from all their friends, and we moved into a huge house with our entire team. Those early months in Spain had me managing *a lot*. I quickly developed a craving to think about something else.

I started learning about astrophysics. It first caught my attention through a YouTube video that found its way into my feed. Next came TED Talks, lectures—whatever I could get my hands on. Higgs boson fields, dark matter, dark energy, gravity as a function of time, all of it. If you want to feel like you and your problems are small, try contemplating the cosmos. I'm not sure why it was astrophysics for me, but it wasn't a problem I was working on or something I had to manage. It was fascinating, and it cultivated wonder.

Psalm 104 reads like that. Another inclusio, this psalm opens and closes with "Bless the LORD, O my soul" (vv. 1 and 35). It is a call to the speaker's entire being to worship and celebrate God. What is it that inspires this effusive praise? It's something like what I felt when I read about dark matter.

The psalm vividly depicts the created cosmos—the moon and the mountains, the earth, sky, and sea, from lions to leviathans, wine to waterfalls. God has made it all, and the psalm depicts God and humankind as inhabitants of this ecology of benevolence. Both psalmist and God rejoice in what God has made where wonder gives way to worship and wild delight in a cosmos too vast to contain.

It's not cosmology alone, but curiosity that ignites wonder. We are made for wonder. To investigate. To follow our inklings. The world is wide and wonderful. What are you curious about these days?

If you've always wondered how different trees get their shape, go find out. Perhaps you find culture facinating. Good! Get a book, make a friend, watch a lecture. If there's anything you've always wanted to know more about, what's stopping you?

Follow your curiosity; let it open you up and widen your view.

Wisdom

Wisdom, it seems, comes from three places: directly from God, reflection on experience, and observation of the world around us. We can ask for the first and work on the second, but the readiest source of wisdom is to simply look around and pay attention. One function of learning is learning how the world works.

The Proverbs reverberate with this command. Get wisdom. Get understanding. Above all else, get wisdom and understanding. How? Listen. Watch. Consider. Remember. Pursue.

As we open our minds to God and let wonder expose us to more of the world he made, wisdom enables us to begin to discern connections, patterns, the warp and woof of reality. We will learn the rules, and we will learn what to do when the rules don't seem to apply. We will grow, not just informed or educated, but wise.

Worship, wonder, and wisdom. As we cultivate the practice of learning this way, we come to use our minds and to see God in the world. We begin to see the world with God as he sees it.

Focus

Learning is one of my strengths. It has a downside.

When the Covid-19 outbreak in China first happened, my supervisor was the vice president of global strategy and operations. He was going on sabbatical which meant that by the time the Covid numbers in Italy had become scary, I was effectively the vice president of global strategy and operations. I was responsible for hundreds of field staff scattered all over the world as travel bans started springing up with no warning and lockdowns started. My full-time job became trying to figure out what was most likely to happen next, which meant a lot of learning. Three weeks in, Spain was in hard lockdown. One adult in my house could walk our dog for twenty minutes once a day, and apart from that it was the six of us on top of one another for months.

Once the initial travel chaos had settled and we had people mostly where they belonged, the conversations about likely economic collapse began. For our organization to forecast and prepare, we needed to have some idea how long restrictions might hold. More learning.

By the time we had developed a plan to face the economic turmoil, George Floyd died in police custody. The Black Lives Matter protests followed and riots came next. My kids and my community wanted some guidance on what to say, what to do, what to think, how to process the moment. More learning.

Even before racial justice issues exploded all over the US, I was flash blinded. I had held my eyes open to torrents of information with little break for too long (apart from a rigid weekly Sabbath that probably saved me). My mind was starting to show the signs. My attention span was short, and I was constantly hungry for more data. When I wasn't actively thinking about something else, when my mind was in neutral, it swerved immediately to Covid or to issues of race and political theory. The learning was good, and it positioned me to help, but it was too much without check or governance, and it became the background noise in what used to be a quiet mind.

I took notice of the internal noise and set some limits on when I would learn, how often, etc., and my mind calmed. That lasted until September 2020, when I fell into the rabbit hole of American election politics. It became difficult to think or talk about anything but Covid-19 or the 2020 US Presidential Election. I recognized it again and reinstituted some focus practices to help me remain master of my mind.

You may not struggle with the news. Maybe it's work emails, or like many caring people who love deeply, it's the constant streams of pain or need expressed on social media from a thousand "friends" that you can't really help.

Focus practices are the abstentions of cognitive exercise—the way of negation, of refusal, of removal. Focus practices help you by eliminating the unnecessary or unhelpful. You decide what things you will not give attention to this quarter, either because you can't stand to do it, or you can't do anything to change it. Similarly, you can decide when you won't think about certain things, like the news, email, or your to-do list. For example, stopping social media an hour before bed and not picking it up again until an hour after your morning prayers can limit the effect of being connected all the time.

The difference between a quiet, poised, insightful mind and the frenetic mind of an anxious, wired internet monkey is the difference between knowing how to focus and actually choosing practices to protect your ability to focus. Focus practices help you steward your most precious power, your attention. Your ability to pay attention and to think clearly from a quiet and open mind is crucial to your cognitive health. You can protect that ability by deciding that you won't give your focus away or let it be captured.

Play

Play is essential to humanness. All focus and no fun makes you dead. Other creatures play, and most do it better than we do. Otters, for example, or this camel I once saw play soccer with a yoga ball. Play isn't unique to humanity, but we are perhaps never more human, more unselfconsciously ourselves than when we are at play.

In my house and in our community, we play board games, card games, word games, and sports. And occasionally tag. When we play, we are joyful together, with one another apart from our burdens, even if for just a moment. How can we weep together if we've never laughed together?

My wife and I developed a habit of playing a game together every Sabbath. Sabbath is for praying and playing,[1] and we do both. We play with the kids, too, but we always get at least one game in, just her and I.

---

1 Peterson, "Good-for-Nothing Sabbath."

In anxious days I think it's a way we protect one another from falling down the hole of our own worried thinking. In happy days, it's just pure fun.

Play, like Sabbath, is intentionally unproductive. It doesn't go anywhere or do anything. It's precisely for that reason that it's so essential to our mental health. We come to ourselves when we play and remember that we are who we are, not what we do. It's critical to lay our burdens down regularly, and to not only remember but also to act like we're not the center of the universe. When we play, we use our minds to stop taking ourselves so seriously, and it helps us receive ourselves and each other as gifts.

5

Emotional

Notice, Interview, Manage

In this chapter we'll:

- Learn to NOTICE our emotions without judgement or excuse as a primary source of intelligence
- Consider how to INTERVIEW our emotions for what they can tell us about our desires so they can become assets in our discipleship
- Explore means to MANAGE our emotions to fit our circumstances

Your emotions never lie.

Twenty years ago, I might have excommunicated myself for that statement. I grew up in a theological tradition that believed somehow that original sin had made liars of our hearts but had left our heads untouched. Reason and logic could be trusted, and we never bent those to our twisted wills, but our emotions always lied, and emotion itself was a sign of weakness. Emotions corrupted the system. We manipulated emotions with altar calls and quivering voices while our consciously held beliefs kept us terrified of them.

> Your emotions are always 100 percent accurate regarding how you are experiencing yourself, the world, and God.

But your emotions are a deep and penetrating intelligence whose designer and maker is God himself. Your emotions are always 100 percent accurate regarding how you are experiencing yourself, the world, and God. However, they are not necessarily accurately describing you, the world, or God. Your emotions are simply telling you the truth about how you actually see things. Granted, it is not wise to obey your emotions (my tradition had that part right), but neither is it wise to deny or ignore them.

If we are to make progress with Jesus in the healing of our own souls and the healing of the world—sanctification and mission—we have to become braver and more competent when it comes to our hearts. In fact, the Apostle Paul would contend that both sanctification and mission hinge on this very thing.

In Ephesians, Paul describes in detail something he prays for the letter's recipients, which includes us. Paul seems to pray a lot, but when he tells us what he prays he appears to have two things in mind. First, he's letting us know what he's requested from God, so we can watch for it almost like you would a package that you know is coming. Second, because God has designed the cosmos to include human will, sometimes the things Paul asks God to do for us and in us require our agreement and even sometimes our participation. Paul tells us what he's prayed for, so we can watch for it and reach for it. Paul's prayer in Ephesians 3:14–19 is as follows:

> For this reason I bow my knees before the Father, from whom every family in heaven and on earth is named, that according to the riches of his glory he may grant you to be strengthened with power through his Spirit in your inner being, so that Christ may dwell in your hearts through faith—that you, being rooted and grounded in love, may have strength to comprehend with all the saints what is the breadth and length and height and depth, and to know the love of Christ that surpasses knowledge, that you may be filled with all the fullness of God.

This prayer is a series of *that's* and *so that's*, a cascade of provisions and consequent possibilities. When dealing with cascades of causation, it's best to start at the bottom and work your way back to the top.

Paul's ultimate aim is that we "may be filled with all the fullness of God" (v. 19)—God suffusing every corner of our beings. It has always been Paul's plan (and God's, for that matter) to have a people so uniquely God's, so steeped in his essence and character, his goodness and his power, grace and truth, that to experience God's people was to experience God.

This is not where most of us live. So how do we get there? We go up the cascade. To be God-soaked people in the world, we will have to experience the love of Jesus in ways that outstrip our ability to explain or even express.

Paul's desire is that we know (*gnosis* in the Greek—experiential knowing) what it's like to feel the tremendous love of Christ for us in all its height and depth and breadth and fullness. This knowing is more than emotion, but it does include emotion. This knowing is to be done by all the saints and with all the saints. We need one another to be able to experience love beyond where our minds can carry us. We are each already rooted and grounded in love, but there is a vast and undiscovered country whose edges we'll never find and whose depth we'll never fathom.

How are we to know such a love? To experience the love of Christ in all its amplitude, we will have to know him in our hearts, in all our cellars, closets, and corridors. The phrase is, "that Christ may dwell in your hearts through faith" (v. 17). This is the first *that* in the cascade, the linchpin in the system. Since Paul is writing to Christians, he can't be speaking of the initial moment when Christ comes to live within the believer at conversion. So what is he speaking of? Whatever it is, it's got to be very, very hard work because Paul prays that through his Spirit, God will give us strength deep in our cores equal to the effulgence of his own beauty and power. That's a lot of backup, and for us to need that much strength, dwelling with Christ in our hearts must be quite a job.

This is no surprise. Anyone with any self-awareness knows that our hearts are complex places full of twisting passages and blind alleys, locked rooms and shadowed corridors. No one gets through childhood unscathed. Our sins, the sins of others against us, and the sin that permeates human society wound us in particular places, and we wall up those parts of our hearts. We lock them tight against being seen, being known, and being hurt again. But we will never be God-soaked where God isn't welcome. Christ can bring no light to the room we keep shut, and no healing to the wounds we won't suffer to be uncovered. Nor can he unleash the gifts locked in those rooms or the powers we have never known ourselves to have, unless we let him dwell in those rooms with us. It is as we let him hold residence as king in the whole of our hearts, that our whole hearts can carry the fullness of God to the ends of the earth.

This level of surrender takes faith. "That Christ may dwell in your hearts through faith" (v. 17). As Jesus slowly, patiently moves into more and more of our hearts, it takes faith to keep saying yes. The New Testament word for faith is *pistis*, and it refers not primarily to cognitive assent to confessed beliefs but rather to trust and loyalty. It is always oriented around a person rather than a proposition. Christ takes up residence in more and more rooms and cellars in our hearts as we keep choosing to trust him when he knocks on the locked doors and as we keep choosing loyalty to our king over self-protection and self-deception.

This is hard work. It requires outside power flushed into the deepest parts of us, down below the wounds and masks. There, we can draw upon that power to cooperate with Jesus as he un-haunts our hearts. This is what Paul was inspired by the Spirit to pray. This is God's intention for you, and for the world. To receive this kind of whole-heartedness, we need facility with the Scriptures, of course, but we also need facility with our emotions. This kind of fluency is nurtured as we notice, interview, and manage our feelings.

Notice

The first step toward emotional thriving is learning to notice our emotions. We want to observe without judgement or excuse. The question is *What do you feel?* not *How are you feeling?* or *Why are you feeling that way?*

How is a question that tends to elicit answers like good, bad, fine, okay, etc. None of those are feelings. So, in answering that question, you're only noticing if what you're feeling is alarming you or not. Decoding *why* we're feeling what we're feeling is above most of our pay grades. The human heart is complex, and there are hidden currents under the surface that lead to the emotions we notice. Noticing isn't analysis; it's just paying attention.

But noticing goes a long way. Secondary emotions like general anxiety and background anger are usually dashboard lights—indicators that you're actually experiencing other emotions you're not paying attention to. You can go looking for why you're anxious and never find the cause because often the anxiety is just your brainstem insisting that your cognitive mind please take note that you are having other emotions. However, once you've noticed the actual emotion, much of the anxiety fades away. Your feelings are designed to help you live your life wholeheartedly, so when they get their message across, they often stop shouting.

My team recently organized a conference for disciple-makers scattered all over the world. They work in some tough places that need communities filled up with all the fullness of God. Part of each day was given to professional care from a team of counselors, coaches, spiritual directors, and the like. At the end of the week, the care team reported that a trend across our people was low emotional vocabulary, and the best thing we could do for them would be to increase their ability to recognize and name their emotions.

Enter the emotions wheel. An internet search will provide you with twenty different options, but they're all basically the same. Usually listed near the center of the wheel are some basic emotions like fear, anger, joy, shame, etc. Further out toward the rim are some more nuanced variations of these. In the fear wedge you might find nervousness and worry. Joy might be subdivided into elation, contentment, etc., and anger into irritability, frustration, and rage. You can start by holding the feeling you're having in your heart. Look at the wheel, find your way from the general to the specific emotion that seems most like what you're feeling, and name it to yourself, to your friend, and to God. Likewise, you can start with the specific emotion you know you're experiencing and work back toward the center, so you can be a little more honest with yourself. For example, you're not just irate; you're angry. Or perhaps that gentle feeling of contentment can let you know you're actually happy for the first time in a while. The wheel, like any good tool, makes a hard job easier by putting some leverage in your hands.

For example, a few months ago my wife noted that I seemed irritable, and had seemed so for some time. She asked would I, perhaps, like to cut it out. I recognized what she had noticed, but *irritable* didn't quite capture it. I've long been friends with my emotions wheel, so it didn't take long to recall that irritability is in the anger family. What other flavor of anger might it be? Within ten seconds I realized that I was feeling *frustrated*—that my desire to do good was being blocked, hamstrung or opposed in literally every direction. Noticing and naming it properly didn't solve the problem, but since it was named it didn't need to shout anymore, and it stopped leaking all over my kids and other innocent bystanders. I could, in fact, cut it out.

We sent this simple tool around to our people and incredible things started happening. Anxiety levels dropped. People found themselves suddenly able to make themselves understood, and much less likely to resent their teammates for not understanding them. Vulnerability, while remaining risky, was no longer a blind leap in the dark. Best of all, many became better disciples of Jesus.

Interview

When we interview our emotions, we are doing just that, asking them questions. We're not conducting an interrogation, trying to get to the bottom of it, or relentlessly investigating until we solve our feelings. It's an interview, and again the question isn't *Why?* but rather *What else?* What else can this feeling tell me about myself and how I'm experiencing my situation, and what can it tell me about what I want?

In the Gospels the question Jesus asks more than any other is *What do you want?* Knowing what we want—no matter if it's good, bad, or indifferent—is an essential part of following our Master as he shepherds not only our actions, but our desires as well. Our emotions are primary clues to what we want, and they give us our most honest windows into our desires as we seek to answer our Teacher's question.

When I get or have something I want, I am happy. When I don't, I am sad. When I'm grieving, I've lost something I want, and when I'm afraid, it might be because I anticipate its loss. When I'm jealous, someone else has something I want. When I feel I shouldn't want something I do want, I feel shame, and when I'm angry, it could be because someone or something won't let me get what I want.

> Knowing what we want—no matter if it's good, bad, or indifferent—is an essential part of following our Master as he shepherds not only our actions, but our desires as well.

Of course, each of these emotions could have other reasons behind them, or at least complicating factors. Nevertheless, following an emotion back to a potential desire at least allows you to raise the question, what deep desires might be undergirding or giving rise to this emotion? This isn't quick work, and we rush it at our peril. Like tearing weeds up but leaving the roots, in our panic to create distance between ourselves and the emotions we're not proud of, we put off the old man with haste and disgust (Eph 4:22). Instead, we need relentless understanding and patience. Surely, envy must be put away, but before we fling it from our sight in hopes no one else notices our jealousy, it serves us to notice what it is the other person has that we want. Envy is sinful; desire itself may not be. Similarly, the wrath of man does not work the righteousness of God, but a man's good desires thwarted can give rise to that anger.

Take my aforementioned frustration as an example. On a Wednesday after midday prayer, I sat at my desk and asked the question, "If frustration is the anger you feel when someone or something is preventing your action, what else can the frustration I'm feeling right now tell me about what I want?" I sat with my frustration as hospitably as I could—no poking or prodding, no insisting it leave—and slowly I became aware that I wasn't feeling actively opposed, but rather like others' decisions, knowingly or not, they were putting me in positions where I couldn't do the good I wanted to do. This nuance was key, as it led me to answer Jesus's question, "Jesus, I feel poorly positioned to do the good in my heart. I do not know for certain that what I want to do is what you want me to do, so can you help me clarify that? And if these desires have come from you, as I think they have, what might I do to improve my position to act on them, and what should I leave to you?"

These questions weren't all answered. I'm still living some of them, but I'm living them consciously with Jesus, and they are providing the vividness and creative tension I need to discern my way forward. Noticing and interviewing my emotions facilitated a heart-level conversation with God which provided a discernment window as I continue to follow Jesus.

Sometimes our emotions are a little more unruly and present themselves at inopportune times and at inappropriate volumes. They flood us and demand attention. In other cases, the opposite happens, our emotions seem hard to access, and we go numb. Flooding and numbness can both be frightening, but neither is helpful. So we must learn to manage our emotions.

Manage

We can't control our emotions directly. When we try, the best we can do amounts to suppression with a little self-deception to cover our tracks. But while we can't control them, we're not completely at their mercy either. Mastery of our emotions is a matter of management not muting. Management is best done indirectly, and unsurprisingly, through the other five dimensions of our souls. We can manage our emotions with our spirits, our bodies, our connections to others, and with our minds.

As followers of Jesus, we are indwelt with the Holy Spirit. As clean as Western Christians like to keep our Trinitarian theology, Paul was a little freer with mystery, going so far as to say, "The Lord [Jesus] is the Spirit" (2 Cor 3:17), and "Thus it is written, 'The first man Adam became a living being'; the last Adam became a life-giving spirit" (1 Cor 15:45). Without spinning off into modalism, we can safely say that all that Christ somehow resides within us. Ergo, "in [Christ] the whole fullness of deity dwells bodily, and you have been filled in him" (Col 2:9–10).

Put another way, we have someone else dwelling inside us, and he has his own emotions he can bring to our experience. When I am feeling something about a situation, he is feeling something about that situation too. Because of my relationship with him in my heart, I can access his feelings as well as my own as I turn to him in submission and trust. I find it best to keep this simple, praying, "Jesus, I'm feeling x about this. What are you feeling?"

I also find this is most helpful in managing my emotions when I pair it with a physical strategy. Slowing my breathing, paying attention to inhaling and exhaling from my diaphragm, and sometimes even counting the breaths. As cliché as, "Take a deep breath and count to ten" has become, it does work. When there is no lag between the feeling and the outward reaction to the situation that gave rise to that feeling, there's no room to manage it. Breathing gives time, but it also physically instructs your system to relax a little, and to downshift out of heightened alert.

We can also make use of our relationships to regulate our emotions. When we see something big happen—say, a car jumps the curb and crashes into a sidewalk café—we subconsciously gather data from two sources. First, we look where the noise and chaos is coming from to see if we are in immediate danger. Then we look at one another to see how big a deal this is. We get that data from one another's faces, and sometimes from the tone of voice people are speaking in. This is what undergirds both phenomena like mass hysteria and daily encounters like a parent speaking in a soothing voice when a child falls off her bike. We are accessing a social system within us for regulating intensity of emotion. So, when I'm in a meeting and I'm finding the train of the conversation increasingly infuriating, I can look around the room and see if I can read what others are feeling. If they're calm, collected, and unperturbed, my anger may not be erased, but the cue from others will help me disconnect from the emotion enough to consider the possibility that I brought something into the conversation that's impacting my experience. I can then effectively downregulate the anger and decrease its power to directly control what I say or do next.

While we can't think our way into different emotions, we can use our minds to regulate their insistence and create reasonable doubt concerning what they're telling us. Social scientist Joseph Grenny has demonstrated that feelings don't emerge immediately from a stimulus or activating event, but rather from the often unconscious narratives our minds create to make sense of or interpret the stimulus. Something happens (my normally compliant kid directly disobeys), and in the blink of an eye my mind writes a story to make sense of what I'm seeing (my kid is being willful and disrespectful on purpose). Then I experience emotions (anger, hurt) not about what the kid is doing, but about the story I wrote about what she was doing.[1]

But what if she didn't hear me? What if she had received contradictory instructions from her mom moments before? What if she heard me, but because she's eight and lives in her own little world of unicorns and pixies, it didn't even register? In any of those situations, I'd have different feelings. So, the feelings aren't about what she's doing, but about the narrative her actions live in—the narrative I write.

I can manage that emotion not by denying I had it, or by beating myself up for it, but by simply noticing the narrative I wrote and choosing to entertain the possibility that there are other stories that could make just as much sense, if not more. I'm thinking my way, not to a different emotion, but to a more generous story. The emotion follows naturally.

None of these strategies are aimed at stuffing, denying or silencing emotions. Your feelings are an incomplete but deep and powerful intelligence. They always tell you the truth about how you are experiencing yourself, the world, and God. Even if they wind up being wrong about any or all of those things, they're one hundred percent accurate about how you're perceiving them, and this intelligence about your perception is invaluable.

Trying to change your feelings directly is impossible, trying to silence them is to throw a gift back in God's face, and trying to wrangle them into something you're more comfortable with amounts to insisting your internal advisors tell you only what you want to hear. Rather than any of these approaches, managing our emotions is a matter of retaining control of the ship while we listen to our advisors and keep command of the captain's table. We do not master our feelings by silencing them but by listening for what wisdom they can bring us.

---

1 Grenny, *Crucial Conversations*.

6

Relational

Discern, Invest, Grow

In this chapter we'll:

- Explore how to DISCERN which of our many relationships should be primary in a given quarter
- Think about how we want to INVEST in those relationships in ways that match our design
- Consider which relational skills we most want to GROW that will help us make our best investment in those key relationships

Many of the people I serve are working in cultural contexts foreign to where their worldviews and systems of communication were formed. As a result, emotional intelligence and spiritual maturity are not enough to cross the distance and help them root in novel contexts. If they're to thrive where they are, they'll need a more robust suite of relational skills than most, and they'll need to attend to the vibrancy of those connections to their new homes.

To a lesser degree, this holds true as well when people come from very different family systems and are trying to make a go of a marriage or a team. Routinely landing in the top four reasons workers leave the mission field early are marital strife and unresolved team conflict. Creating understanding is hard. Creating community is harder, still. Wear and tear here can become catastrophic if we don't give this part of our souls adequate attention.

This has always been easier for our colleagues from more collective cultures to embrace. They know that relationships often determine individual outcomes. How I am relating to you is part of who I am, and I must steward that part of me like I steward all the other parts of my soul. But we can't steward all our relationships equally, especially now that virtual relationships have left us more connected and lonelier than ever.

Discern

A few years ago I had a brush with burnout. I wasn't working too much; I was enjoying what I was doing, and my co-workers were easy enough to get along with. I was exercising four days a week, regularly checking in with my emotions, being careful to play and to rest, and I was enjoying my relationship with God. So where did the burnout come from?

My role within the organization had changed. I had moved, during the early days of Covid-19, from a clearly defined set of relationships to a vague set of responsibilities and little sense of to whom or for whom I was responsible. This would have been okay for a little while, and in all honesty, I enjoy less defined assignments as they give me more room to innovate. But this went on for a few months, and the burnout snuck up on me. No one's fault, but in the absence of a clear external rubric—something outside of myself that helps me decide whose needs are top priority—everyone's needs became top priority. The inability to discern which relationships were most important in the moment left me unable to invest meaningfully in any of them.

> A good plan to thrive relationally will include an intelligent, purposeful way to discern which relationships are most important for you to attend to right now.

Would this have gone differently in some other, non-Covid year? Maybe. But what I learned was that even if you have the rest of your vectors pretty dialed in, you can't transformatively love everyone all the time. You need a way to prioritize regardless of how much chaos is in the system.

A good plan to thrive relationally will include an intelligent, purposeful way to discern which relationships are most important for you to attend to right now. Life happens in seasons, and nothing is in bloom all the time. While there will be a few relationships (family, closest friends, team) that will always take priority over others, even within that circle, some relationships will need more from you than others to keep being healthy. One kid needs more time this fall than another. This summer it would be good to invest extra energy in your marriage. Your friend at work has shown little interest in the gospel or in you, but another coworker has been curious about your practice of prayer or your references to Jesus.

That you intentionally try to discern is more important than how you discern, but how still matters. Household relationships should always take priority. No one dies wishing they had missed more of their kids' lives or had paid less attention to their spouse. There needs to be some way to account for the fact that some relationships are almost entirely virtual, and therefore usually less real. Social media can make you privy to a million sorrows you can't help with, and you need a way to determine how much of that you'll carry because your relationships with the people you actually live with pay the bill.

Listening prayer is a critical discipline for this—ask God directly, perhaps every quarter, which relationships he'd like you to pull to the fore (knowing that others will therefore recede for a while), and then sit quietly to see who or what comes to mind. Of course, there's room for numerous other voices and desires to make themselves heard in that silence, but there's also room for the Shepherd to speak.

In tandem with listening prayer, I've found collective discernment to be invaluable. I'll ask my core community to listen with me, or I'll bring them my thoughts about where I feel invited by Jesus to lean in, and I'll let them ask questions, challenge, or give additional thoughts to consider. I'll take that back to Jesus and have another conversation while holding those thoughts or challenges up to him to see what I see. Then I will make a not-final kind of final decision about how I'll focus my relational energy that quarter.

There are, of course, other discernment windows I could look through, and the Spirit always has room to change things as time unfolds. But having a practice of intentionality regarding how I'll prioritize my relationships keeps me from simply putting out fires, following the loudest voices, or being paralyzed by all the needs around me.

Invest

The happiest people in the world have a few things in common, one of them being they are investing in the relationships most important to them.[1] We are made for generous community, made to be together and made to love one another. Our souls thrive as we give to those most important to us.

What do we give? What are the currencies of investment? Time is one. Quality time, quantity time, passing the time—each of these serve

---
1 Kelly, *Rhythm of Life*, 14.

different purposes, but they hold in common the message *I am with you.* I want to be with you. You're worth being with. Whatever good happens in time spent together is built upon the foundation of having been chosen by someone.

A few years into our time in Central Asia, I began to feel a need for more local relationships. I tried to spend time in the neighborhood markets but nothing clicked. You only went to the tea houses with someone, so hanging around in one to make friends was a no go. Eventually, I found an Aikido dojo halfway between work and home, and I joined. I quickly learned that if I wanted to move from curious outsider to one of the guys, I'd have to spend time with the other students outside the dojo as well. With middling language and little in common, I didn't really expect much to happen, but time invested mattered. Soon, two of those men became some of my closest relationships in the country, and those friendships did more to root me there than anything else. Time is the evidence that you've chosen someone.

Curiosity is the evidence that you see them. If time is the first currency of investment, attention is a close second. Simone Weil, a modern mystic, said, "Attention is the rarest and purest form of generosity."[2] We give no gift of ourselves so pure and so selfless as simply paying deep attention to another.

> Attention says I see you.
> You're not invisible. There's beauty to behold in you, and I like what I see.

In a planning meeting for a conference I run with my mentor, Jim, he asked the room to just encourage me with what they appreciate about me. The room was maybe 30 percent women, but the four people who spoke up were all women. They said kind things, but the fourth mentioned what she saw in the room. She said, "I notice that everyone who spoke is female. I think what I most love about you is that you see us. You pay attention to us. We're not invisible, and you're not afraid to see us." God, I hope that's true, but what I know is that I felt seen in that meeting, and it put strength in me in a moment when I desperately needed it. Attention says I see you. You're not invisible. There's beauty to behold in you, and I like what I see.

---

2 Weil, "Letter to Joë."

These investments can be made on the fly, of course, and sometimes the best investments of time and attention are the ones we don't plan. But it's curious how infrequent these investments become when we don't plan. The easiest way I have found to make these deposits is to build them in. Morning prayer together, curious questions at dinner, date nights, monthly calls with staff—these all go on the calendar, and if I just show all the way up, I'm likely to make an investment in someone I love. Few things lead to strength in my soul like seeing someone I love flourish at my touch. So, I plan for it.

Grow

5DThrive is an approach to Christian anti-fragility and not just resilience. It's not enough to just manage our relationships. We want to become better at them. We want to increase the strength and skill with which we approach the task of loving our neighbors. We want to grow relationally.

My friend Aidan and I were at a friend's birthday party and the topic of zombie apocalypses came up. That's normal, right? Aidan joked that he'd be the first to die in an apocalyptic scenario. He couldn't fix things, didn't know cars, and couldn't build stuff. But I knew better. Aidan could lead. Aidan could take a room full of strangers and make them a small army. More than that, Aidan understood, could help others understand, and could help them make themselves understood. Aidan had what people call soft skills—the stuff that actually matters. Two in particular stand out.

Aidan knew how to ask curious questions. A curious question is an open question—not a question you can answer with a yes or a no. It invites the other to actually say something. It's usually not a why question, as these can come off as a challenge or as an invitation to prove a point. A curious question isn't opening a debate but rather inviting revelation. It's not a leading question as it's not trying to get anywhere. Curious questions are after deeper awareness and understanding, so they create a good space to be seen. Finally, curious questions are genuinely curious. Aidan also has good cultural intelligence—he is good at covering the distance between himself and someone very different from him. He has grown both of these skills over time.

The key is to have a plan to grow, and to keep working on the plan. How might your relationships benefit from a little more skill on your part? Where could a small investment of energy in this direction now lead to deeper and richer thriving for your soul in the days to come?

In these last five chapters we've considered how to intentionally invest in our own thriving in each dimension of our souls. We've looked at each independently, always aware that each is part of a single whole, but considering each one at a time, like we might consider the various component systems of a car. But once we close the hood, the systems have to work together as a unit, and they have to work well enough to carry the car and its passengers safely where they want to go. Let's get into that next.

7
Thriving in Real Life

In this chapter we'll:

- Examine how the specifics of our real, everyday lives must be taken into account as we plan to thrive
- Reflect on the place of suffering and adversity in thriving
- Consider the role of community in thriving

It's possible to thrive, even in chaos. Especially in chaos. But thriving usually only happens when we plan for it, and even then, anyone who's ever made a New Year's resolution knows that the best laid plans often fail. For our thrive plans to work, they will have to take into account at least three things: the specifics of our actual lives, the inescapability of adversity and human frailty, and our connections to other people.

Real Life

In our community we train people to thrive so they can do the work they're called to do vibrantly and for a long time. We want them to thrive for their own sakes, because we love them. But because we love them, we want them to be able to bring whole-souled service to the world and to express what's in their hearts through vividly lived lives with as little encumbrance as possible. Thriving supports and supplies good work.

> Thrive first. Make your thrive practices some of your big rocks.

How much time and effort, then, should go into thriving in a real life with real jobs and real demands? This is a common question, and I like to answer it with two basic principles: investing in the asset first, and Minimum Viable Progress (MVP).

Thrive first. Make your thrive practices some of your big rocks. Budget time, money, and attention to these practices before you allocate resources to productivity. In entrepreneurial language, pay yourself first. Practically speaking, we encourage our people to devote 10 percent of their work hours to high-quality thrive practices, and an additional

10 percent of their "off-work hours" to thriving. For members of our community who have less control over what they'd view as working hours, we still encourage at least 10 percent of their off time be allocated to purposefully supporting their own thrive.

We insist on this. Diminishment of your capacity leads to negative effects on what's important to you and your mission in the world. Increases in your vibrancy, presence in the moment, health, and resilience all lead to more of you being brought to the good works God has given you to do with your time on the earth. Since your time is limited, you can't spend it all trying to thrive, but you can make it the first thing you do. Likely no one in your life is going to ask you to invest in yourself before you look after their needs, but a good friend might, and a good leader certainly will. In any case, it's on you to budget your bandwidth in ways that make thriving more likely.

How do you know if you're budgeting enough time or energy to thriving? This is where the principle of seeking Minimum Viable Progress (MVP)—is helpful. When I select practices for my thrive plan, I remember that I'm looking to move myself steadily, incrementally up the thrive continuum away from sickness and toward fitness in each dimension, and I'm aiming to do so with enough momentum that if I hit a bump in the road, I'm not likely to go tumbling backward.

Perhaps a useful way to think about MVP is to consider the ditches to either side. Imagine a man who works out for three hours a day, meets weekly with his counselor and his life coach, attends eight seminars a year on topics that tickle his fancy, and takes a five-day spiritual retreat every month. While it could be argued that this guy is investing seriously in himself, it's also obvious that this is way too much. He's here to love his God and his neighbor, to make disciples, and to do good works. But he has ordered his life—whether from narcissism, anxiety, shame, or something else—entirely around himself. This is not the way to go.

Conversely, we could imagine a woman somewhere who thinks she eats well and tries to stretch when the pain and tension in her muscles gets to be too distracting. She takes a walk once or twice a week when she can, and sometimes when the kids are quiet and the house isn't too messy, she sits down and tries to pray or to notice what she's been feeling lately though usually this effort is interrupted by a text message or a friend in need. She is doing something to cultivate vibrancy and vigor, but is it enough and are the actions she's taking the right ones to get her where she wants to go? Likely not.

Each month, when we do our vector checks, we notice where each dimension is headed and how much momentum we have. Remember, vectors have direction and magnitude, and each quarter when we assess if our Thrive plan is working and make necessary adjustments, we are considering whether or not we are actually making Minimum Viable Progress in each dimension. If a particular dimension is consistently lagging, then we must reconsider our practices and try, with prayer and counsel from our close community and sagacious friends, to discern what else we could do or what we could do differently that would make the difference.

As I write this, it is January 9th. Each quarter our team reexamines our thrive plans and makes adjustments that reflect the season we are entering, the specific terrain of our lives, our interests, invitations we might be sensing from Jesus, and the trends in each of our dimensions across the last quarter. In a few days when we next meet, we'll be sharing our thrive plans with one another and asking for feedback, resourcing, encouragement, and even a little accountability. As an example, here is my thrive plan for the first quarter of this year.

- Spiritual
    - Withdraw
        - Early morning prayer and reading the Lectionary Scriptures
        - Quarterly forty-eight-hour solitary retreat
    - Gather
        - Friday night Sabbath dinner/House-church
        - Weekly Sabbath day
        - Daily praying of the Hours as a household
        - Team meeting
        - Monthly spiritual direction
    - Obey
        - Reflect frequently on words/impressions given by Jesus, how I've responded, and how he has met me in the response
        - Prayer of Examen

- Physical
  - Eat
    - Eat real food
    - Limit refined sugar and processed carbohydrates
    - Take my vitamins
  - Move
    - Strength/conditioning (weights, calisthenics, martial arts, walking) four to five days/week
  - Recover
    - Stretching after every workout, and before bed as needed
    - Seven and a half hours per night of sleep or more
    - Weekly Sabbath day
- Cognitive
  - Learn
    - Doctoral study
  - Focus
    - Radically limit news and YouTube, and remain off social media
    - Contain messaging and emails to two windows per day
  - Play
    - Read novels
    - Weekly Sabbath day
    - Play games with my wife, kids, and some friends at least weekly
    - Bi-weekly date with my wife
- Emotional
  - Notice
    - Prayer of Examen daily
    - Bring the feelings that come with me into prayer to God and name them aloud
  - Interview
    - Journal
    - Talk with my spiritual director regularly, and with a few key friends when opportunity arises
  - Manage
    - Practice diaphragmatic breathing
    - Notice the narrative
    - Practice a delay between others' behaviors and my speech
    - Strength/conditioning four to five days/week

- Relational
  - Discern
    - Family—Try to get a bead on what each member of my household most needs, and doesn't need, from me right now
    - Direct reports—Notice interactions with each other
    - Other colleagues—Notice who is asking for the help I am best suited to provide
  - Invest
    - Family—Extra time with my wife, listen carefully to each kid daily, keep the Hours
    - Direct reports—Help them use relational intelligence
    - Other colleagues—Listen, teach, consult, and do not take responsibility for what they do with it
  - Grow
    - Employ relational intelligence insights in team meetings

This may look like a lot, but a closer examination reveals that the whole plan is held together by a shorter list of core practices that address several dimensions at once. Things like regular exercise, the Prayer of Examen, Sabbath observance, praying the Hours, and spiritual direction appear multiple times in the plan. The actual list of activities isn't so long, and the activation energy necessary to get started isn't that significant. Once these practices become habit, that activation energy decreases as these practices become routine in the best sense.

Now, as an individual, I'm spiritually contemplative, intellectually a little intense, and very physical. This is probably evident in my thrive plan. Others may not enjoy heavy weights and fight training, and I am utterly disinterested in running and distance swimming. Some may find a solitary, silent retreat terrifying but recognize their need to regularly and intentionally incorporate worship music. The trick is to work with the Spirit and with people who know you well to discern what kinds of practices are best for you and then to measure the efficacy of those practices quarterly to see if they're working and what kinds of adjustments are needed. Some friends and colleagues in different life situations have offered their current thrive plans as additional examples, which can be found in the Appendix on page 243.

Adversity and Weakness

When the pandemic was gaining steam and the lockdowns were just starting, I made a few YouTube videos roughing in the bones of 5DThrive for my audience because I knew that the world they'd be living in soon was about to have a lot in common with the kind of world I had been serving for years. A few days after the videos went up, my friend Marie wrote,

> Mark and I watched your video. Maybe we suck, but we are just too overwhelmed to even know where to start. I've been sick for months and have had to stop my treatments because of the Covid thing, and Mark's workload has nearly tripled. I know some people are out of work, so we should be grateful, but it's still hard. The kids aren't doing great, and now I'm homeschooling them with the only curriculum I could find quickly, which is exactly as awful as it sounds. Do you have some kind of "Thriving for Dummies" or "Thrive Weak" kind of course you could send?

Later I'll share what I sent her, but her question brings other questions to the surface. What about suffering? Chronic incurable illness? Psychological disorders that God doesn't seem to heal instantly? Aging and irreversible decline? Sudden calamity?

What about the inevitability of weakness in a fallen world?

The spiritual tradition I grew up in seemed to worship weakness and view strength with suspicion. In a sense, this is understandable. We hear of how when the Apostle Paul was afflicted with an acute and chronic condition, he chose to celebrate it because God had told him that God's strength was made complete in weakness. We sing songs from our childhood, "Little ones to him belong. They are weak, but he is strong." And no doubt, this is true. We are frail and easily broken. In a world where almost every other creature has fangs, talons, claws or venom, we are hairless, clawless, and largely helpless.

It makes sense to accept our fundamental frailty, and when God makes up the difference, acting through those frail places in ways that evidence his presence with us for the world, it only makes sense to celebrate that. But celebrating weakness and worshipping weakness aren't the same thing.

I think we lose our way when we uncritically accept a dichotomy that the Scriptures do not suggest—the idea that for God to be strong we must be weak, that our created and God-given strength is to be set in opposition to God's uncreated strength, or that to intentionally grow stronger is to necessarily place our faith in the strength we are cultivating. Here, some words from a man acquainted with weakness, with strength, and with God will prove clarifying.

In Psalm 18, David talks about strength in three ways, and they are not mutually exclusive:

1. David says that God has made him strong. God trained David's hands for war and his fingers for fighting and makes him strong enough to bend a bow of bronze.
2. Further, God lends his strength to David's and acts with David as David faces off against impossible odds and insurmountable obstacles.
3. Finally, in situations that totally outstrip David's capacity, when he's besieged and helpless, God acts in his own strength on David's behalf and delivers David without David's aid.

We are, perhaps, most familiar with the third. Stories of God acting on his people's behalf fill the pages of the Bible, but the Scriptures are also a story of God making and maturing his people, growing them from sheep into shepherds, and raising them from infants into grown children who are capable of partnering with him in the family business of saving the world. He is strong when we are weak, but he is also strong when we are strong. While we should never place our faith in our own strength, we should still receive it and use it for the flourishing of others.

In Psalm 18, David is strong in particular ways because God has made him so. He made David to be a warrior, a poet, and a king, and these are the ways we see David's unique strength expressing itself. As Israel's king, it's good news to God's people that David is strong. No one needs a power-hungry leader, but weak leaders are just as dangerous. David is stronger still when God multiplies the force of David's deeds, and this is also good news for God's people because David rules Israel with God, who ultimately is his people's king. Strength is good news.

Weakness, though, isn't necessarily bad news. Weakness isn't to be feared or judged. As men and women made of dust, we must accept our frailty, but we must never seek it or hide behind it. The same man who chose to celebrate his weaknesses never once commanded his audiences to be weak or to cultivate weakness. Rather, he repeatedly says,

"Be strong" (Eph 6:10–11; 1 Cor 16:13–14; 2 Tim 2:1). Weakness is to be accepted when necessary. Strength is to be cultivated whenever possible.

Still, where does that leave us when we are weak? I know a number of people with crippling, progressive diseases, and others with melancholies that may never completely lift this side of resurrection. Some of them are very dear to me, and some of them are very wise. The wise ones vigorously pursue increased vibrancy and vigor in the dimensions of their souls not afflicted by their illness, and they seek to slow the progress of their diseases as much as possible. For them, thriving in an afflicted dimension is a matter of resisting its effects with perseverance and working to live within unwelcome limits without being totally limited by them.

Other people in my world—people like Marie, who asked for a "Thriving for Dummies Handbook"—might not have a crippling illness, but they have been, for the moment, overcome by events. I remember reading once that plane crashes don't usually happen because one thing goes wrong. Rather, a number of small errors and minor malfunctions coincide catastrophically, and the plane is overcome by events. In these cases, I suggest a field-expedient 5D Thrive Plan. Stripped down to a bare minimum, a plan like this probably won't serve to see you forward to deeper development and wider horizons, but it will see you through, and when life settles a little you can add what remains.

A field-expedient thrive plan retains all three aspects of spiritual thrive, and one aspect of each of the other four dimensions. When my friends find themselves overcome by events, I encourage them to make a plan with these elements:

- Spiritual: You need to draw close to Jesus any way you can in these times. This will mean finding one practice to help you Withdraw with him, one practice that makes it easier to encounter him when you Gather with others, and one practice to help you review how he has been with you and how you've responded (Obey). The spiritual plan changes the least in the bare-bones version.

- Physical: You need to Move. Fix your diet later. As a bonus, moving will likely help you sleep better. Long walks are best, followed by short, intense workouts. What's most important is that you do it very often, and you make it hard to skip.

- Cognitive: Focus. You already have too much on your mind. Cut out anything that adds to that. Cut out anything that involves scrolling. Scrolling feels for the moment like it's distracting you from your chaotic life, but in reality, it's adding the chaos of other lives to your emotional distress. You have no agency in these other lives at all and you are helpless to change them.
- Emotional: Notice. It may be good to get a counselor in these seasons to help you interview, but most important is noticing and naming the feelings you're having without judgement or excuse. The ones you don't notice become anxiety or anger, and usually are driving every decision you make. If you're in a crisis, that's not the version of you you need to have at the wheel.
- Relational: Discern. Which relationships are really critical? Which of those actually add lift to me, rather than load? In a crisis, you need more lifters and fewer loaders.

This brings us to the third reality we have to take into account when we make plans to thrive—other people.

Community

For twenty-five years, I've been fascinated with the question of how people actually change, and I've devoted most of those years learning how it happens. I've come to the conclusion that lasting individual change is exceedingly rare and almost impossible to predict. Because we are social creatures, it shouldn't surprise us that change doesn't usually follow wanting to change, intending to change, or even learning ways to change. Rather, people change most often by becoming part of communities of change—formative communities.

There are many ways to be in community. Geography, ideology, values, and aims can connect people and pull them into a sense of "us." All communities are, in fact, formative, since the habits that form our souls are caught more than taught, and we catch them from one another. But not all communities are purposeful and profitable in the ways they form their constituents.

Five guys sitting in a basement somewhere smoking pot all day when they could be looking for jobs is a disabling community. Identification with and participation in that circle diminishes them. Of course, patently destructive behaviors aren't the only ways we disable one another unintentionally, but they are the easiest to see.

Similarly, the people who too-often congregate at a dive bar to commiserate and avoid going home to their real lives and real problems, are perhaps an enabling community. Going to the bar isn't a problem but helping one another normalize medicating emotional pain and avoiding key relationships is. Here, enabling is not the opposite of disabling. Rather, it refers to the reinforcement of unhelpful patterns.

If we take a darker turn, it's not hard to find examples of twisted communities. Cults—of dogma and of personality—bend people, and often result in mutant iterations of society. In the last few years, we've seen this happen with the emergence of mob thinking and cancel culture through the proliferation of unthoughtful engagement with social media.

Perhaps most common, though, and most familiar, is the complicit community—home groups and Sunday meetings that let us gather and remain basically unchanged. In these we are all complicit in neither informing nor disrupting one another's behaviors or rhythms. This form of community encourages participation without mutual submission or shared responsibility for one another. Complicit community can be larger and more reinforced such as the case of denominations or even organizations huddling up to mutually assure one another that we're right. These are more dangerous, perhaps, than the other examples because in these, we protect one another's perceived right to not change since doing so reinforces our individual ability to resist change ourselves.

So, while all community is formative in the sense that participation in any community changes the individual and the community, not all community is intentionally so. To be intentionally formative, a community needs certain things. This became evident to me in a conversation with middle leadership in a mission organization that was considering implementing 5DThrive across its personnel. The question arose of how much commitment and how much adoption of the approach would be necessary to garner its benefits. We followed that rabbit and eventually came to understand that formative community is superior to trying to thrive alone or even in independent parallel with others.

We started with the least amount of commitment and adoption possible and worked our way through deepening degrees of engagement. Here's what we asked and what we learned.

- **What if supervisors used monthly calls with staff to ask after particular dimensions of their soul that seem most important to them at the time without really engaging the whole system?**

We concluded that those particular dimensions might get adequate attention, but the others would likely not. Further, the ten people Bob is responsible for would be receiving leadership limited by Bob's proclivities and deficiencies, and the ten people Lucy is responsible for would likewise have the support they receive limited by Lucy's strengths and weaknesses. This was not preferable.

- **What if we introduced the Thrive Wheel schema to the international staff and offered some training as to how each part of our souls contributes to the others (i.e., what if we took an educational/informational approach)?** This angle would likely lead to an increased consciousness among international staff of the different dimensions of their souls and of the fact that they are integrated units. Understanding, however, cannot be relied upon to change behavior or increase engagement. Further, simply understanding the Thrive Wheel without the other elements of the approach wouldn't be enough to help them track progress or scaffold meaningful action.

- **What if supervisors used the vector checks in their monthly calls with international staff?** This would likely result in improved self-awareness among field staff as well as an increase in competency and likelihood to take one another's pulses on teams. Since this is experiential and behavioral, it's apt to stick. However, without the concurrent ability to plan to thrive, awareness alone without agency to effect change is very likely to lead to frustration or apathy.

- **What if we train on the Thrive Wheel, use the vector checks, and teach our people how to make Thrive Plans but don't encourage community-wide adoption of the approach?** In this case, the benefits are significant. In addition to increases in self-awareness across field staff, supervisors are likely to notice trouble spots long before they become significant problems for people. Additionally, equipping staff to create and implement thrive plans would give them significantly more agency and control, mitigating the emotional toll of chaos and empowering them to invest in themselves. However, if this remains completely individual, if there is no sense of shared commitment to one another on these terms, individual willpower is going to flag, and it will be much harder to draft from one another's progress. The fallout of a population failing to thrive in independent parallel with one another is hard to overstate.

- **What if, as a community, we commit to adopt this approach together?** The downside here is the potential to feel like individual autonomy and personal style can be threatened or squelched especially among supervisors. This can be mitigated against by learning how to do this one way together, and then learning how to improvise individually as skill increases. What's gained far outweighs the risk. The community would have a shared vocabulary across teams, regions, and groups which facilitates easier cross-support by field staff. Further, it is exponentially easier to develop personnel (especially emergent leaders) in a context with shared vocabulary and a common suite of tools. The previous four options each improved on the one before, but this option was an order of magnitude better than the last.

In engaging this group in the conversation above, it became increasingly clear to me that for a community to be truly formative it needs:

- A shared intention
- A shared *commitment* of its members to one another and to that intention
- A shared *way* to practice with explicit and identifiable behaviors that let its constituents learn the way as they walk it together[1]

This should not have come as a surprise. As a lifelong martial artist, I've known this in my bones. Traditional martial arts are practiced in a *dojo*—literally, a "house of the way." Practitioners are shaped as they practice that way—be it ju*do*, karate-*do*, ken*do*—not as individuals seeking lessons but in shared community on a path together. The practices they engage contain and transmit the way they are practicing with shared intention and commitment.

---

1 For more information on Christian community, consider David Jansen's *Intentional Christian*.

Christian history reveals similar phenomena in monastic communities which often shared a *regula*—a rule of life. A rule in this sense is not the kind you keep, but the kind that keeps you like a ruler helps you keep your lines straight. By engaging a shared rule of life, which would have some elements common among all, and others specifically tailored to each member, these communities were able to live vibrant expressions of the way of Jesus in eras when much of the rest of the church had totally lost its way.

This kind of community is an ecosystem in which individual people are far more likely to thrive, and therefore more likely to give vibrant witness to Jesus and less likely to flame out decades before they're done. It follows, then, that cultivating such a generative ecosystem is among the greatest gifts leaders can give their people.

8

Leading Toward Thrive

In this chapter we'll:

- Examine two cues to help us lead toward thrive: catalyze and capacitate
- Summarize part one

So far, we've asserted that even in stress and uncertainty, it's possible to thrive, and we've suggested that thriving needs to be holistic if it's to work and to take into account the five dimensions of the human being or soul. We've explored a simple approach to checking in with each dimension of your soul every month, thereby increasing self-awareness, giving nuance to experience, and lowering the likelihood of unforeseen catastrophic collapse. We've unpacked a concrete and balanced way to plan to thrive, including practices that help each dimension of our personalities move away from sickness and toward fitness, and we've hammered out how to make it work in the real world of schedules, adversities, and other people.

Thriving is essential to flourishing, so any attempt at viable self-leadership should include consideration of progressive holistic wellness. But some of us lead more than just ourselves. We lead families, teams, communities, and organizations, and if we want to lead like Jesus, we want to lead generatively.

To be clear, even when we want to lead people in ways that help them become more, we all make mistakes. You can do your best and get key things really wrong. You can do things fundamentally right, and it still may not ultimately affect the outcomes. But most of the time, the more generative your leadership, the more beautiful and fruitful you can expect the outcome to be.

Generative leaders strive to become good, wise, and strong. Good leaders will make it as easy as possible for those they lead to thrive and to grow as they work. Wise leaders know that investing in their people is among the most strategically sound decisions they can make, and they know how to do it. Strong leaders aren't afraid to use their authority—not to accrue more power, but to help those they lead become stronger too.

My leadership ten years ago was not as generative as it is now, and hopefully it will be even more like sun and rain ten years from now. But any time, all the time, our leadership is imperfect. The best we can do is identify what is uniquely ours to contribute to our people and do our utmost to deliver. When it comes to leading our people toward thriving, it's our job to catalyze and capacitate.

Catalyze

In chemistry, a catalyst is something added to a reaction that facilitates that reaction by lowering the amount of energy necessary for it to take place. Catalysts help things get started and keep going without themselves being part of the equation. For example, some of the people I look after work in warzones. They have to learn how to thrive there, and it can be really hard. I'm not there with them, but as a catalyst for thriving in their situation, I'm looking to make it easier to get started and to keep going on the journey toward thriving and to lower the amount of attention, will power, expertise, and energy they have to contribute to that process to make it work.

> Catalysts help things get started
> and keep going without themselves
> being part of the equation.

To be clear, a leader's job is to catalyze thriving not to secure it. Leaders aren't the parents of the led except when we're talking about leading our own children. The people we lead are adults, so they must be respected as adults and expected to steward themselves like adults. For some this is harder than others, so the expectation to do so can create resistance. But at the end of the day, who doesn't want a leader who aims to make them stronger without doing the work for them, thereby robbing them of their agency?

The notion of leading by catalyzing thriving provides an excellent window into the best uses of power. But before we focus on that, let me say that power does not corrupt. People, all people, are in some way or another corrupted by sin. Power can magnify the effect of that, but power in itself isn't evil, and a disparity of power between persons or groups does not necessarily mean evil is afoot. The idea that differences in power are bad or that they reflect a failure of community has more in common with Marx than with Jesus. A story from my days in Central Asia may help here.

Earlier I mentioned my Aikido dojo in Central Asia. As the only American there, I was something of a novelty, so I occasionally found myself invited to tea after class with the sensei and a few of the senior students. Now, to understand this story, it's important to know a little about the culture in the dojo and one point of grammar.

In this particular dojo, the sensei was the founder and teacher. There were other instructors of lesser rank who taught classes, the most senior among them being my instructor who was called the *sempai*. At this point in our Central Asian odyssey, my grasp of the local language was pretty good, but I still had a few artifacts that were hard to shake. Chief among them was a proclivity to always use the informal *you* when speaking to people, even in the rare cases where my social station called for the formal *You*.

On this particular evening, the sensei had been engaging me in a lengthy discussion of something or other in front of all the senior students, and I had repeatedly made just that mistake. In typical local fashion, he confronted me on it indirectly.

"I once met a British fellow," my sensei remarked, "who said in England they only use the formal *You*, never the informal, even when speaking to clear inferiors."

The change in topic, thankfully, wasn't lost on me, "Oh, sensei! I'm so sorry! I've been calling you *you* this whole time instead of *You*, haven't I? I apologize. I meant no disrespect! This is a part of the language that is still awkward for me."

"My British friend spoke English. You speak English in America, don't you?" He wasn't buying it.

"No, sensei," my sempai jumped in to save me, "I've been to the US. Everyone walks around smiling like idiots and calling one another *you*, regardless of their power. In America, they believe that everyone is equal." I felt a flash of pride as my teacher and friend made the assertion that we Americans understood that all people are created equal.

After a long pause, my sensei sat back and said, "Well, that's the stupidest thing I've ever heard. Some are older; some are younger. Some are rich, and some are poor. Some are taller; some are shorter. Some teach, and some learn. Some are smart, and some are, well, not. The only thing, the one thing, no two people can ever be is equal."

This notion of power gradients being inherent in all relationships isn't unique to my sensei or even to his people. Cultures fall on a continuum of comfort with the reality that in any given situation some people have more power than others. But in high power distance cultures and in low power distance cultures, the incontrovertible fact of the distance remains, and to ignore it or pretend it isn't so is negligence. As leaders, even in basically flat structures, we usually have more power/influence/say than those we lead. The question is one of how we use it.

In his beautiful book *Playing God*, Andy Crouch contends that power is for flourishing:

> Here is what we need to discover about power: it is both better and worse than we could imagine. Power at its best is … the one swift stroke of the machete that opens a coconut for the honored guest. It is a source of refreshment, laughter, joy and life—and of more power. Remove power and you cut off life, the possibility of creating something new and better in this rich and recalcitrant world. Life is power. Power is life. And flourishing power leads to flourishing life.[1]

Sometimes an appropriate use of power is the catalyst someone needs. A year after the leadership team I served with took over responsibility for our particular group of international workers, we held a conference designed to help them thrive. In a short talk—which a friend began calling my "You Will Thrive, So Help Me God" speech—we strove to help those we lead know that this is where we put our foot down. This is what we are using our power to insist upon. We don't insist on much else, really. Just this. They will use their best energy to invest in themselves. They are each intrinsically valuable, and their vibrancy is of utmost strategic importance. We would use what power we had to remove any guilt that might remain about taking care of themselves. The boss said thrive, so thrive. When power is used for flourishing, authority feels like grace, and that's good news.

John 15 as Seen in Midlife

I have come to believe that midlife is for the inner world what puberty is for the body—a period of pronounced and protracted awkwardness and angst that gives way to a maturity and competency otherwise unavailable. So much can change categorically in this period. At least that's how

---

[1] Crouch, *Playing God*, 25.

it's going for me. One example of that change is the radical difference between how I used to hear Jesus in John 15, and how I hear him now.

John 15 is the well-known "Vine and Branches" chapter. Abide in me, Jesus says, and as I abide in you, you'll bear much fruit (vv. 4–11). I'm telling you this so my joy can be yours, and your joy can be full. It's the Father's good will that you bear much fruit. He paints a picture of a verdant, vibrant life—a life in which the endless, uncreated joy of the Son of God becomes our own, and that joy becomes the predominant emotional experience of our lives. His words paint a picture of lasting impact—fruit that remains. This, for any follower of Jesus, is the dream—joy within and fruitful work without, all interwoven by intimate connection with God in Christ.

I would get a little nervous when I read it in my twenties and thirties. To be clear, I'd feel the draw. I'd see the logic, and sense how this was at the center of things. But at the same time, there was always this nagging fear in a back closet of my heart that Jesus was measuring me and telling me that if I couldn't see fruit that remained, it was because I wasn't connecting properly with him, and if I didn't step it up, I'd find myself pruned. This doubt, this pressure to produce never made it to the level of conscious thought. Instead, it presented itself as a rush to read past this passage or an urge to break it down into manageable steps I could take to ensure I'd bear the fruit that God was after.

> Productivity and fruitfulness
> are not the same thing.

But a good old-fashioned midlife crisis can do wonders for muddled thinking. It turns out that when Jesus said, "By this my Father is glorified, that you bear much fruit" (v. 8), he was telling us something God wanted *for* us, not *from* us. The fruit is the part God would worry about, so we didn't have to. And in any case, productivity and fruitfulness are not the same thing.

I see this passage very differently now, and it affects the way I lead. Let me share with you what maybe should have been obvious all along. Jesus says he's the vine and you are a branch. So, imagine a branch. At one end the branch is connected to the vine, and at the other it's connected to its fruit. Now take a moment and consider the first several verses of John 15. How many of the imperative verbs (verbs that constitute a command) ask you to attend to your connection to the vine, and how many ask you to attend to bearing fruit? You might be surprised when you learn that all of the imperative verbs orient your attention and energy toward your thriving in Jesus, and the effect is fruitfulness.

But if you survey the popular missions literature, the vast majority is written to how to more effectively bear fruit. In some cases, it's even reduced to measures of productivity. Teams measure engagement by measuring efforts at the fruiting end of the branch, apparently assuming, often incorrectly, a vital connection to the vine. But continually turning people's attention to outcomes is the opposite of what Jesus seems to do here. There is, of course, much to be gained in considering the wisest ways to use our time and learning from the experiences of others in contexts like ours. But if we are to lead like Jesus, we must cultivate in our leadership of others a predisposition to catalyze attention to their connection to life and to trust that the desired effects in their ministries will come.

Practical Catalysis

One way we catalyze thriving in our staff is by including a discussion of their most recent 5DVector Checks in each of our monthly calls. Knowing that their thriving will be one of the first things we ask about makes it very likely that they'll have thought about it before we talk. This is further assured by the Monthly Check-in Tool[2] they fill out and send to us before the call. The simple act of routinely focusing on thriving in our interactions with staff is catalytic because when leaders train their focus on something, followers tend to follow suit.

But as important as the monthly vector checks are, the three questions we ask afterward are perhaps even more important.

> *Question 1: What part of your vector check do you most want to talk about?*

This question forces them to consider the vector check as a whole, notice the interplay between dimensions, and determine what is most important to them. Further, it respects their agency and gives them some control over what part of their soul we explore together this month. The 5DVector Check isn't a crowbar designed to allow leaders forced entry into their staff's inner worlds. This question allows the staff member some say over what part of them gets the most attention.

---

2 See Appendix on page 243.

That's not to say that we might not ask about another dimension in the same call, but we are very unlikely to push. We might express curiosity and invite them to say more about something that stood out or simply notice aloud what captures our attention. We may even express some concern if appropriate, but leaders cannot force thriving—we can only catalyze it, and questions are far more energetic than mandates.

> Question 2: *Where have you seen Jesus most active in you this month, and where would you like to see his action moving forward?*

5DThrive is not a self-help tool. It builds self-awareness, and it helps us consider how best to participate in our own ongoing restoration in a holistic way. But the approach is predicated upon the assumption that, as followers of Jesus, we are seeking strategic human flourishing *in him*. So, as we engage in thrive practices, we are doing so as apprentices of Jesus and looking for burning bushes within us where God might be striking up a conversation we maybe never saw coming. 5DThrive helps us practically follow Jesus by increasing the acuity of our attention and care of our own souls as he works to shape them for freedom.

Each month we try to catalyze vividness around the questions, "What is Jesus doing in you, right now? What might he be inviting you toward next?" Once they've noticed their souls and have a decent map of where things are going, they can use that map to track the activity of the one who is perpetually saving them. Tracking Jesus amplifies their own ability to cooperate in that endeavor by helping them show up to Jesus as he lives in them ever more fully. This practice further catalyzes gratitude, joy, and attentive obedience to Jesus in the events of our real lives.

Sometimes, though, the road is hard, and the way seems dark. We all have seasons when we just feel broken everywhere and can't seem to catch a glimpse of the Teacher through the unknown crowd. In these moments, leaders might gently adjust this question: "What part of your soul feels most in need of restoring right now? What part of you would you most want Jesus to touch, right now?" Often, we make their answer a prayer that either they pray, or we pray for them. In the darkness, we try to catalyze thriving tomorrow by kindling hope today.

> Question 3: *How can I help you?*

The leadership Jesus embodied and taught is servant-leadership—where the king puts on the servant's garb and washes his people's feet. The easiest way I've found to identify what my people need from me is to ask them.

Some leaders try to act like servants by always getting the check, clearing the dishes, or being the one to sacrifice the most in every encounter. But sometimes that amounts to service-performance more than actually serving. If you really want to serve someone, first attend to what *they* think they need rather than what you think they need. In any case, asking them to think about it is a fantastic way to help them find the gaps they might have missed.

The kinds of help with thriving that people in my line of work usually need tend to fall into two categories: issues with their teams and issues with their competencies. Sometimes someone can't seem to thrive because of unhealth in their primary team, unresolved conflict on that team, or rarely, a team leader who might not take a particular dimension seriously and undermines their efforts to grow there. More often, though, they just don't know how to thrive in a particular dimension, and they need to be taught.

Both cases are matters of capacity. Either their own competencies and capacities for flourishing need to be developed, or their environment fails to support that developement. This leads us to our next coaching cue.

Capacitate

Leaders set and clarify expectations. Grace-filled expectations can feel like good news, but if those we lead lack the capacity to fulfill an expectation—even a generous, life-affirming one—that invitation to thriving can feel heavy, confusing, and intimidating. In these cases, it's critical that we serve those we lead by nourishing their capacity to thrive, both by addressing needs in the individuals themselves and in their particular environments, so their ecosystems can support their thriving.

Investing in Individuals

I grew up in a very emotional home. Emotional, but not emotionally intelligent. Emotions like anger, fear, and sorrow hung thickly in the air, but were never addressed, except to assign blame. In fact, talking about your feelings was usually discouraged as weak, "psychobabble," or New Age. We knew the Bible. We were solid students in school. We knew how to eat right and exercise, but emotions were a blind spot.

This emotional incompetence was baptized, canonized, and vigorously reinforced by our theological tradition. Feelings were to be distrusted, ignored, or even renounced as inherently sinful. We weren't alone in this conspiracy either. Southeast Michigan is known for the kind of blue-collar stoicism that can work year in and year out through brutal Great Lakes winters without batting an eye. Between household, church, and local culture, I was well and truly destined to have a hole in my emotional capacity.

Most often, the obstacles to thriving that individuals face lie in the way certain dimensions of soul were ignored, decried, or mismanaged in their families or communities of origin which leads to a blind gap in capacity. These gaps can present across a spectrum from resistance, to unfamiliarity, to urgent felt need. Leaving resistance for later, let's consider three examples where capacitation was called for.

1. Amy had endured a tough and even traumatic few years. She had been using an emotions wheel over the past several months and had become increasingly comfortable with her feelings. But in a monthly call with her regional leader she mused, "I'm learning to notice and name my emotions, and I think that's helping, but I don't know what to do with them from there." Her leader suggested a resource to help her interview her feelings to discover her underlying desires. After checking it out, Amy messaged him, "Thanks for the suggestion. Good food for thought."

2. Alan works in an overpopulated post-Soviet city. The stress of his job at a local high school, irritations with corrupt immigration processes, and the constant press of millions of people running roughshod over an infrastructure built for a fraction of that number accumulated over the years, and he felt it in his body. He didn't grow up exercising or eating right, so he had no idea what to do or where to start. Fortunately, he remembered working out for a few months with his former team leader, who is now his regional supervisor, and in their monthly call he mentioned needing help with a program to increase his physical thriving. A week later, Alan had a diet and exercise plan that fit his life—a plan he knew he could follow because he had experience with almost all the exercises from when he had trained with his team leader.

3. Charis has been an avid student of the Bible for decades, so she wasn't expecting what happened when her colleague suggested

they use part of their team meeting for something he called Right Brained Lectio. He gave everyone a sheet of paper and some colored pencils and instructed them to doodle or draw while a familiar passage of Scripture was read slowly through four times. Being a serious Bible student, she wondered what the silly coloring was about, but played along with an open mind. As it turned out, that's exactly what happened. The act of using the artistic and spatial portions of her brain gave the Scriptures access to the emotional centers of her soul in a way exegetical study never had. She found herself deeply moved, and heard Jesus speak to her during the exercise. She remarked later in her usual understated way, "Thanks for that. I was surprised at what happened. I wasn't expecting that."

What these examples have in common is the way a leader or a teammate helped a colleague move meaningfully toward thriving by trying to enhance their colleague's capacity. It didn't take much, but what was offered was enough to cover the gap in capacity.

What they don't have in common is even more interesting. Alan was the only one to actually ask for help, and this is significant since the capacity development employed in his case amounted to a significant change in how he lived his daily life. If he had received that same advice unsolicited (indeed he had, years before), it wouldn't have produced nearly the same effect.

Neither Charis nor Amy asked for help, but the outcomes with these two situations are very different. Amy received, unsolicited, a resource that she reviewed on her own. Charis, on the other hand, experienced something that, while also unsolicited, was welcome and easy to receive because she experienced it in the context of a shared practice. Charis's response was, "Thanks for that. I was surprised at what happened." Amy's was, "Good food for thought." One had a tiny, life-altering experience, and the other might remember the conversation next week, but probably not.

What constitutes the difference there is shared experience in the context of a simple, explicit, shared practice. Remember, people learn in the following order: (1) experience, (2) express, (3) explain.

What we actually, personally experience, we come to be able to express. In the act of expressing what we saw, felt, sensed, and heard, our experience is reinforced and is codified as part of our story. As we reflect on that experience and the implications we discover as we express it, we slowly come to understand it well enough to explain it. That's how we learn to swim, ride a bike, and literally everything else.

Recall, too, that most approaches to capacity development run in exactly the opposite direction: (1) explain, (2) express, (3) experience.

We describe the mechanics of change to people (explain), and expect them to say that they understand and will try it (express). But we leave them completely unsupported and demotivated at the very point where learning happens—experience.

The resource Amy's leader sent her explained how to interview your emotions to help you follow Jesus. This knowledge will do absolutely nothing for Amy until she uses it, and she's not likely to try it on her own until the pain of not being able to move past merely noticing her feelings is acute enough that it drives her from the disinterest of unfamiliarity to a desperate willingness to try anything.

> Capacity development, therefore, is best done through explicit practices aimed at engaging people where the gaps in their competencies lie.

Leading people through discrete practices that build thriving in a specific dimension, the way Charis's colleague and Alan's regional leader did, allows them to experience both the practice and the potential effect and leaves them positioned to continue benefiting from the capacity-building experience on their own. Alan worked out with his team leader. Charis explored the Scriptures emotionally with teammates, but they both experienced change by participating in a clear practice with others. Capacity development, therefore, is best done through explicit practices aimed at engaging people where the gaps in their competencies lie.

Investing in Ecosystems

Developmentally rich, shared experiences play a big role in a little gathering called the NextGen Leaders Conference—an effort birthed and spearheaded by some of my dearest friends, Jim and Sterling O'Neill. One of the central goals of the conference is to equip young leaders to take care of their souls, because healthy, beautiful souls can engender vibrant communities that, in turn, can heal the world.

A couple of years ago, one of the conference organizers and I were debriefing the most recent event, and almost as an aside he said, "All we can do is help put these dear people back together, try to get some water to their parched hearts, and then send them back into environments caustic to their souls." He was talking about churches and mission agencies.

Just last week my friend Dan said to me, "Mission organizations have this tendency to inadvertently chew their people up." This has been my observation as well. Christian organizations—I'd wager most organizations—probably don't choose to create a debilitating atmosphere as a key strategic outcome. So why does it seem to happen so regularly?

My undergraduate work in biology gave me a healthy respect for the role an ecosystem plays in the development of the individual organisms within it. An ecosystem is made up of individual species, all living together in a kind of functional web of production and predation. The ecosystem shapes and is shaped by the individuals that comprise it, such that it's impossible to understand how either individuals or ecosystems function without understanding the other. The health of each depends on both.

Organizational cultures are like the ecosystem to the individuals that work in them. Organizational culture certainly includes the explicit, intentional culture. Things like core values, stated priorities, and *we believe* statements fall into this category. Explicit culture is important, as it describes for the community what it should ideally feel like to be part of that community, but the reality is usually not the ideal.

Culture isn't merely, or even primarily, contained in core values. Culture is "how things get done around here." Beneath the explicit culture is a deeper reality, an implicit momentum composed of the accumulated oversights, compromises, and blind spots that make up the rest of the culture—the hidden curriculum. Sometimes the implicit culture in a missional team or organization is patently toxic and destructive, but more often, it's simply diminishing to souls and frustrating to those who wish to make progress. In fact, most of the missional faith communities I've worked in or consulted for have beautiful explicit cultures, and the hidden curricula haven't been monstrous or evil. Rather, they've simply been unintentionally complicit with entropy and unintentionally unfriendly to souls.

An example of unfavorable conditions growing in the shadow of an explicit cultural facet in one organization I love is the value they place on field autonomy—the responsibility and prerogative of each field of service to manage itself. The explicit value, in my view, is very good, as I've seen the opposite in many organizations choke out initiative, innovation, and cultural relevance in the specific places where people are working. The team on the field knows the field the best and should have enormous latitude in discerning what Jesus is inviting them to do and how he's leading them to do it. This autonomy is often accompanied by an unconscious expectation that leadership maintain a hands-off posture. But it's this unconscious expectation that gives rise to two issues that can arise in the shadow of a good idea like field autonomy: perception aversion and benign neglect.

When regional leaders disengage from teams on the ground, usually because the teams are running well and being reasonably well-led, those teams grow accustomed to not being really seen. To avoid taking a high-touch/high-control approach to field teams, leaders at higher levels can default to a low-touch/low-control kind of engagement. But in that low-touch environment, an aversion to accountability can grow as well an anxiety that no one outside our team is seeing what's going on in here. Every team has dysfunctions and disease, but so much unhealth can grow where no one ever looks. No one wants their unhealth unearthed. We're all prone to covering our shame even when there isn't reason to, so perception aversion starts to make us dodgy and defensive. Autonomy becomes isolation, and that's good for no one.

Likewise, when a field team has responsibility for itself and its members, regional leaders can forget that they are not alone in that responsibility. Autonomy in this case can predispose the organization and its leaders to a kind of benign neglect. Care becomes reactive instead of proactive, and resources are allocated to putting out fires instead of to building strong people. Leaders go undeveloped except when they're doing a bad job and require remedial development which leaves the high-capacity personnel to scrape together what they can on their own to develop their innate potential. No one plans to engender a reactive culture that fosters weak personnel who are likely to start more fires. No one intends to hamstring the community by neglecting its leaders' development in favor of staying out of their business. But what begins as an appropriate desire to give field teams freedom, unconsciously devolves into giving them nothing unless they ask for it. By then, of course, it's usually too late and it's limited to what they know to ask for. The motive is benign, but the result is neglect.

Regardless of what we say we value, this is how things get done around here. But this is not all we have in our ecosystem—not by a long shot.

There are, of course, many other good explicit and implicit facets to being us. But the ecosystem is preventing or depressing the individuals' ability to thrive, and therefore requires adjustment through careful reflection and cultivation of the kinds of things we want growing in those spaces.

For example, leaders could set an expectation of transparency for teams and make it easier to be perceived by simply setting a cadence of regular, low-intensity check-ins with field staff in which they experience being perceived and affirmed. Likewise, shifting from a reactive to a proactive stance on member care and leader development would require a change in resource allocation, but would result in people getting care in time, individuals becoming more resilient, and leaders being developed as or before they are desperately needed, which deepens the community's leadership bench and increases its potential for vibrancy and agility in the future.

Adjustments like this help to prevent the ecosystem from muting its individuals' ability to thrive and multiplies their chances of thriving by making the ecosystem itself more generative. That's how leaders build capacity in ecosystems that then engender vibrancy and wellness for their members.

When You Lack the Capacity to Capacitate

No one is a master of all five dimensions of the soul. I'd wager few really ever master one. Sometimes people need capacity development that you're not able to give. They need answers to questions that you can't answer. Fortunately, you don't always have to know. You just have to know someone who does. Referral is often the very best thing you can do for someone.

Capacitation does not always demand that you're the one delivering the help. I'm a spiritual director, but I don't do direction for my direct reports as that creates an ethical bog. However, I will still bring my spiritual direction competencies into conversation—much like a doctor never stops knowing medicine just because they choose not to be someone's primary physician. Even though I could provide that kind of professional care to my staff, I don't. I do, however, know several other gifted spiritual directors,[3] and I'll often refer my people to them.

---

[3] Member care can be defined as: The continual and systematic application of resources into the life of the mission worker before, during, and after their assignment to ensure they have the inner resources to withstand the stresses of their work and its context.

I also know quite a few talented, skilled counselors and psychologists, as well as educational specialists and family therapists. All of these people are resources I can call on to build my staff's capacity to thrive. There are also many excellent books, videos, and courses that can be very helpful if applied at the right time—when desperation or curiosity gives rise to a question one of those resources can answer. Building capacity in our personnel demands that we know *some* things, and that we know where else our people can go when they need more than we can or should give.

Even if you're a therapist, you're not *their* therapist. You can't be. You're their leader. As leaders, it's important that we remember that our relationships with those we lead are not primarily therapeutic. They may well be healing in nature, but this healing happens on the way. It's not our primary relationship, and when we blur those lines, all sorts of entanglements and unmet expectations occur. It's critical to remember that you're their leader, and that power differential is enough to make any other relationship confusing.

> Generative leaders help people thrive,
> and thriving people change the world.

What you can do is catalyze and capacitate. You can use your power to keep questions of thriving before their attention and to make room for them to be able to attend to their souls. You can build their capacity by connecting them with resources and helping them cultivate the competencies they need to become vibrant witnesses to the ever-generous life of Jesus. You can tend the ecosystems they work in, cull the soul-diminishing tendencies in implicit culture and replace them with practices and postures that support their efforts to thrive. In short, we can lead like Jesus. Jesus leads us generatively, formatively, using our real lives with him to heal our souls and make us more, and then leading us back into the world to do the same. Generative leaders help people thrive, and thriving people change the world.

Summary

It's possible to thrive, even in chaos. To thrive, an organism must metabolize its environment, both nutrients and stressors, and turn them into growth and fruit.

The human organism is a soul—an integrated, embodied being. While it's impossible to completely separate the different facets of a soul, it's helpful to think about our humanity as a system of interdependent dimensions—the spiritual, the physical, the cognitive, the emotional, and the relational. In order to nurture thrive in all five dimensions, we need to cultivate awareness and make intelligent choices. We can do this through monthly 5DVector Checks and by building and executing 5DThrive Plans which comprise practices selected to promote Minimum Viable Progress in each dimension. For these plans to be effective, they must take into account the actual realities of our lives, including the particular adversities we face and the people we live with.

Generative leaders have the ability and responsibility to foster vibrancy and fruitfulness in those they lead by catalyzing and capacitating thriving. By investing energy in these two ways, leaders serve their people as they seek to thrive in place. This enables them to bring their whole souls to bear on the work God has given them and on the task of becoming all God has dreamed for them to be. In so doing, soul tending leaders heal the world by promoting strategic human flourishing in Jesus among those they lead as they, in turn, serve a needy world.

This service in the world happens in the context of real work, but that work happens in a world rife with chaos and arrayed to unravel us. If we are to bring the strength we gain to bear on the task of serving the world in our work, we must learn to integrate the disparate parts of our lives into unified expressions of beautiful obedience to Jesus. So, it's to the task of integrated work that we now turn.

Part II
Work | Trunk

Introduction to Part II

The people who love you—including God, your friends, and hopefully your leaders—want you to thrive. We're also looking to thrive so we can bring the most awake, vibrant, vigorous version of ourselves to the calling God has created us uniquely to pursue. We thrive, at least in part, in order to do beautiful, lasting work.

> You're an individual made in God's image,
> and your dignity as such makes the pursuit of your flourishing
> worth it; but we're after more.

Thriving

It's possible for otherwise healthy, thriving people to still break. Those fractures tend to happen in predictable places. You know them already. Family. Team. Integrated identity. Burnout. These, for sure, can be avoided in large measure or mitigated by learning to thrive. But sometimes it seems like the stronger we are, the more quickly we break in these places. Conversely, when these places are reinforced and integrated, our power seems to multiply. This is especially true as we bring our newfound vibrancy to our work, so next we will consider *how* we do our work.

Work

My high school physics class taught me that work equals force times displacement. This is a useful definition. If I push a wheelbarrow ten meters, I have done work. If you push a pencil across your desk, you've done work. If together, we push against a parked tractor trailer, we will expend huge amounts of our energy, but we will do no work. No displacement—no movement, no distance covered, no work. Work is the application of force that also gets something done.

If force isn't transferred efficiently to the object you're trying to move, it's possible to fail to get work done, or to get less work done than you'd expect given the force you're applying. Imagine if you use a bunch of dry spaghetti or a pool noodle as a lever. With the spaghetti, the force can't produce work because the lever breaks. The pool noodle doesn't work because the lever isn't rigid, so force is lost as it leaks out through the flexibility of the implement. Fracture and leakage. Many of us fracture, and most of us leak. This has a frustrating effect on our work.

The people I lead have many different jobs. The specifics of each person's work is unique, but we should all approach that work in a similar way. How does work contribute to thriving or foster glory in ourselves and others as lights in the dark? To answer this question, we must consider the unique position our work occupies between thriving and development.

Our task now is to consider and explore how to lead ourselves and others from thriving toward strategic human flourishing. This task demands that we steward the strength and vitality we gain through our investment in ourselves and our connection with Jesus and that we somehow direct that strength simultaneously toward doing good and becoming more. To do so, we must purposefully integrate the various parts of our real lives into one coherent expression of strength and beauty. Our ability to leverage our newly cultivated strength to do good work—to not just expend effort but to actually get somewhere—is dependent upon how well we can integrate those parts.

Let me offer a few examples.

Bracing

I enjoy strength training, and in particular three compound barbell lifts that comprise the classic expressions of raw strength: the back squat, the deadlift, and the overhead press. I won't bore you with descriptions of how these lifts are performed, except for a key detail that helps illuminate the necessity of integration in the expression of strength.

These three lifts aren't cosmetic movements. They are prized for their ability to make you truly strong. In different ways, they each require you to use every single limb, and nearly every muscle in your body. They don't isolate a body part or even half of your frame, but demand that you successfully integrate and coordinate the top and bottom halves of your body and all four limbs in order to perform them safely and successfully. To be sure, lighter weights can be lifted without this integration, but when there is significant weight on the bar, there's no way to move it correctly without connecting the whole body.

It's the integration of your diverse parts that prevents injury and makes force production possible. You can move heavy weight and not get hurt if you're strong and integrated. In fact, the argument can be made that you're only really as strong as you are integrated. Strong parts only make a strong whole when they are adequately integrated and coordinated.

We brace by taking a large belly breath and cinching the muscles of the abdomen down against it. This technique creates significant intra-abdominal pressure, making your trunk rigid and giving your limbs something firm to leverage against, facilitating the transfer of force from your legs through your trunk to your hands and into the barbell. This allows work to happen. Without this rigidity, the best one can hope for (with heavy loads) is failure. The more likely outcome is force leakage, fatigue, and severe spinal injury. Without insisting on integration, we can't do as much work as we'd like, and when we can, it is often with significant risk.

Breathing

This isn't only the case when you're trying to do something really hard once or twice like deadlifting twice your body weight. Integration of your whole body is also critical for effectively producing smaller amounts of force repeatedly like when a fighter throws punches. None of the punches are maximal efforts, but every one of them is intended to make contact and do damage. For a punch to be effective, it usually has to be part of a combination of punches.

The power for punches comes from the legs. The legs drive the feet into the ground and leverage the fighter's body weight against gravity. The arms are not where the bulk of the power comes from. Certainly, some of the force in a punch comes from the muscles of the upper body, but the vast majority comes from the legs and especially the rotation of the hips. The purpose of the arms is to deliver the power generated by the legs through the hands into specifically chosen targets on the opponent's body. Force comes from the legs and hips; speed comes from the arms, and this combination produces a powerful punch.

But only when they combine. How is this combination achieved reliably and repeatedly? By breathing in a very specific way.

Fighters breathe from the diaphragm freely and fully when not giving or receiving strikes. But when they throw punches, they'll inhale once and exhale tiny blasts of air through their noses or through clenched teeth and hiss a little explosion with each strike. If you've ever seen a fight or watched a boxer train, you've heard the sound. There are multiple purposes for the explosive breath which include tensing the abdomen in case a counter shot is thrown to the body, and simply regulating breathing to avoid gassing out early in the fight. But by far the most important purpose of the fighter's breath is to integrate the top and bottom portions of her body at the moment the blow lands, allowing her whole body to contribute to producing the force being delivered in the blow. In effect, it's exactly like bracing in weightlifting, but for fractions of the time, over and over again. A fighter learns to breathe in a way that allows perfect integration of all the moving parts of his body, repeatedly and reliably, in order to make every punch count.

Integration

A well-known biblical example of integration is found in Ecclesiastes 4:12, "A threefold cord is not quickly broken." A rope is made by twisting individual strands together, multiplying tensile strength and resistance to abrasion. Integrating the individual strands makes the whole stronger than the sum of its parts.

Designed integration doesn't only multiply the ability to pull but also the ability to hold things up. Many species of trees have trunks and root systems that work together, sometimes even growing together into integrated buttresses and structures that allow the tree to hold up massive systems of fruiting branches whose weight far exceeds what the individual parts of the trunk would be able to hold up without integration. These trees have been designed to hold up whole ecosystems through integrated biological architecture.

When God makes trees, he designs them with integration in mind. The expression of strength and application of power are dependent not only upon how strong we are, but also upon how well we can hold our strength together in concerted and directed efforts without coming undone in the process.

Our prior discussion of thriving included the assertion that entropy is real and that things come undone by themselves. Our efforts to thrive are investments against that gradient. Likewise, in a cosmos where entropy is undeniable, we must expect predispositions toward disintegration. This is especially true at the key points where we are trying to gain leverage and apply useful force—in other words, we should expect tendencies toward disintegration wherever we try to do good, lasting work.

Thus, intelligent, adamant, relentless attention and investment of appropriate energy is necessary. Without it the strength we gain learning to thrive leaks away through faulty seams, or worse, we come apart at those seams as the very strength we've cultivated breaks us in the middle. When we live integrated lives, more of our effort goes toward the desired effects, and less energy is lost. Integrated lives are more fruitful lives, and we make these integrations in our work in the world.

In the following chapters we will explore four key integrations:

- Integrating your work with God's work
- Integrating your vocation and your ministry
- Integrating your oikos and your mission
- Integrating yourself and your communities

Certainly, there are other integrations we could discuss. But these four are the places where I've most often seen people fracture. These are, in my opinion, the critical junctures that must be attended to, invested in, and woven together if we are to avoid catastrophic injury and if we are to multiply the power Christ is giving us to effect lasting change in the world.

9

Integrating Your Work and God's Work

In this chapter we'll:

- Look at the examples of Paul and Jesus regarding coworking with God
- Examine the contemplative stride
- Consider practical guidance on cultivating this integration

God is at work in the world, holding the cosmos together, upsetting entropy, renewing creation, saving the day, and making the sad things come untrue. We all have parts to play in the restoration of all things, but we only can play them to the degree that our work is aligned with his. Perhaps the most significant losses of our energy occur when our efforts are uncoupled from his. Two ways this disintegration is most obvious is when we spend our limited energy working where God isn't working, and when we attempt God-sized stuff with human-sized batteries. In both cases we wind up exhausted and God's intentions to use us are, for the present at least, unrealized.

It's critical to remember the goal of our work in the world: obedience and fruitfulness. As we noted in chapter 2, we seek a beautiful obedience—not the reflexive obedience of slaves, but the reflective obedience of sons and daughters, actively engaged in their Father's business. Here a distinction must be made: activity does not equal obedience. It's possible to stay busy, even pathologically so, with things God never asked you to do.

This is easy to get wrong, though. We know that inactivity doesn't usually equal obedience, so we make the logical leap that if we get busy with good things, we will be doing what pleases the Father. But the Father is pleased by obedience. Not because he's an insecure tyrant, but because he's calling the plays and the goodness he wants to give to the world is tied to our intelligent, listening cooperation. Beautiful, reflective, loving, discerning obedience is the sign of life that matters.

If our work is to yield fruitful, beautiful obedience, we'll need to discern what God's actually up to in our contexts, to identify our unique part in what he's doing, and then to do that *with him*. When we integrate our work with God's, we find God working with us.

The Example of Paul

In the opening portions of his letter to the church at Colossae, Paul spends some time helping his readers understand why he's writing them and how to understand his work. He says that he focuses on a few key activities—proclaiming Jesus, and warning and teaching those he comes in contact with—in order to be able one day to present people to God complete in Christ. Paul has discerned what God is doing in his context, and he's even identified the part that is his to play.

"For this I toil," he says, "struggling with all [God's] energy that he powerfully works within me" (Col 1:29). Paul knows that God is at work in the world, and in him. Further, God is doing both with all his might. Paul, therefore, cooperates with that direction and energy and brings all his might to bear on it.

The church I grew up in used to warn us, "Be careful not to work in your strength but in God's. If you're struggling, you're probably not working in God's strength." The idea was that life with God's infinite strength was supposed to be effortless for us. But that doesn't seem to be how Paul sees it. Rather, like a fireman has to almost ride a firehose with his full weight and all his strength, we must also work—really toil and strive—even when we're working with God. It's both human and divine to work hard.

Paul's hard work, however, is with the dynamic and wild power of God who personally works inside and alongside Paul as Paul works alongside him. This is the kind of integration of our work with God's that can and must become normal for us. Too much is at stake to waste time pursuing our own ends or working disconnected from his power.

The Example of Jesus

> My Father is working until now, and I am working … Truly, truly, I say to you, the Son can do nothing of his own accord, but only what he sees the Father doing. For whatever the Father does, that the Son does likewise. For the Father loves the Son and shows him all that he himself is doing …

I can do nothing on my own. As I hear, I judge, and my judgment is just, because I seek not my own will but the will of him who sent me. (John 5:17, 19–20, 30)

Jesus clearly lived in a universe in which his Father was perpetually working, and Jesus located his work within and alongside that work. "My Father is working until now," he said, "and I am working." Jesus didn't appear burdened with the responsibility to start something—he came to join a game that was already afoot.

Indeed, Jesus didn't seem to think he *could* do anything on his own, but he saw that the only effective, lasting work he could do was the work the Father was already doing. "The Son," he said, "can do nothing by himself." If that is true for the Son of God, how much more is it true for me and you? But what the Father did, the Son also did. Jesus describes a dance of dependence, a coordinated cooperation so close that to see one move was to see the other move.

This kind of synergy was possible because Jesus had his eyes open. God *showed* Jesus what he was up to. He didn't make Jesus track it down or figure it out. He showed him. Why? Because he loves him. The Father shared his deeds with the Son not to position the Son for more productive labor but because of fierce affection for him. "For the Father loves the Son and shows him all he does."

The picture painted is of a working, showing, speaking God, and a working, seeing, listening Jesus. Jesus was limited to what he saw and heard from the Father, in part because that's all that will work, but also because of what motivated him. Jesus wasn't working to answer questions about himself. *Am I enough? Is this enough?* He wasn't working to fulfill noble personal ambitions. *I will show them the way, and I'll be king, and save the world.* Jesus wasn't working from an individual drive, but from a shared, relational generativity. "For the Father loves the Son and shows him all he himself is doing. ... I seek not my own will but the will of him who sent me" (John 5:20, 30). Jesus was capable of this kind of tactical harmony with the Father because he wasn't working to satisfy something in himself but from a desire to make God's relentlessly generous heart happy.

This generous and generative working relationship isn't exclusive to Jesus and the Father. Quite the contrary, in fact. It's supposed to be normative for us. John builds his gospel narrative around several key themes one of which is the notion of Jesus as *sent*. The word *sent* and its derivatives occur almost sixty times in John's presentation of Jesus.

As John begins to conclude his gospel, he gives us a scene in which Jesus speaks to his gathered friends, prophetically announces the impartation of the Holy Spirit, and says to them (and to all the readers of John's gospel), "As the Father has sent me, even so I am sending you" (John 20:21).

With these words, John connects Jesus's understanding of himself as sent from God, and the work attached to that vocation to our understanding of ourselves. We are to know ourselves as, among other things, sent by Jesus into the world. The relationship Jesus had with the Father, we now have with the Father and the Son by the Spirit he gave us. Now the Father and the Son, by the Spirit, show us what the Father is up to. He's always been working, right up to this very day. He loves you, and he wants to show you what he's doing, so you can join him in it. As you continue to integrate your work with his, trusting his love, his lead, and his voice, your desire becomes increasingly to make his great, generous heart happy. And that's good for everyone.

The Contemplative Stride

What Jesus describes in John 5 is not dissimilar to something Elaine Heath has called, "A contemplative stance." She describes a way of life in which we show up, pay attention, get involved, and release the outcomes. It's a way to live responsively to the Spirit in the normal grind of daily life.

Some of our lives are rarely very normal, though. For many reading this book, normal was left behind some time ago for something a little wilder—a life of pilgrimage in the hard places. People like us need a contemplative *stride*. Here's how an adaptation of Heath's stance might look for people in motion on the raggedy edges of the world.

Show All the Way Up

To integrate our work with God's, we'll need to be wide awake and fully in the moment. God is at work *here, now*. So that's where we've got to be. To do that we'll need to show up to God, to ourselves, and to our contexts.

When we show up to God, we want to show up to him as he is, not as we fear him to be, think him to be, or wish he would be. God's not an idea or a range of possibilities. He's infinite, yes, but not variable. God is as he is, and it is with this God that we have business. The more work we do to align our sense of God with that of Jesus, the easier it's going to become to tune in to him in the moments of our lives. Likewise, as we attempt to tune in more frequently and with greater focus, our souls begin to get the groove of connecting with him, and it becomes second nature when we most need it to be.

When we show up to ourselves, we need to show up to us as we are, not as we fear ourselves to be, think we are, or wish we were. This practice is always hard because none of us knows ourself completely. Every human heart is a mystery even to itself. But if we can be as honest as we can about what we're feeling in a given moment, we position ourselves to be led and blessed by God. God only leads us from where we actually are and blesses us as we actually are—not where or as we're pretending to be.

It's useful to notice resonances and resistances. When we check in with ourselves, we may notice excitement, drawing, desire—resonance. Or we may notice dread, combativeness, repulsion—resistance. In either case, there is something worth looking into. Curiosity will draw us toward resonances, but it's just as important to go looking where we fear we'll find a dragon, because dragons hoard gold. As Jordan Peterson says,

> Why would a dragon hoard gold? Because the dragon represents everything that you're afraid of. What's embedded in everything you're afraid of? Absolutely everything that you need to find. Run from what you're afraid of, run from exactly what you need to find. Dragons hoard gold because the thing you most need is always to be found where you least want to look.[1]

> We can't skim across the surface of the water; we must dive.

When we show up to our context, we must show up to it, as much as we can, as it is, not as we fear it to be, think it is, or wish it were. This is especially true when we wander far from home, in cultures very foreign to us, and when we return home after such a journey. When we cross cultures, and when we cross back, we must go deep. We must live where the locals live. Shop where they shop. Grieve where they grieve, and celebrate where they celebrate. We can't skim across the surface of the water; we must dive. And when we dive, we must eschew the scuba suit and the safe air supply. We must strip down to our bare essentials and free dive until we grow gills. The contemplative stride invites us to show up as we are, with God as he is, to where we are as it is, without defense or delusion.

---

1 Peterson, "Why Would a Dragon."

Pay Attention

Once we've showed up, we must wake up. We can live large portions of our lives on autopilot, but we don't have to. If we are going to find where God is working in a situation, we must pay attention. This attention costs us something. It's a resource. We can only spend so much of it in a day or a week. Our reserves are limited, so if we're to have enough attention left to pay when an opportune moment arises, we'll have to grow our reserves and learn to steward it carefully. We must protect our attention from meaningless distractions in the off hours and learn to focus it at will.

But where should we direct our attention? I've found it helpful to first focus on seeing the people around me. This seems obvious, but it's amazing how many people we can walk past in an hour and never actually see them. I was a resident assistant in college. My RA partner and I looked after a dormitory of seventy-two young men. My room was in the middle of the hall, and one evening after a long day of classes, I closed the door of my room behind me and realized I couldn't remember walking from the dormitory door at the end of the hall to my room. What's worse, I knew I had spoken to at least three of my guys in the hall just moments before, but for the life of me I couldn't remember which ones or what any of us had said. I was on autopilot.

The next day I decided to purposefully make eye contact with everyone I passed in the dorm hall, no matter what kind of hurry I was in or what sort of day I was having. This one decision, this tiny habit, made a world of difference in the depth and quality of my relationships with my men and in how I prayed for them. The thirty second walk from my door to the end of the hall sometimes lasted five minutes, sometimes less, but I was paying attention, so when God showed me things, I was able to see them.

Sadly, I haven't always paid that kind of attention. You probably haven't, either. In her masterful book *Strengthening the Soul of Your Leadership*, Ruth Haley Barton observes, "*Many* of us are choosing to live lives that do not set us up to pay attention, to notice those places where God is at work and to ask ourselves what these things mean."[2] Our ability to pay attention is often tied to the kind of pace of life we choose. Barton asks,

---

2 Barton, *Strengthening the Soul*, 62.

> How much paying attention am I doing—really? Do I have enough give in my schedule to be able to turn aside when there is something that warrants it? Could it be because I am moving so fast that I do not have time to turn aside and look? Do I even have mechanisms in my life that create space for paying attention, so that I don't miss the places where God himself is trying to communicate with me?[3]

These questions come from Barton's reflections on the encounter between Moses and God in the burning bush in Exodus 3.

> And the angel of the LORD appeared to him in a flame of fire out of the midst of a bush. He looked, and behold, the bush was burning, yet it was not consumed. And Moses said, "I will turn aside to see this great sight, why the bush is not burned." When the LORD saw that he turned aside to see, God called to him out of the bush. (Exod 3:2–4)

Barton suggests that we pay attention to burning bushes both without and within. Something in our situations, surroundings, or conversations catches our attention. It shimmers differently, the words ring deeper. It piques our curiosity and invites us to stop what we were doing and focus here. Why? Because it could well be God, but we won't know unless we "turn aside to see."

"There seemed to be a cause-and-effect relationship," Barton posits, "between Moses' willingness to pay attention and God's willingness to speak."[4] This conversation for Moses amounted to a restoration and clarification of vocation, a demonstration of miraculous power, and direction for the rest of his life. For the Hebrew people, it led to their salvation from slavery and eventual settlement of the Promised Land. Such a huge change, and God was pleased to start it with a curious flicker on a hillside. Imagine what might *not* have happened if Moses hadn't paid attention.

But where do we look for these burning bushes? I've used this analogy with many friends along the way who are learning how to lead by discernment. I encourage them to look and listen for signs of desire. Desire is the human heart's receptor site for God. In the Gospels, as we've noted, Jesus's most frequent question was, "What do you want?" If we are hunting for where God might be at work, a great place to look is desire.

---

3 Barton, 62.
4 Barton, 60–61.

Desire sometimes looks like longing, or ambition. Sometimes it sounds like nostalgia, or reveals itself in what you miss or grieve for. Recall in chapter 5 how we learned to interview our emotions to see what they might tell us about our desires. We can do the same thing with the people we talk to. A curious, truly non-leading question is almost never ill received, and we can notice desires that well up within our own hearts as we enter others' lives.

> Desire is the human heart's receptor site for God.

In this way we can narrow the field somewhat from everything assaulting our overwhelmed senses to the people in front of us. From there, it narrows more to the expressed needs or desires, and finally from among those expressions, we may find something that glints or sings to us a little differently. We may find a burning bush. This is not always God at work, but it often is. In any case, if Jesus is to be believed, we need not worry too much about getting it wrong. It's God's job to show us which bushes he's lit up. It's our job to be paying attention.

Listen and Obey

Once we've paid attention and are actually tracking what's happening inside and out, and once we have some sense of what God *might* be up to, or at least suspect we've caught his scent, what must come next is action. We must attempt obedience.

Obeying is more nuanced than getting involved, pitching in, or making a contribution. Obedience implies relationship between the one who obeys and the one being obeyed. It assumes that the work will be done according to the intent of the one giving the instructions. When we get involved, we aren't trying to make our mark. We're trying to make his. As Jesus said, "I seek not to please myself but him who sent me" (John 5:30, NIV).

To obey we'll have to listen for what he wants us to do. The instructions may come as words but more often as an impression. Sometimes there's a bright convergence of a biblical teaching, present need or opportunity, and a distinct pressure or drawing in the heart to act. There can even be an overwhelming compassion that demands action, as we'll see happened often with Jesus. We need not fear missing it if we have been paying attention. Our confidence isn't in our ability to hear, but in his ability to make himself clear enough for our glad cooperation.

We must also be listening for what *not* to do. Here I don't only mean foibles and missteps, but also good, intelligent, sensible contributions that we could make, but are being led not to. This kind of talk can raise anxiety about doing it wrong, but it needn't be a fearful thing. God hasn't given us a spirit of fear, so fear is never useful in discerning how to obey. God isn't guiding us into the obedience of toddlers in a minefield, but of adult children enjoying a marvelous dance. He leads; we follow, but there's so much room for creative expression. In *The Contemplative Pastor*, Eugene Peterson assures us:

> We do not learn our relationship with God out of a cocksure, arrogant knowledge of exactly what God wants (which launches us into a vigorous clean-up campaign of the world on his behalf, in the course of which we shout orders at him, bossing him around so that he can assist us in accomplishing his will). Nor do we cower before him in a scrupulous anxiety that fears offending him, only venturing a word or an action when explicitly commanded, and at all other times worrying endlessly of what we might have done to offend him.[5]

God is glad to lead, and he shows us what he's doing and tells us our part because he loves us. We can be glad to follow, to listen, and to obey, because we're not robots or slaves, but sons and daughters, working elbow-to-elbow with our magnificently competent Father. We are artisans in the family business of making the world beautiful again.

> God isn't guiding us into the obedience of toddlers in a minefield, but of adult children enjoying a marvelous dance.

Release the Outcomes

Western spiritual leadership is sometimes approached like business leadership with a dash of Jesus to baptize it along with some pithy remarks about how leaders serve. We are trained to focus on outcomes. *Where are the results?* This question is not without wisdom. If something is patently not working repeatedly, then it certainly deserves some scrutiny.

---

5 Eugene Peterson, *Contemplative Pastor*, 107.

But success in kingdom endeavors can't be measured by outcomes. Too many wills are involved, and too many different timelines are in play—none of which are to be violated. Some of God's intentions are for right now, so the results will fruit presently. Some of his intentions are for much later, and success will look very much like failure.

> Some of God's intentions are for right now,
> so the results will fruit presently.

I was having lunch once with a dear friend. Perplexed and anxious about the apparent lack of fruit in my evangelistic efforts at the time, I worried aloud that I might not really have anything to offer the wider missional conversations I was being invited into. He said something—I don't quite recall what—and I wondered, *When am I going to stop measuring outcomes and start measuring obedience?* What if success is a matter of doing what Jesus says, no matter how costly, dangerous, absurd, or mundane? What if his role is to aim and to measure, and ours is to do our small and indispensable parts?

Beautiful obedience is ours. Outcomes aren't. Just as the action is initiated by God, it will also be brought to completion by him.

You may have noticed I wrote that last sentence in the passive voice. Americans hate the passive voice. My friends in Central Asia loved it. I edited a newspaper for one of the government ministries while I lived there, and the majority of my toil was to transform passive voiced sentences into robust, active statements.

Ancient Greek has a third option. Eugene Peterson, again in *The Contemplative Pastor*, lets us in on the middle voice. While we don't have a direct equivalent in English, we do have an example—the phrase *to counsel*. I can counsel a friend (active voice). I can be counseled (passive voice). But I can also *take counsel*. In this case—the middle voice—I can participate in the action that another initiates and completes. Peterson suggests the middle voice is where we live our lives with God:

> In prayer, I do not control the action. That is a pagan concept of prayer, putting the gods to work by my incantations or rituals. I am not controlled by the action. That is a Hindu concept of prayer in which I slump passively into the impersonal and fated will of gods and goddesses. I enter into the action begun by another, my creating and saving Lord, and find myself participating in the results of the action. I neither do it, nor

have it done to me; I will to participate in what is willed. ... Prayer and spirituality feature participating, the complex participation of God and the human, His will and our wills. ... We neither manipulate God (active voice) nor are we manipulated by God (passive voice). We are involved in the action and participate in its results but do not control or define it (middle voice). Prayer takes place in the middle voice. ... At our human and Christian best we pray in the middle voice at the center between active and passive, drawing from them as we have need and occasion, but always uniquely and artistically ourselves, "participating in the results of the action."[6]

The contemplative stride takes place entirely in the middle voice. We show up and pay attention to what God has initiated. Then, we obey and trust the Spirit to guide us aright and keep our senses tuned for additional instruction. Finally, we carefully discern when our scene in the drama is ending, and we let the play go on and release the outcomes to the show's writer, director, and star.

> The contemplative stride takes place entirely in the middle voice.

We see this pattern repeatedly in Jesus's life. One excellent example is recorded in Matthew 14 and Mark 6. Jesus and his students are awash in desperate people and in the midst of ministry so busy that they don't have time to eat. It is in this time that Jesus received news that his cousin, John the Baptist, had been beheaded.

Jesus shows up. He shows up to his students, to their fatigue, and to their need to step away and rest. He and his students get in a boat and leave the effective work they were doing and set sail for the other side of the lake where they hope to rest, recover strength, and perhaps grieve.

But the crowds have other plans. They see where the boat is headed and run around the lake, outpacing Jesus and his friends just enough so that they, and their needs, meet the weary workers on the other side. When Jesus steps off the boat, he has the option to stop showing up, to withdraw, and to recoil. But he doesn't. He stays engaged and he pays attention to what's in front of him. A crowd running around a lake is out of the ordinary, like a burning bush, maybe.

---

6 Peterson, *Contemplative Pastor*, 103–5.

Matthew and Mark both say, "When he went ashore he saw a great crowd, and he had compassion on them" (Matt 14:14). Mark adds that he perceived them like sheep without a shepherd. He saw them, and he saw their need, and a burning bush within was lit. The term here is *splagchnizomai*, and it refers to a deep, nearly irresistible, compelling compassion felt viscerally in the gut. It's a powerful term, and the synoptic Gospels (Matthew, Mark, and Luke) are peppered with it. The earliest adherents to Jesus and his way remembered him as a man compelled by compassion. For Jesus, this compassion amounted to directions from the Father. As Terrence W. Tilley puts it, "if only God or God's empowering and empowered agent is the only subject of this particular verb in the New Testament, *the power of such compassion must be divine.*"[7]

So, Jesus obeys this direction from within. Mark says he teaches the crowd many things. Matthew says he heals their diseases. The compassion carries on through dinner, and sets up one of the most significant miracles recorded in the Gospels—the feeding of the five thousand.

But when dinner is over, Jesus leaves. Both writers tell us he does so, "immediately." He sends his students away in a boat, dismisses the crowds, and hikes up a mountain to pray. Finally, the solitude he was after in the first place. What's of note to us here is that there's no external signal that it's time to go. He teaches, heals, feeds, and releases the outcomes. He doesn't explain to the crowds the significance of the miracle, or what it means. He doesn't ask them to stop chasing him. The compassion is satisfied; the instructions are complete, and Jesus lets it go and moves on to solitude, silence, and the next burning bush.

Some Practical Help

The example of Jesus in John 5 provides a few clues as to how to live and work deeply enmeshed and integrated with God and his work in the world.

Perhaps the first, and most obvious, is the primacy of discernment. We must become perceptive, attentive, and likely to see and hear what's afoot around us. Strategy is important, and we can see the curves and lines of carefully laid plans especially as we trace the work and travels of Paul in the New Testament. But strategic thinking, though necessary, is never sufficient. We must be able to see beyond, within, and under what first presents itself to us. Further, we must be able to discern which needs and opportunities before us are actually where God is working

---

7 Tilley, *Disciples' Jesus*, 156 (emphasis in original).

and inviting us to join him. In a world that overwhelms our senses and decimates our attention spans, this kind of sensitivity doesn't come naturally and must be intentionally cultivated.

> But strategic thinking, though necessary,
> is never sufficient.

This leads us to the second clue. Jesus practiced a life of deep engagement and radical withdrawal. We see this in the example above. He deeply engages with the crowds, and then he attempts to withdraw with his students to rest. When that fails, he deeply engages again, but then sends the crowd *and* his students away and withdraws totally. I think this is instructive for us because we rarely make the most of solitude even when we can make the time and space for it. We get alone and quiet, and then we check email, social media, and messages. We withdraw partially, and then consequently engage partially. We are never all the way in either gear. This leaves us idling at best, but more often grinds us down.

When Jesus is alone, he prays. A brief survey of the Gospels reveals a stunning frequency with which significant decisions or changes of direction are preceded by protracted periods of solitary prayer. Discernment *happens* in the noisy crowd, but it's *practiced* alone on the quiet mountain.

Finally, the role of emotion in divine guidance needs to become more vivid. The Jesus of the Gospels is a deeply emotional man, and those emotions were very often a source of guidance. This is not to say that all emotions are guidance, and indeed some emotions are never guidance. Nor is it to say that emotionalism equates to discernment. In the New Testament, the heart was understood to contain the mind *and* the emotions, and to attempt discernment while ignoring our feelings is to try to listen with one ear plugged and one eye shut. It's unnecessary and counter-productive. Better we become competent and sensitive to the Father with all the powers he has given us, so that we may integrate those powers with his own.

Perhaps you can see the obvious overlap between the practices that support spiritual and emotional thriving outlined in the first part of this book and the competencies necessary to the integration of our work with God's. As we proceed further in our discussion of integrated work, these points of overlap will continue. This overlap is to be expected since we seek to thrive in order to do the good works that God has foreordained that we should walk in.

10
Integrating Your Vocation and Your Ministry

In this chapter we'll:

- Look at the problem of integrated identity
- Consider how a shift in focus can help integrate vocation and ministry
- Examine how a vivid, public obedience can lead to shared practice and new disciples

"*Fact!* You study martial art."

The way Vefa was vigorously mispronouncing *fact* in her Russian accent sounded like I was in a lot of trouble. It was hilarious, but I kept a straight face.

"*Fact!*" she continued, "You have more than one master degree. *Fact!* You type very fast with all finger of both hands. I have you! We know who you are now! You are CIA!"

Well, there it was. *Fact* thrice over. In front of my entire intermediate English class, Vefa had brilliantly deduced from my hobbies, education, and typing acumen that I was working for the CIA.

"Vefa," I let some of the amusement creep into my voice, "you think I'm a *spy*? I live here with my wife and a bunch of kids. What brought you to this exciting conclusion?"

"You think I have not seen movie? In movie, American spy always know martial art, always have much education, and always type on computer using all fingers. Different people do these things, yes, but no one except spy do all of them." She had me there. But what she said next left me breathless. "Besides, why else would you come here, and *stay* here, in our broken, corrupt little mud puddle country? How you pay bills with this little school? You make no sense."

This happened a lot. Many of the cross-cultural workers I know have been confused for intelligence agents at least once. It's no wonder. People think in categories, so when we appear, having descended on the wings of the morning from the heavenly city of America, and we go about our daily lives with our odd schedules and apparent immunity to hunger and calamity, they are left bewildered by us.

We, in turn, are left with a wall of confusion and suspicion between us and the people we're trying to engage. *Fact.*

Integrated Identity: Everyone's Problem

Conversations like this get bundled into something called *integrated identity*. It's not the sole purview of cross-cultural workers—indeed, most followers of Jesus could use some help here—but cross-cultural workers need to have a clear, understandable, integrated identity.

Countries can be placed in one of two categories. Limited access countries and open countries. The terms are inadequate to the complexity they describe, but let's use them, anyway. Limited access countries are places you can't get a missionary visa. It's illegal to proselytize (their term, usually) and sometimes illegal for locals to be Christians. Christians are still the most persecuted population on the planet, in large part due to the governments of these countries. Conversion (again, their term) usually comes with some form of censure, and often with imprisonment, torture, or death. Some of these places are impoverished, and some incredibly rich. Access to the country isn't limited so much as access to the gospel is.

Disciple-makers in contexts like these obviously don't live there as missionaries. Rather, they start businesses that contribute economically and materially to the country. Or they get hired in existing businesses and organizations, occupying roles they are uniquely fitted to fill, due to their international experience and/or being native speakers of a major trade language, like English, French, or Chinese. Most often, they have portfolio careers, meaning they hold a few part-time positions with different enterprises to pay the bills.

In the past, people would instead cultivate something called a *platform*—a way of being in the country legally but was rarely what it appeared to be. The industry parlance for this approach is *job-faking*, to be contrasted with *job-making* (starting a real business) or *job-taking* (getting hired at an existing local company).

Platforms had their perks, for sure. They give you immense control of your time, and allow you a lot of freedom to do what you came to do. When people move to a limited access country in hopes of making the gospel more available to people so they can choose to follow Jesus or not, they want to spend their time talking with people about Christ's kingdom and demonstrating it with deeds of love and power. They may not want to spend their time negotiating deals, filing legal briefs, or teaching chemical engineering. This is understandable.

But what isn't understandable is who they are to their local friends. Workers lack an identity that holds their deep desires and their everyday lives visibly and comprehensibly together. Instead of a secret identity, they need an integrated identity—a self-understanding and a consequent self-presentation to the world that is truthful, hides nothing, and makes sense.

This is just as true in open countries. Open countries are those places where you can practice whatever religion you want. You might get mocked, disowned, or misunderstood, but you probably won't get maimed or killed for following Jesus. Conversion is usually viewed as a personal choice, and foreigners can move there as missionaries or religious workers. Being a pastor doesn't end in a prison sentence, though it's often the end of your ability to make disciples.

When I was a pastor, the single greatest obstacle I faced to making disciples was the fact I was a pastor. I'm not suggesting being a pastor is bad, but it presents significant obstacles, the chief among them being the things I could *say* to my congregation far outstripped the things I could *show* them because the way we passed most of our waking hours was so different. Their day jobs looked nothing like mine which crippled my ability to model a vivid companionship with Jesus in the workday world.

Ray, a local friend of mine in Central Asia, once commented that foreign workers were professional meeting-havers. He said they call meetings, go to meetings, have meetings to work out what was discussed at the meetings, and tried to start Jesus-meetings. He said they met like it was their job. He said this in contrast to *my* workday. I taught at a university and a local international school, and I ran a language acquisition consulting business on the side. Ray could understand this. I had a job and a side-hustle, and also met with Ray weekly to help him grow as a disciple of Jesus. I held a portfolio career in part because we needed money, but mostly because it allowed me to model a discipleship that I never could as a professional minister.

Is that to say full-time Christian workers are doing it wrong? No, absolutely not. But whether you work as a professor in a limited access country or as a pastor or missionary in a more open context, both environments present challenges to your ability to make disciples. They either limit what you can say and how much time you can give to saying it, or they limit what you can show because your day-to-day life is so different from the lives your hosts lead. In both cases, the question of how to integrate your vocation and your ministry—your day job and your disciple-making—becomes central.

From Making to Being

An organization I work closely with describes itself as a community of disciple-makers from all professions. I like this description for several reasons. First, I appreciate the emphasis on "all professions." We are all called to obey Christ's commission to disciple the nations not just those among us who are clergy. I also like that it emphasizes the actual commission given to us by Christ before his ascension, that is, to make disciples. Focusing our efforts down to actual obedience to our King's command is wise. It can keep us from spending our energy on missional-ish exploits that don't actually bring people into glad obedience to Jesus.

However, I think we would be well served, especially as we think about integrating our vocations and our ministries, to take one step back from *making* disciples to attend more vigorously to *being* disciples. This shift has greatly simplified my attempts at integration regardless of where I live or how much freedom I enjoy.

> I think we would be well served, especially as we think about integrating our vocations and our ministries, to take one step back from *making* disciples to attend more vigorously to *being* disciples.

At a conference in Ontario, I heard Dallas Willard describe discipleship as "vivid companionship with Jesus." I love that. Weaving together my day job and my calling becomes increasingly effortless as my companionship with Jesus becomes increasingly vivid to me and to the people watching me live. As my apprenticeship to Jesus gets sharper, more vibrant, and more visible, the problems of integration seem to disappear.

To be clear, I'm not talking about a vivid presentation of your discipleship, but rather the presentation of a genuinely vivid discipleship. We aren't trying to *look* good in public. We're trying to *become* good in public and letting people look, but this only works if our companionship with Jesus actually is becoming more vivid. A city set on a hill can't be hidden, but it can be shrouded in a fog of mediocre, half-hearted religiosity. Let's avoid that.

I think the trick here is to lean hard into our identities as disciples. The Scriptures tell us we have several wonderful, essential identities. Names like *son, daughter, priest,* and *beloved of God* should occupy the very center of our self-understanding. But it's easy to be cataclysmically wrong about these. Perhaps you weren't loved well as a child. Or you were abused or abandoned by your father. Perhaps religion was used to stifle your heart instead of to guide it. By themselves, these are tragedies. Imagine how the tragedy is compounded when you try to view God, or to understand how God views you, through the cracked and mottled lenses these tragedies left you with. The core truths of who you are become lies about you and about God. You need someone who knows better and is committed to helping you know it too so that you can be free of the stories you're trapped in—the stories that mute the glory inside you. What you need is a teacher.

I'm convinced that this is why Jesus came to us as a rabbi. When he walked the earth, Jesus made one invitation: Follow me. Become my disciple. Join the community of people who, together, are learning from me how to live their lives as I would. Whatever our misconceptions might be, Jesus is the authority on what God is actually like. Jesus can teach you how to be loved, led, and parented by God. *Disciple* is not our only identity, and it may not even be the most important, but it's certainly the first, and it's how we learn the rest of them. As we explicitly understand Jesus as our teacher and ourselves as his students, he shapes our understanding and experience, and our discipleship becomes more authentic. The more vivid our companionship with Jesus is to us, the more vivid it will be to others.

A Public Obedience

Again, this is not about being nice people. It's a matter of finding out what Jesus thinks and how Jesus feels about everything and then explicitly attaching your opinions, decisions, and contributions to that. Men were typically promiscuous where we used to live in Central Asia. Routinely, I'd be invited to go solicit prostitutes with men in the neighborhood, and sometimes even colleagues at work. It would have been easy to just say, "No thanks," or even, "No thanks, I'm a Christian, and Christians don't do that."

Instead, I chose to blame Jesus. "You guys know I follow Jesus the Messiah, right? Yeah, so in the Law, God said that a man should love his wife and only sleep with her. Adultery is destructive to the man, the woman, families, and the whole community. Jesus the Messiah said even entertaining it in my mind is destructive. So, no guys, I can't go with you. I love my wife. I love my kids. I love God, and Jesus said that adultery and love don't go together. I even love you guys—you're my friends and neighbors—and if I went with you, I'd be helping you hurt yourselves. I can't do that."

It wasn't long before I was known in the community as "the guy who only sleeps with his wife." When people asked why I so limited myself, those who knew me would say, "Jesus said."

These encounters aren't openings to promote Christian dogma and ethics, but opportunities to testify to being taught by Jesus in the here and now. To be more than pretense and religious lecture, we have to be people who really are regularly, with adequate intensity and focus, setting the words of Jesus before our attention. When someone is your teacher, their words are so often within you that they come out of your mouth as your own. This is how the disciple becomes like the teacher, and this is how we bear fruit.

As we genuinely understand ourselves as students and apprentices of Jesus, we expect him to be teaching us in the here and now. We choose, as students, to hold his words before our attention, with adequate frequency and focus, so he can use them within us to alter our attitudes, orientations, thinking, and actions. A more public discipleship makes for more opportunity to give an answer for the hope that is in us because it engenders more questions. Further, we can give those answers with meekness and humility because we aren't coming at our friends like people who know how they should live. We're bearing witness to the fact that we're presently being taught how to live.

Sharable Practices

Beyond what we say and how we explain our choices, there are still other ways we can make *how* we follow Jesus more vivid and visible and more experientially rich for ourselves, our households, and others in our lives. Here are a few that have worked for us.

Our household's "discipleship dinner" is really just dinner with a few carefully chosen practices woven into the meal we have together every day. You'll recall that we share what we're grateful for, listen attentively to one another, and read from a family devotional. Much of the time, it's *The Jesus Storybook Bible*. Why? Well, my kids can't connect with N.T. Wright or Teresa of Avila just yet, and I can't connect with most children's Bibles. We aren't *pretending* to connect emotionally with the words and works of Jesus, we're connecting and letting that connection be seen by the people we invite to join us for dinner. Friends, neighbors, and colleagues from work can catch a glimpse of what following Jesus could entail—how it might look and feel to practice his way.

Julie, our longtime friend, follows Jesus and keeps *namaz*, kind of. It's likely *namaz*—the Muslim practice of praying at five set times in the day—was borrowed from the early Christian Liturgy of the Hours. Julie has an app on her phone, an alarm that sounds at each call to prayer. She spends a good deal of her time with Muslim friends, so when the bell chimes, she asks her friends if they'd like to pray with her. She reads the Psalm for the day, and they pray. Julie prays in Jesus's name. This particular habit is immensely powerful in taking the unfolding conversation Julie is having with her friends about Jesus out of the realm of idea and dogma, and into a practice in which they can directly encounter him. Little by little, Julie's discipleship can host theirs.

If you don't live or work in a majority Muslim context, praying *namaz* wouldn't be of much practical use, but praying the Hours could be. As far off and odd as it may sound, imagine the potential effect of being at lunch with a colleague, hearing your phone chime, and announcing without preamble or apology, "Ah! It's time for midday prayer. You're welcome to join me. I read a Psalm and pray for someone I work with. If you'd rather not, I'll just step away for a moment and we can pick this up after?" At best, a colleague prays with you at lunch. At worst, she has something to ask you about, and you have an opportunity for a gracious, salted answer.

This orientation toward sharable practices is rooted in how the Eastern world views conversion. In the West, we seem to unconsciously assume conversion goes *believe, behave, belong*. You can see this in the way we handle baptism or church membership. A person professes to believe certain things about Jesus. We ask them to wait a while to see if their conversion was genuine—we monitor their behavior. Then, when we're satisfied with the first two, we baptize them or stand them up in front of the congregation as new members, using ritual to communicate that now they belong.

The Eastern world knows the opposite is actually more true—belong, behave, believe. You're marked somehow as *us* and not *them*. You're born into a community, hired into a company, accepted into a martial arts school, etc. You belong. As such, you join us in doing what we do in the ways we do it. You keep our cultural norms, operate according to our rules, practice our katas and disciplines. You behave. Eventually, as your identity as one of *us* begins to inform your identity as *you*, and as the carefully crafted practices have time to teach you another way to see and experience the world, you come to find that you actually believe what the practices embody and the community confesses to be true. By belonging and behaving, you come to believe.

This is why, I'm convinced, Jesus left us with two ordinances and not a list of dogmas. We are his people, gathered in his name; we belong. We do these things in remembrance of him, in obedience to him; we behave. As we inhabit these rich, deeply experiential practices together, our faith is stoked; we believe.

Praying for people in Jesus's name is even easier than inviting them to pray with you. It has become axiomatic in missions conversations that praying with people in Jesus's name is typically a fruitful practice especially in Muslim communities. But *especially* doesn't mean *only*, and I've been told numerous times that you can't just offer to pray for someone on the street or over lunch in the West. I don't buy it. Let me tell you a story.

In August of 2018, our daughter, Haddiye Joy, died in the womb. It crushed us. It decimated our hearts and rocked us in our foundations. After the horrible three days in the hospital delivering her remains, my wife found a little motorized car being sold on a local online marketplace here in Spain. She wanted to bring something happy home for one of our other daughters. It was a small thing. Silly, even, but sometimes you just do the next good thing and keep trying to move forward.

We drove to a town nearby to pick it up. The British woman selling it was visibly distraught. We weren't in any shape to help anyone, but broken hearts can sometimes sense each other, so we asked if she was okay.

She had two kids. The younger girl, a brand-new baby, had a rare genetic condition that made it very easy for her skin to blister and break. They call these kids "butterfly babies" because they are so fragile. Many of them suffer their whole lives and die very young.

We had nothing to say. She knew about our stillbirth and felt bad to even mention her grief and worry. Right there on the street in Spain, we asked if we could pray with her. She started crying and nodded yes.

We prayed broken phrases and remembered aloud that Jesus could heal because he had, and that Jesus was stronger than death because he rose. We asked. We just said please. We wept together, she thanked us, and we left.

Weeks later we saw a post on social media. Strangely, the story had changed. Now, her daughter found herself in the less than 1 percent of cases that spontaneously heal. The doctor had no idea why. We did. What's more, this woman's faith had been rekindled and she was exploring the notion of God again.

I am still learning from this story. I'm learning to show up to people with my whole heart, even when it's broken. I'm learning that praying in Jesus's name *is* proclaiming Jesus's name. And I'm learning that I can still contribute when my confidence is rocked, when I have more doubts than answers, and when my faith has taken damage and feels very small. It turns out, that's all the faith it takes. Sometimes broken faith is what broken people need. If they need a hero, it's Jesus and not me.

This is how we integrate our vocations and our ministries. We treat God like he's God, especially on the job, and we treat people like we're all just people—frail people made of dust who could probably use prayer. When we treat people like the things in their hearts matter to God, we're doing what Jesus did when he incarnated the Father. People see God's heart toward them in us when we *act* in the ways Jesus acts toward them. Our light shines before others as we imitate our teacher.

> Let compassion make you bold
> and see what happens.

This integration is less about being a disciple-maker on the job, and more a matter of viewing your day job as the place you're being apprenticed by Jesus. You're a disciple on display. Be honest and forthright, and let the winsomeness of your simple candor make up for the occasional awkwardness. Let the words of Jesus abide in you by taking him seriously as your teacher, and yourself seriously as his student. Become obsessed enough with Jesus that you bring him up naturally and invite people to interact with what Jesus said and did. They don't have to agree to study

John's gospel with you. They just have to stay in the conversation when you share what has your attention.

Pray. Pray visibly, not so people will think well of you, but so people can spot God in your line of sight. Find some culturally acceptable way to be a little odd on this point, so they can spot it as part of an apprenticeship to Jesus. And pray for them at any chance they give you. They are glorious, and they are only dust, and every bone in their bodies knows both of these things to be true. Let compassion make you bold and see what happens.

11

Integrating Your Oikos and Your Misson

In this chapter we'll:

- Explain the myth of work/family balance
- Explore the biblical concept of households and their integrative missional potential
- Discuss extensive practical guidance on cultivating missional oikoi

The early days of our work in Central Asia were characterized by language study and attempting to make a go of living in an extremely foreign place. The fact that my wife and I were basically focused on exactly the same things most of the time made it easy to keep in step with one another. Since our children were five and two, and we were homeschooling them, there weren't really any forces that were pulling us in meaningfully different directions.

But once formal language study was past, a third child entered the mix. The age spread became more complex, and things began to change. I was out of the house a lot, teaching in schools, tutoring private English students, and making disciples where I could. Joy was carrying the vast majority of the homeschooling, and running the house we utilized to encourage and care for other workers.

This much divergence may not have been a threat to our sense of unity by itself, but the cultural environment exacerbated a bifurcation of our lives. Culturally, women stayed home, and men stayed out to all hours of the night. Grandparents raised or helped raise kids, so it wasn't a totally crushing load for women in the best of cases, but we didn't have grandparents around. If I wanted to have relationships with my family, *and* with the men among the people we had come to serve, there simply wouldn't be enough of me to go around. Further, our marriage has always been a partnership. She's who I want to work with. I don't want to work and then come home to a separate life, and I really didn't want my kids to grow up watching their daddy make constant compromises with work or with them because there weren't enough hours in my day.

Conventional wisdom approaches situations like this in search of an illusive, mythical creature called work/life balance. I tried hard to strike this magical balance. I used a day timer and a ream of graph paper and a hundred-thousand good intentions, but my kids' needs wouldn't stay static long enough to form a rhythm, and the local environment wouldn't allow for the predictability I needed to plan balanced days. The demands in both directions—work and family—were enormous and welcome. But in trying to work both, neither could flourish.

I should have seen that coming. I was a biologist once, and I know that the clinical term for when an organism's internal processes reach balance is death. Balance does not give rise to life. Homeostasis—the intricate management of perpetually shifting dynamic *imbalances*—does. Balance is what happens a little while after something stops living.

My freshman physics course taught me that if I apply equal force on an object in opposite directions (balance), the best I can expect is nothing. It won't move at all. If you succeed at achieving balance, it's because you've achieved nothing else. But more commonly, if the force is great enough or applied long enough, the object is torn in half. This was happening to me. The more strength and vigor I brought to the twin endeavors of my heart—my family and my work in the world—the more I came apart. The only way I knew to avoid catastrophic tension snapping me in two was to bring less than my whole heart to all that I did. Disintegration here looks like rupture or a half-hearted life, and I don't know which is worse.

Enter the Oikos

As is often the case when Jesus is leading me to alter my perspective, not long after I became aware of my discontent with the pursuit of balance, I encountered a convergence of a longing in my heart, something I was studying in the Scriptures, and some insights from some new friends.[1] This time the convergence was around the biblical concept of the household—in Greek, the *oikos*.

In the world of the New Testament, the oikos was the basic unit of society. The word, which literally translates to "house," refers to the nuclear family, members of the extended family, servants and employees, the

---

[1] I credit much of my thinking on the topic of *oikoi* (the plural of *oikos*) to Robert J. Banks, Roger Gehring's *House, Church and Mission*, and Jeremy Pryor's work on Family Teams. After more than a decade of experimenting with and teaching the notion of household mission, it is impossible for me to adequately parse out which insights came first from whom and which pieces are my own synthesis and development. Let us leave it at this: I credit what's helpful to them, and I take responsibility for whatever is not.

family business or economic engine, and the physical plant in and from which all of the household's activities flowed. Everyone in the household understood their identity to be bound up with that of the household, and the work of each contributed to the shared wellbeing of all. With this structure, work/family dichotomies would have been much rarer, and when they existed less severe, as children spent a lot of their time serving with their parents while being apprenticed in the household trade.

For example, when Peter responded to the invitation from Cornelius to come to his home in Acts 10, Cornelius' household believed the gospel and received the Holy Spirit. This was likely an event that included upwards of thirty people. Similarly, when Paul started the church in Philippi, he basically evangelized two households (Lydia's and the jailer's) before he was run out of town. Just these two groups comprised enough people and enough social engagement and subsequent influence to multiply and sustain a discipling presence in that city for years to come. In each of these cases, the oikos included extended family, key people who were not related, the house they lived in, and the way they paid the bills.

The household was also a primary social unit in the Old Testament. Take for example Joshua's famous challenge, "Choose this day whom you will serve ... as for me *and my house*, we will serve the LORD" (Josh 24:15, emphasis added). In Joshua's day, that wouldn't have meant him, his wife, and his 2.5 children. It would have been a larger, more complex social unit with greater leverage to influence its community. Abraham's household, as another example, at one point included three hundred fighting men, so the total number had to be well above that.

The oikos isn't observable merely in biblical settings. In fact, while the nuclear family is arguably the core unit of functioning societies, it's only in the last century or so that any society has been affluent enough to allow such a small social unit to be financially viable for the majority of its people. Throughout most of human history, we've been living in somewhat larger groups which has allowed us to apply greater leverage to the questions of living and living well with less force. Today, in places or at times when the nuclear family falters, falls on hard times, or is inadequate to survive, something like oikoi emerge again.

But for most of us, the majority of our lives is lived in nuclear families, and then our lives are split between work and home life.[2] What benefit does an exploration of households in the New Testament

---

2 This is, of course, with the obvious and important exception of single people, who are a critical part of any society, and are especially necessary to the propagation of the way of Jesus. Singleness and households will be treated later.

hold for us? And how might it help us unlock the enigma of work/family balance in a way that doesn't neutralize or cleave us in two? For that, we'll need to look into one house in particular.

The Household of Stephanas

> Now I urge you, brothers—you know that the household of Stephanas were the first converts in Achaia, and that they have devoted themselves to the service of the saints—be subject to such as these, and to every fellow worker and laborer. (1 Cor 16:15–16)

Here, at the end of a long and rather difficult letter, Paul leaves the church at Corinth with a visual aid that will help them imagine and embody what he's been trying to teach them. Usually, Paul offers himself as such an aid, but in this case his credibility has been damaged by profiteers. He even mentions that he had asked Apollos to go instead, but for whatever reason, Apollos wouldn't go. Paul chooses a local example and holds them up as examples to follow and even to "be subject to."

This exemplar isn't an individual or an amorphous collection of individuals, but a household. When Paul wanted the Corinthian believers to know how to be disciples and how to be the church in that city, he pointed to an oikos.

What's special about this oikos?

And to every fellow worker and laborer. (v. 16)

The first thing to note is the last thing Paul mentions. This phrase can be translated a number of different ways. The idea in all of them is basically "and to those who work this way with them." The house of Stephanas appears to have been part of a network of such households.

Indeed, churches in Paul's day were essentially city-wide networks of believing, disciple-making households. Most of the functions of church life were carried out at the household level with all the oikoi in the city meeting together regularly for worship, mutual edification, and the Lord's Table.[3] This is why all of Paul's explicit ethical teaching (i.e., 1 Timothy, Ephesians, Colossians) references relationships typical of households but is silent on professional ministerial relationships. There are no instructions for how to deal with your worship leader, for example, but repeated admonitions for how to live out household relationships (even problematic ones like slave/master) in transformative ways.

---

3 Lim, "God's Kingdom as Oikos."

The church was less an educational club and more an alternate society which modeled what normal human relationships could be in God's kingdom.

They have devoted themselves. (v. 15)

The word *devoted* here can also be rendered *addicted*. It connotes a total allocation of will and effort, a conscious decision sustained long enough and with adequate intensity that it becomes something you almost can't help but do. It becomes intrinsic to the group's identity—both internally (how individuals in the group understand themselves as part of that group) and externally (how the rest of the community understands the group). They have found their mission; they've committed, and they've executed on that commitment over time.

The subject is *they*, not *he*. For Ancient Roman households, decisions of which god to worship or faith to practice were made by the head of the house—typically the male who owned the house or business in and from which the oikos worked. When Stephanas decided to follow Jesus, so did his household. But passages like Hebrews 6, 1 John 2:19, and the letter to Philemon indicate that even once a householder had decided that his (or her) house was to follow Jesus, individual members of the house might well dissent.

A contemporary parallel isn't hard to imagine. Mom and Dad follow Jesus, and the kids do, too—until adolescence. Then, suddenly, little Johnny is an atheist, or Susie is a Buddhist. Or, more commonly, Johnny and Susie go to college, and once they're out of the house, they just stop practicing their parents' faith altogether and opt for the dominant religion of their culture: secular consumerism.

Contra to this narrative, the entire household of Stephanas had discerned a shared calling, a house mission, and every member of the team seemed to be pulling their weight. Examples of this kind of total engagement in a shared mission range from the Kennedys' choice to influence American politics, to the Rockefellers' decision to shape financial markets and amass great wealth, to the immigrant family running the little restaurant they live above.[4] We know what it looks like when a house has a mission to which it is devoted, and we've seen how the target of that devotion determines the kind of people that household grows. Stephanas's household had a mission, too.

---

4 Pryor, "How the Biblical Family."

To the service of the saints. (v. 15)

Stephanas's household looks after God's people. They have dedicated themselves together to the care of the believers around them. They've made the success of others' stories the plotline of their own.

For clarity, allow me to draw a false contrast. This household hasn't devoted itself to the success of local church programs, but to the care of the saints. The dichotomy is false because the early church had no programs needing volunteers or building projects needing funds. Though anachronistic, the contrast is, I hope, helpful in that Stephanas didn't have to lead his household to back his local Sunday gathering's project of the month. Instead, he had to lead his household to discern what part of God's heart was theirs to steward together, and where they should focus their time, talent and treasure. This goal is a different matter altogether, and one far more exciting to me as the head of a household.

This house also works in concert with a network of such households. Perhaps some of them are also aimed at the care of the saints. Such speculation isn't useful to build dogma upon, but it's helpful for inspiring the imagination to conceive of previously unimagined possibilities. What might it look like if churches stopped being primarily ministry service centers and became instead networks of vibrant, focused oikoi?

Finally, Paul offers this household and its compatriots as examples of how to be the church. He tells us to model our lives after them and even to let them lead us. Paul offers what, to modern imaginations, is a radical alternative to how we see church, disciple-making, and family.

Some may legitimately point out that the oikos as described in the New Testament was a social structure specific to a time and place different from our own and therefore shouldn't be prescribed as how we should live now. That is a fair critique.

I think that argument may be weaker than it at first appears, but let's allow it to limit us to this: What if the oikos provides a readily available solution to our problem of disintegration at the place where work and family meet? If we can envision a configuration of work and family to be pulling in the same direction, we could actually get somewhere. If everyone in the household understood wage earning, school, ministry, care of the home, care of one another, and care of others outside the household as part of one shared mission in which everyone plays a part, we might find integration at this point much easier.

What if the picture Paul provides gives us what we need to escape the fool's errand of balancing work and family and instead provides us an alternate way to structure our lives and our stories? This is certainly what it did for me.

The Vagabonds

As we prepared to leave Tennessee for Central Asia, we started writing monthly newsletters to people who wanted to know what we were up to and partner with us in those endeavors through prayer or financial backing. We needed a catchy title as well as a way to identify ourselves in these missives that wouldn't create security concerns for us later. The government of the country we were moving to wasn't exactly friendly to the gospel of Jesus as King, so a layer or two of anonymity wouldn't hurt. I was struck simultaneously by Paul's assertions that apostles—sent ones—are the last of all, "the offscouring of the world." I was also acutely aware of how much time my family spent on the road, traversing most of the Eastern US in search of people to partner with us financially and in prayer. The notion of being happy vagabonds, peripatetic Jesus nomads, seemed apropos, so our monthly missive was named *The Vagabond Way*.

Since we left Nashville fifteen years ago, we've lived in eight homes, sometimes moving as often as three times in a year. The wandering, the rootlessness of place, though not of relationships, has become part of who we are, and knowing who you are is essential to being a functioning household.

Essential but not sufficient. Speaking as a dad with below-average natural parenting talent and above-average ambitions to change the world, just knowing who you are as a household is far from enough. Having a shared identity but lacking the requisite skills to live into it together is a recipe for rupture.

When the work/family tightrope act had just about wrung me out, I happened upon a talk given by Jeremy Pryor, in which he unpacked how biblical households could be a viable model for how we approach work as families.[5] In particular, he suggested a role for fathers that I hadn't considered before. What if we viewed our families as our primary teams? Each family member had a role to play. Breadwinning, running the house, helping with the family's chosen ministries, preparing to carry on the family's mission in further generations, etc. The head of house might

---

5 Pryor, "How the Biblical Family." The video quality has degraded over time, but Jeremy has developed his thoughts considerably in his work on Family Teams, which at the time of this writing can be found at familyteams.com and on YouTube.

function as the team coach, keeping the game plan clear, helping team mates function as a team and not merely as individuals, developing each player and encouraging them to bring their best to the game.

I started discussing my discoveries, both biblical and practical, with my wife, and we began to experiment with some real-world applications.

A House Mission

We find ourselves in the stories we inhabit. The human brain is a story-making machine. We understand *everything* narratively. The people in my house needed a story that made sense of what we were doing, and why we were doing it. We didn't want to say, "Because God called us here to do things," as that would paint God as the reason for all the sacrifices the adults were making, but the children were paying for. What, then? What is the story the Vagabonds find themselves in?

To find out we consulted our hearts and our constitutions—what moves us and how we're made. By *us* here I'm referring to the adult members of the household, which in our case at that time was me and my wife. These are the questions we explored. I offer them here, neatly and in an intelligent order, but our process was more trial and error, stumbling in the dark and barking our shins on the furniture.

First, *What do you want?* God leads us, aims us, and makes the best use of us by our desires. Not *all* of our desires, of course, but guidance can usually be found in something we really want to do. So, what are some of the deep longings of your heart? When you die, what do you want to have done or been? For example, Joy and I had always wanted a house—something like Schaffer's L'Abri or Tolkien's Rivendell—where people like us could be trained, known, healed, taught, and sent back out gladder and more dangerous for having been with us. Knowing this didn't mean that's what we had to do right then, but it helped us zero in a little on what our household might be.

Next, *Do you have a sense of calling, and if so, how would you articulate it?* The Apostle Paul talks about calling in three ways. He says we have been called to Jesus Christ. That's true of every Christ follower, and it's forever. He also uses the word to refer to being specifically sent to a place, like being called to preach the gospel in Macedonia (Acts 16:6–10). This calling wouldn't be permanent like the calling to Christ, but it would persist until he had finished his assigned task in that place. Another use of the word *calling* refers to the special contribution God is asking you to make with your time on earth. Paul was called to be a preacher and a teacher of the Gentiles (Rom 15:15–16), and this calling persisted throughout his life.

When we were hashing out our household mission, we had a vague sense of calling. We felt called to serve the whole church in the whole world. Not just the world, but the church in the world. Also not the church in just one place, but the whole, global church as it was manifested in specific localities. Perhaps even more specifically, we felt called to help the church help the world. This little bit of clarity suggested that we might not be lifetime workers in one place but might instead have a career in multiple countries. The story we crafted would need to suit such a journey.

We also had some clarity on my sense of calling. We were pretty sure I was an apostle (with the smallest possible letter *a*). Ephesians 4 says God has given apostles, prophets, evangelists, shepherds, and teachers to the church to equip the saints to serve. I grew up in a tradition that insisted that apostles and prophets don't exist anymore, so it took me a while to wrap my head around this self-understanding. (If you're from a similar tradition, then feel free to skip this paragraph. No hard feelings.) I knew in my DNA that my calling involved architecting spiritual communities, working on liminal edges of things, and going where no one has gone. Further, my task would always involve helping catalyze synergy between the other parts of the body.

Joy was less clear about her sense of calling. She knew she felt called to be where there was less access to the gospel and that her burden from the Lord was for the church as a community. The coming years would bring more clarity on her calling, but we had enough to begin. The whole church in the whole world. My apostolic calling, and her calling to healthy community. That's what we knew, so that was enough.

From there, *How do you love?* When you love someone and feel compelled by that love to act on their behalf, what kinds of things are you doing? Providing counsel? Fixing their car? Cooking a meal? Listening compassionately? Cheering them on? When you love, what does it look like? For me, it usually looks like seeing them deeply and saying *yes* to what I see. It often involves a little teaching, or clarifying, but just enough to activate them and take them off the leash, so they can freely do the beautiful thing that's in their heart to do. For Joy it looks like making room. Sharing space. Doing practical things together, so deep matters can rise to the surface unhurried and be considered without fear or shame. Joy makes welcome the stranger, and then she protects them like family.

One way to zero in on how you love is to ask, When I love someone, what is it I most often want for them? Conversely, when someone's situation really bothers you, when you find their group or church or team really frustrating, what is (or isn't) happening that bothers you? Joy wants people to have a place, to belong, and to find healing and meaning with others. She gets frustrated when groups talk community, but people won't actually live their lives vulnerably together. She gets really frustrated when the in-group keeps outsiders out, intentionally or not. I find myself frustrated when communities are configured in ways that deactivate or diminish their members, or when the status quo is given as a reason to avoid frightening but necessary change. Similarly, what I most want for people is that they're known in community, feel loved as they are, and are fully developed and released to cause all the right kinds of trouble in the world.

> Perhaps even more interesting than your individual gifts, what happens in those gorgeous moments when your powers combine?

Finally, *How are you strong?* What are your gifts, natural and spiritual? When people come to you for help, what is it they most often ask for? When you're most alive serving people, what is it you're doing? How has God made you each uniquely strong? My dominant gifts are teaching and leadership. Joy is a born shepherd of souls with acute discernment and hospitality skills. I'm good at seeing what could be and believing it could be when not many others would. Joy is the best at seeing what is and is insistent that the dreams I dream become practical and tangible. She is masterful at the practical.

Perhaps even more interesting than your individual gifts, what happens in those gorgeous moments when your powers combine? When you're in a state of flow together, and you're more than the sum of your parts? One thing we noticed in each place we've lived is that communities seem to spring up around us. It's what happens almost effortlessly when our gifts, desires, and proclivities toward love mingle. This isn't something to ignore when attempting to discern a mission for your household.

I was an architect, a teacher, and an activator. Joy was a healer, a host, and a friend. We felt deeply that we wanted to work together closely, to create a space between us that would be developmental in effect for those who would spend time with us. This healing, developing, friendly homespace, where people could be and discover and become who they truly were, and then be released back into the world stronger, more alive, and more beautiful—this was our house's mission.

We could feel it vividly. To imagine it set our hearts beating faster and electrified our blood. We could sense the "yes and amen" of Jesus on it. It was very good. However, practical contours were less clear, and trying to convey it to our children (then aged 7, 3, and 1) was a wash. If we were to make a team of our household, we'd need something more than a beautiful dream. We'd need words.

A House Motto

"Winter is coming."[6]

House Stark occupied Winterfell, their ancestral home in the far north. Their task was to remember and to live as though winter was coming, and to keep the Wall and its forces in good order and to provide a defense against the terrors in the frozen expanse further north. Those words, "winter is coming," seemed to hold within them the readiness, the sense of duty, and the stern realism every member of House Stark needed to discharge their responsibilities and live out their house's purpose.

I've only read one of George R. R. Martin's fascinating novels, and I've never seen the show that spun from them, but at just the time we were needing a way to simplify and codify our house's mission, a friend had recommended *A Song of Ice and Fire*, and I was captured by the idea of a house motto.

We tried *Bless and Build*, and it stuck. *Bless* seemed to resonate with much of what Joy wanted for people and wanted our house to do for them. It even harked back to a charge a childhood friend of her family would give them, "Be blessed, and be a blessing!" *Build* carried the ideas of architecting developmental spaces, and even building competencies and capacities into people, which matched me nicely. Further, it connected to our shared calling to build the whole church in the whole world.

To be honest, we didn't work long on the motto. It sort of sprang out of my mouth one day, and it worked. It was short, clear, imperative, and the alliteration made it easy for the kids to remember. The benefits were instantaneous and surprising.

---

6 Martin, *Song of Ice*.

First, nothing gives the sense that you're a team like a cheer or a victory chant. When people we wanted to care for were coming over to the house for dinner, we'd circle up, assign responsibilities like helping to set the table, choosing toys to freely share with their kids, cleaning up the dining room, and so on. We'd give them a very brief primer on who these people were and how specifically we wanted to encourage them that evening. We'd pray for the family and our efforts to help them, and we'd break out to our tasks with, "Hands in! One, two, three, *Bless and Build*!" I'm not a psychologist. I don't know why this stuff works on kids and middle-aged men, but it does.

More importantly, the words provided a pre-conversion ethic rooted in identity we could use to guide our kids' behavior. The Apostle Paul roots his ethic partly in eschatology, but primarily in identity. Paul enjoins the Ephesians, "For at one time you were darkness, but now you are light in the Lord. Walk as children of light" (Eph 5:8). He roots the behavior he expects from them in their new identity. He doesn't say they're darkness but should be light, that they're bad but should be good. Nor does he say they are *in* the light, or had been *in* darkness. The kind of thing they are—their identity—has changed, so they should act like it.

Such an assertion makes sense when someone has become a follower of Jesus. But before such a conversion, it rings with moralization. The motto helped here. Before we could say, "You're light in the Lord, so walk as children of the light," we could say, "You're a Tanner, House Vagabond, and the Vagabonds *Bless and Build*. This is who we are, who you are. So, act like it."

One kid wrecks another's Lego project. "Hey buddy, when you did that, were you building or destroying? Right, but we build. What could you do now to build? Could you help him fix it? Do you think that would also help build your relationship?"

The aggrieved kid calls his brother a butt-head. "Pal, calling someone a mean name with anger in your heart—is that blessing or cursing? What do you need to do now to make that right?"

"Sweetheart, when you make that appalled-to-the-point-of-outrage face when your brother chews too loudly, how do you think he might feel? It might not be cursing him, but is it blessing?"

Make no mistake, we don't always do it like that. We do it much worse more often than we'd like. But the words help with the trees and the forest, with the specifics of training the kids *and* with the story we're training them in. They know the game they're playing, and they're learning to play their positions. This makes all the difference between apprenticeship and mere catechism. Having a house mission that's clear enough that the kids can contribute creates a context in which we can apprentice them in the family business of blessing and building.

House Rhythms

Everything at present tends toward entropy. The things we weave together come apart, unless we routinely shore them up and keep them in sync. This principle is no less true for our households. We need touchpoints where we can intentionally weave our lives together, and we need these touchpoints to form the rhythm we live by.

> Having a house mission that's clear enough that the kids can contribute creates a context in which we can apprentice them in the family business of blessing and building.

My household has evolved clear daily and weekly rhythms. Every day we observe morning and evening prayer together, and every day these are largely the same. There is, of course, some variation in the Scriptures we read, the praise we offer, and the petitions we lift, but we do them at the same time every day, in roughly the same way. The sameness, far from making it boring or rote, provides incredible stability and predictability. The behaviors we repeat intentionally are the things our children come to believe to be true. Say prayer is the center of life, and it matters little. Pray without ceasing, and you've taught the whole lesson without uttering a word.

Every day we also make discipleship part of our dinner together. Every dinner is largely the same. We say grace, and Joy asks what we're grateful for. Again, a gratitude practice, which copious research has shown to be incredibly helpful in living a happy, productive life, is best taught by practicing it and not by talking about it. We share what we're particularly grateful for that day as we load our plates, and we manage chaos while we eat. Near the end of the meal one of the kids gets one of our favorite family devotional books, and someone reads a selection for the day. The kids clear the table and wash the dishes, and it's done. It's a tiny investment with a tremendous potential return.

Weekly we observe a Sabbath day. We kick off our sabbath with a special Friday Night Sabbath Dinner. We follow a simple liturgy. There's almost always some Scripture to reflect upon together, and we make it routinely special with the plates, cutlery, and dessert choices. We are celebrating together the end of a work week, intentionally entering into the Sabbath rest promised and given by God. On Sunday mornings we have a special breakfast which usually winds up being brunch. It's something sweet that we normally wouldn't get for breakfast, but the important part is the Special Plate. Whoever gets the Special Plate gets a huge pancake, they get to eat it *before* their protein, and the rest of us get the pleasure of telling that person something we appreciate about them. The team is celebrating its players.

In Central Asia we also held a weekly House Team meeting. We'd discuss how the routines of the week were working out and what needed tweaking. We'd talk about the work we'd each have in the coming week. We'd make a plan for tackling these together, praying into them for one another, and thinking about how to help each other succeed.

This short set of rhythms has allowed our family to remain a team, a working unit, through four major job changes, a deportation, six months of displacement living out of a van, an intercontinental move, four schools, three painful tragedies, and even the onset of puberty. Rhythms allow you to make what's most important routine, so you never fail to execute on your highest priorities together.

Singleness

I'm not single, and I wasn't single for long, so I'm not going to pretend to understand what you might be thinking right now if you're single. I'd hazard a guess that you might be wondering if you should've skipped this chapter.

Let me tell you a story.

Mira was reinforcing a point from *The Jesus Storybook Bible* to her boyfriend, Milo, at my dinner table. Mira and Milo were nominal Muslims, raised in the city where we served most recently. Mira came to dinner often and sometimes brought Milo. Each time, they overheard me discipling my four children at our table after dinner.

As the head of my house and a good host, after reading the stories to my children, I'd carefully explain them to our guests in the local language, since it's rude to talk past someone and not include them. Since Milo spoke better Russian than the local language, Mira would reiterate and share with him the beauty and goodness of Jesus whom she hadn't even met. This happened without ever having to navigate the awkward social obligations that would have come with me preaching directly to them over the meal. It was incredible.

This nearly effortless discipleship of a young Muslim couple was only possible because Julie, a single American woman in her thirties, lived with us in our home as part of our household. We had entered this arrangement carefully and with prayer while aware of the unique challenges Julie faced as a single, young woman in a Muslim country and also aware of my family's needs at the time. Mira was Julie's friend long before she was ours, and it was the freedom that came with Julie's singleness, combined with the testimony of a redeemed family and a Godward head of the house, that provided a context for Mira and Milo to have repeated, rich, and textured exposure to the gospel and its effects on multiple generations of people who were all at my table.

This goes way back. Jesus did this from Simon Peter's house. Paul did it from Aquila and Priscilla's house. As we noted before, Paul's entire practical ecclesiology assumes that the church is built with oikoi. For Paul, the church isn't *instead* of family, or *other than* family. It's Family*Plus*.

Remember, in the New Testament, house churches aren't miniature versions of big-church. They're a full house being transformed, activated, and networked to fill communities with Christ. In Colossians, Paul unpacks a rich Christology, and then he teaches us to live Christ out in the complex relationships of a household.

"Okay, fine," you might say. "Singles and families living together might make sense back then in Paul's time, or in other cultures, but it's not practical for people from the West." I vigorously disagree. If it worked back then, and it works "over there," it probably works here and now. In fact, it may just offer an alternative story of singleness and of family life that could challenge false assumptions that have crippled the mission and the spiritual formation of the church in the West for generations.

There are obvious benefits. Singles get lonely, maybe more often than married people. Humans are social creatures and designed to live in multi-generational social groups. Because of the profoundly individualistic cultural narrative in the West, we assume lonely people need to get married. But sometimes, people aren't lonely because they need a spouse. They're lonely because they need a family. Some of us are called to be single, but we're not called to be alone or to exist in some weird limbo between sitting at the kids' table or with the grownups. One can be a single, contributing adult without being alone.

Living together as a household requires vulnerability and the surrendering of significant freedoms while purposefully making room. This attitude is required of everyone in the house. These three practices, are deeply resonant with the texture of the gospel. When we open ourselves, embrace limits, and make room every day for each other's gifts and weakness, we model the gospel in ways that let the world experience Christ at depths we can't explain it to them. Further, those postures can uncouple us from pursuits that run deep in our blood and counter to Jesus's dreams for our own hearts—pursuits like clinging to life, misunderstanding liberty, and worshiping happiness.

> When we open ourselves, embrace limits, and make room every day for each other's gifts and weakness, we model the gospel in ways that let the world experience Christ at depths we can't explain it to them.

Practically, living this way can unlock significant resources (time and money) for ministry. Having Julie in our home meant after a long day teaching at the university I didn't have to decide whether I was going to go create relationships with seekers or spend time with my children. Julie could cast the line, and the family could land the fish. Sometimes, the single member(s) of a household can forego building their careers for a while to focus all their time and attention on making disciples while the family with whom they live can play a strong supporting role and provide the context to teach people how to live in God's family. Alternatively, everyone can work, minister, and expand the network of people the house can touch while diverting funds that would have gone to two or three house payments into worthy causes.

Sure, not every family is cut out for this, and probably no family is at every stage of life. The same is true for singles. There are parts of our souls that can be healed living this way, and other parts for which this lifestyle is the wrong prescription. But for most of us, practicing hospitality, vulnerability, and submission to another's needs in this way could re-activate our homes and increase their reach in the world, diversifying the paths by which the transforming love of Jesus can penetrate the deep places of our hearts.

Likewise, single people who aren't being invited by Jesus to move in with a family can still live into their place in God's family by looking for ways to integrate more completely with other single colleagues or with families they become close to. As with all things relational, this will require patient discernment, some shared rhythms to commit to together, and forbearance as everyone is bound to disappoint one another significantly along the way. These disappointments will likely highlight family-of-origin dysfunctions (we all have them) and provide safe opportunities to heal from minor traumas and negligences that otherwise could have plagued us for our whole lives.

We can draw new maps for family and singleness if we're willing to experiment a little. I'm convinced it will only take a few households with enough heart and moxie to strike out into waters too long forgotten and to see how Jesus meets us there.[7]

A Clarification

I'm not suggesting this is how you *must* live if you are to integrate your household and your mission. I'm offering a way that I know it *can* work, described vividly in the New Testament and borne out by my own experience over a decade of observation.

We have tried to use the oikos as the blueprint for our integrated household. We've identified a mission, simplified it with a motto, and instituted rhythms so our house can function like one team with one shared goal. You don't have to do it like we have, but you can. You have to do *something* about the fact that to chase balance is to chase a myth, and a dark myth, at that, as balance is another word for cell death.

Living life as an integrated household means *sending* mom or dad to work, not just letting them go, and praying for them to work like kingdom people, with salty, gospel-rich conversations along the way. It means sending the kids to school, to learn academics from their teachers, and to learn how to be kingdom people from Jesus in the context of unbelieving friends. When oikos and mission are integrated, work and family are part of the same thing—Christified households enacting the benevolent reign of Christ on earth in real time.

As a leader checking in regularly on my people, I know that attempting a work/family balance is, at best, going to render them neutral, and at worst will rend them in two. I need to know that they're integrating the two, and I'm interested to know how. We aren't supposed to live fractured lives.

---

[7] I published much of this section previously as "Family Plus," *Spirit of Revival*, March 15, 2018.

I also want to know how their strategies change as their lives unfold. When we moved to Europe, for example, our lives became more separate than ever before, and this arrangement persists in the States. There's nothing for that. Much of our work is remote, and we have kids aged 3 to 20 with three in school and one in college. Julie doesn't live with us anymore. A lot must be recalibrated.

I'm sitting down more with my two older kids, trying to cast a vision for a multi-generational legacy. Wouldn't it be great to be known as the family that blesses and builds? Wouldn't it be such a win if whenever someone heard that a Tanner went to this school, or worked at this factory, or was a police officer in this town, they knew that it was likely to be better because we were there? Conversations evolve and become more complex with less correction and mandate, and more visioneering and invitation.

12

Integrating Yourself and Your Communities

In this chapter we'll:

- Discuss how to avoid three common mistakes when integrating with a host culture
- Examine three questions that are crucial to ask and answer when integrating with a team
- Introduce three rules for generative conflict

Alice moved with her husband and young son to India. Six months later, she gave birth to a little girl. Her husband worked for an international company, but they took the assignment in India in hopes of using his profession to create inroads toward sharing their faith and making disciples.

They chose a house that matched his salary which made for comfortable lodging but significant separation from the people they moved to engage. His work was done in English, but they took Hindi classes on the weekends, and they tried to utilize the cultural training they received before they left the US. They put in the work, but at the end of three years they were lonely, disconnected, and felt like failures. He transferred back to Arizona, and they closed that chapter of their lives with confusion and a lot of disappointment.

Archie left the UK around the same time and joined a humanitarian team working in Iraq. The team had seen a lot of turn-over in recent years and had even lost its team leader to visa troubles. Archie came to his new assignment with high hopes of community and camaraderie, but he found himself consistently confused in interactions with his team. He had team mates from three different countries, and there seemed to be a lot of unwritten rules of engagement. Nothing was explicit, but every misstep seemed to have significant relational consequences within the team. Eventually, more energy was going into keeping the team at peace than into the work the team had come to do. Four years in, the team dissolved, and Archie was faced with a choice: return home to the UK or try another team. Disappointed and even injured by his experience with his team in Iraq, he couldn't muster the optimism to hope his next team would be better and opted to go home.

The thing these stories have in common is how Alice and Archie integrated their lives with others'. In Alice's case, failure to integrate adequately with her host community led to loneliness, isolation, and frustration. For Archie, a failure to integrate with his team—or for his team to integrate as a team at all—led to the same result.

We've considered the importance of integrating our work with God's, our households with our mission, and our vocation with our ministries. But we are not islands. We are doing all these things ensconced in the communities among whom and with whom we serve. We must attend, as well, to how we integrate ourselves with our communities.

Integrating with Our Host Cultures: Three Common Mistakes

Most of the people I work with have had some training in crossing cultures. Either it was part of their college degree program, or they've taken training as part of preparation to move overseas. In many ways, this training proves helpful, but it can also create a false sense of competence. Knowing about buoyancy and hydrodynamics doesn't make you a good swimmer, and knowing how culture works doesn't necessarily lead you to thrive and to work gainfully in a new one.

When people leave their home culture to live among a host community, the psychological stress can be astounding. The struggles I've witnessed, in myself and in others, integrating with a host culture tend to be associated with three mistakes that many cross-cultural workers unknowingly make. Disciples of Jesus who don't leave their home culture make versions of these same mistakes, so recognizing them can be helpful for everyone.

Mistake #1: Confusing Cultural Awareness for Cultural Intelligence

I had excellent cross-cultural training before I moved to Central Asia. Many, perhaps most, of those who move cross-culturally with the intention of blessing their host community, being of service, and helping people follow Jesus have had at least some training. They've studied cultural dynamics like power distance, short-term versus long-term orientation, masculinity versus femininity, individualism versus collectivism, values of indulgence versus restraint, and how much a society avoids uncertainty.[1] They've considered the people they are moving to serve and have explored whether they are motivated by shame and honor, guilt and innocence, or fear and power in relational contexts. They've read up on the history of the country they're moving to, have learned how they dress and how they greet one another. They've learned whether shoes are worn indoors or not, how to behave differently toward men and women, and which parts of the body are considered honorable or unclean. They know stuff, and they think that knowledge will translate directly to competency. Worse, they often assume it already has.

The misunderstanding that knowledge about culture equals competence in that culture is one of several assumptions that get us in trouble when we first try to cross cultures.[2] Another false assumption is that international experience directly translates to cultural intelligence, when in fact, mistakes made repeatedly in international encounters can become permanent habits and actually erode cultural intelligence.

The reality in cross-cultural adjustment is that it's not merely a matter of trying to apply what you learned once in a cleverly designed training. It's an ongoing dialogue with your host community, and within yourself. This dialogue serves you so much better than simply knowing some stuff. Knowledge alone predisposes you to a fixed mindset whereas the deliberate cultivation of a growing intelligence by nature lends toward a growth mindset. And a growth mindset is what you'll need if you want to truly become understandable to your hosts.

If you desire to integrate with your host community, you'll need to do so as a learner who brings with you more curiosity than comment and more cultural intelligence than mere cultural know-how.

Mistake #2: Seeking to Be Understood More Than We Seek to Understand

There's a prayer attributed to Francis of Assisi in which he asks God, "Grant that I might seek not to be understood, so much as to understand." This should be the prayer of every language student on the planet and everyone in a human relationship. But more often than not our desire to get our point across, to be heard, and to extend our will outweighs our willingness to be patient, to listen, and to seek first to understand.

---

1 Explore Geert Hofstede's six dimensions of national culture for more about this.
2 Cultural Intelligence Center, 9.

Nowhere is this more evident than how we are prone to approach language acquisition.

We leave our homes, our people, our cultures, and we jump out into the unknown. We go armed with a plan, a mission, and a story in our minds of what we are setting out to do. The first step is to gain the ability to communicate, so we look to learn the language, but what this usually means is that we try to control our environment using language. We try to find a language school so we can start speaking. Understandably, we want to be able to order food, pick up our mail, pay our water bills, and converse with the nice police officer who pulled us over for reasons totally lost on us. We start learning grammar very quickly, and we are asked to produce—to speak or to write—quite soon. Usually, we use a book or written text to do this.

This would all be fine and good, if that's how people actually learned language. Consider, for example, how children gain fluency in their native languages.

Kids *acquire* language long before they can learn about it. Who learns grammar in preschool? Kids learn language by hearing it, and by listening. Slowly, the body of language that they understand grows, until eventually, given the right situation, speech just erupts. Language is acquired by a long, quiet practice of listening, then, after that, producing. Linguists refer to this as "the silent period"—the time in which language is being acquired but no speaking is happening.

Adults can acquire second, third, and eighth languages this way *if* they will be quiet long enough. For this reason, I always strongly encourage language learners to stay away from programs that have them conjugating verbs, memorizing and producing long lists of nouns, or really speaking much beyond some simple survival phrases at all in the first month of full-time study. If you want to acquire a language, you've got to put a premium and priority on listening. *Listening is the master skill of communication.*

But when we arrive in a new culture, we freak out. Everything is out of our control, and we really want to feel like we are mastering something. Consequently, we choose programs that have us reading sounds we don't even know how to hear. Our accent is awful, and practice makes permanent, so we never sound quite right. We start talking before we know how people go about saying things, so we wind up cobbling together sentences that make sense to us, using their words, but the meaning is totally lost on them. We often speak without communicating because we let our anxiety push us to value being understood over understanding.

But if we want to share the gospel, we've got to be able to communicate, and communication goes both ways. *Listening is the master skill in disciple-making.* You cannot lead someone from a place you don't know, so why would we think we can disciple someone whom we do not at least seek to deeply understand? Put another way, no one wants to talk with you about their hearts—or the wounds and dreams within them—if they don't believe you really want to understand them. How you approach your acquisition of their language tells them if you're there to converse or merely to tell.

This preference for listening to understand is critical if work groups are ever to become real teams and if teams are ever to last as formative communities. We must seek to understand more than we seek to be understood. It is possible to win a conversation and lose a community. *Listening is the master skill in team life.*

I'm noticing this in Jesus's life, too. Every time there's a major decision, he disappears in to the mountains or across the sea to pray. When he comes back, he has some direction from the Father. Do you think he went off into solitude and just continually talked? How did the Father tell him anything if he was speaking the whole time? I'm beginning to wonder how much of Jesus's prayer life was quietly listening. I heard an older woman answer this way when asked on the fly what prayer is; she said, "Prayer is listening to the heart and love of God." Listening, huh? Tony Horsfall, while reflecting on the story of Martha and Mary in Luke's gospel, says Jesus is more interested in Martha's attention than her service. *What if listening is the master skill of prayer?*

So, here's something to think about. How big a role does listening play in your disciple-making? In your praying? In your family? In your ministry? In your teams? How often do you use good, curious questions? Not leading questions, but questions designed and delivered because you're really wanting to understand more about the other person, or more of their point of view? When you're having one of those argument fantasies—you know the ones I'm talking about—how much of that conversation is you asking questions, and how much is you giving them a piece of your mind? What might happen if you flipped the script in your imaginary conversations and used that creative juice to make a list of questions that might help you understand this person you love better?

How much of your language acquisition has focused on listening to understand, and how much has focused on speaking to be understood? This may seem like a small thing, but it sets the orientation of the rest of your relationship with your host community. Why? *Because listening is the master skill of love.*

> If we are to integrate with any community—family, team, host culture—we have got to become people who value understanding above being understood, and we must approach our own development with that priority squarely in mind.

If we are to integrate with any community—family, team, host culture—we have got to become people who value understanding above being understood, and we must approach our own development with that priority squarely in mind.

Mistake #3: Spacesuit Missiology

"It is critical to grasp that the divine Word *became* flesh," my professor insisted vehemently. "It is a terrible, indeed a heretical flaw, to assert that the Word merely *put on* flesh in order to dwell among us, the way an astronaut might put on a spacesuit to dwell amongst the stars—separate, insulated, and other."

The course was *Advanced Christology: The Doctrine of Christ in the Scriptures and Christian History*. An upper-level course in the seminary, it was taught by a genius named John Morrison and attended by only a few of us. The professor continued, "That kind of spacesuit Christology aborts the majority of what Christ did to save us. He did not only die and rise. He first lived with us, as us. The incomprehensible, divine Logos *became* us. Otherwise, we'd still be in the dark. As Gregory of Nazianus insisted, 'For that which he has not assumed he has not redeemed.' He can only save us insofar as he became us."

This assertion resonates with what the writer of Hebrews has to say about Jesus: "Although he was a son, he learned obedience through what he suffered. And being made perfect, he became the source of eternal salvation to all who obey him" (Heb 5:8–9). God became flesh, and that human being became the source of eternal salvation through a process of learning obedience by vulnerability to pain. This is the opposite of merely putting on our humanity. He became our humanity, and only then was he able to become the source of our salvation by not resisting or protecting himself from the experience of being one of us. "For [this reason] we do not have a high priest who is unable to sympathize with our weaknesses" (Heb 4:15). Jesus understands, and indeed went to great lengths and stayed at those lengths long enough to learn how to walk with God the way we would have to, even weak and acutely vulnerable.

It seems as if the actual mechanism of our salvation is Jesus's journey of becoming. To the degree he became, he redeemed. And because he became, he understands and can intercede for us to God, and for God to us. Jesus can reach us, always, because he became us.

How far did he go in his self-subjugation to the limits we live with? "Therefore, he had to be made like his brothers in every respect, so that he might become a merciful and faithful high priest in the service of God, to make propitiation for the sins of the people" (Heb 2:17). In order for salvation to work, he had to become like us in every respect. He lived our lives under the conditions we live in order to give his life to us.

When Jesus says to us in John 20:21, "As the Father has sent me, even so I am sending you," I have to wonder if the same rules hold true for us. Of course, we are not being made high priests in the order of Melchizedek, and our obedience is not credited to those we reach, but I have to wonder, what if the mechanism of the unreached being reached is the journey of *our* becoming? What if we can only reach what we are willing to become? And what if our becoming is limited by the way we allow or don't allow ourselves to experience life from the weak positions our host friends find themselves in?

> It seems as if the actual mechanism of our salvation is Jesus's journey of becoming.

Paul famously said, "I have become all things to all people, that by all means I might save some" (1 Cor 9:22). Well-meaning people have used this statement to make a case for more culturally relevant church services, but I think Paul had something else in mind. Paul was well aware of the centrality of incarnating the message of the gospel. Paul knew that just as the divine Word had to thoroughly become flesh in Jesus to reach us, the gospel would again demand the messenger becoming something he or she isn't yet in order to reach the lost.

How do we do that? For many, it's a matter of adopting local styles of dress, and possibly decorating one room in their houses in a somewhat local fashion. It may mean mimicking gestures and non-verbal modes of communication, learning local idioms, and attending local weddings and funerals. Certainly, all of this is part of what it means to become all things to all people, but Paul himself lays down vividly what it meant for him:

> For though I am free from all, I have made myself a servant to all, that I might win more of them. To the Jews I became as a Jew, in order to win Jews. To those under the law I became as one under the law (though not being myself under the law) that I might win those under the law. To those outside the law I became as one outside the law (not being outside the law of God but under the law of Christ) that I might win those outside the law. To the weak I became weak, that I might win the weak. I have become all things to all people, that by all means I might save some. I do it all for the sake of the gospel, that I may share with them in its blessings. (1 Cor 9:19–23)

Without doing violence to core facts of who God has made him to be in Christ, Paul became his audience. He gave up freedom, and he chose a position of weakness. He neither clung to nor reacted to the culture and privileges of his upbringing, but allowed himself to be subject to the conditions in which he found the people he was trying to reach. Paul did not *put on* his neighbor's affectations. He *became like* his neighbor. How? By allowing the forces that prevailed upon them to also prevail upon him. He chose to be vulnerable to the conditions that shaped their lives, and in so doing, he was shaped by those conditions into the kind of person they could understand. Because he could, even if just a little, understand them, in that voluntary abdication of freedom and privilege. The Word became flesh again, in Paul, and dwelt among the people it was sent to save.

It would be a mistake to come 90 percent of the way and find ourselves lonely, worn out, and ineffectual. Though that is what many, perhaps most of us do. What makes the difference—what makes ministry incarnational and not just international—is what we allow ourselves to become as we refuse to protect ourselves from life as our hosts are forced, and blessed, to live. This is the distance between tolerated outsider and welcome guest. It's the path from inscrutable to understood. We can become flesh and dwell among them, and we all can behold the glory of Jesus as he floods our shared space with grace and truth.

This reality is just as true for those of us who don't uproot ourselves and move to a new country and culture. Even in our home cities, we can choose not to use our power and money to insulate ourselves from what our neighbors are facing. We can choose downward mobility, when it comes to where we live, and especially how we live. Of course, as with those who move cross-culturally, this must be done under the guidance and impetus of the Spirit. But if we are conscious of our natural predilections to put on a spacesuit before we step into the world, the Spirit has more room to help us live a little more dangerously for the sake of the gospel.

Integrating with Our Teams: Three Crucial Questions

In seminary we learned the top three reasons cross-cultural workers quit their fields of service before they feel they've finished with their work there: money, marriage, and team. Those three jockey for position, but they consistently have been the top three reasons for attrition. People run out of money, or they run out of chutzpah to raise it. Couples realize they have different degrees of commitment to what they're doing, or they are under-resourced to sustain a marriage in a challenging setting. And teaming can be really, really hard.

Teaming amounts to organizing people in a way that allows you to do more together than the sum of your parts. A team is a force multiplier, and with all force multipliers, you either get more done or you fracture. Teams are often primary loci for disintegration, but they can be some of the most integrative contexts available to us.

We've had some wonderful team experiences, and I don't think we've ever been on a bad team, per se. Team is what you make it. But we have experienced, and contributed to, some dysfunction and some real beauty in the many teams we've served. Teaming is one of those skills you learn as you go, and even awesome teams are high-maintenance. In the best of times, they require a lot of attention, but this attention has real potential to pay off in significantly expanded reach and depth of impact. Twenty-five years of ministry teaming has taught me to ask three questions and to insist on good answers.

Question 1: To Team or Not to Team?

This is really the wrong question, but I'm getting ahead of myself.

Here's a common refrain. Bob and Jack both find themselves seeking to make disciples in a major world city. They run into each other one day, hit it off, and become fast friends. In time, their circle of friends grows to include Laney, Amelia, and Mark. It's not long before Jack suggests they all form a team to do what they've each come to do—make disciples in one way or another—in their strange new city. Everyone gets along, so they all agree. Not long after, the wheels fall off.

They fall off because as soon as they went from friend group to team, everything gained an order of magnitude in complexity. They were independent operators a moment ago, but now my success is tied to and limited by yours. A bevy of new relational dynamics have been introduced, with implicit and explicit expectations as well as an emerging power dynamic. Someone(s) will lead the team. Who will it be, and do we all agree on the selection? What will leading and following look like? Am I aware of all my family-of-origin baggage that I'm about to work out either *on* my team leader or *as* the team leader?

Just because you live in the same place, and do roughly the same thing, doesn't necessarily mean you should be a team, but it also doesn't mean you shouldn't. I've seen the opposite refrain just as often. Five different independent units in the same city are working on exactly the same thing, and they could actually move the needle if they'd just work together. But teaming remains squarely out of the question because no one wants to give up their independence, their right to call the shots, or their particularly nuanced vision of exactly how things are supposed to go, so everyone works really hard, and nothing really gets done.

A team has a common goal, and the members are supposed to pursue that goal together. That's a degree of complexity and specificity that merely being in the same place and copacetic are insufficient to sustain. Teaming can do more, but it also costs more and involves more than simple relationship.

This nuance has been hard for me to learn. I hate crowds, but I love people. Especially once I've met them. I have an almost naïve ability to believe in people, to expect the best from them, and to want the best for them. I'd adopt every stray worker in the world if I could. This, however, has stung me repeatedly, and I've learned to ask a better question than *Should we team?*

How is Jesus inviting us to be gifts to one another right now? Or, put another way, What is the relationship Jesus is giving us to inhabit together?

Perhaps it's as teammates. Perhaps it's as confidantes who are able to support one another specifically because we don't work on the same team.

Perhaps it's simply as friends who play board games every Thursday and help one another release the compulsion to take ourselves so seriously all the time. All of these are needed. The trick is to ask Jesus exactly how he's asking us to serve one another and to let him decide the answer.

If that's too vague, fear not. As we ask Jesus this question, here are some things we can consider.

> How is Jesus inviting us to be gifts to one another right now?
> Or, put another way,
> What is the relationship Jesus is giving us to inhabit together?

We are each on two journeys at the same time—an outer journey and an inner journey. The outer journey is our missional journey, our work in the world. It's the contribution we're called to progressively make over the course of our lives in the diverse situations and locations in which we are placed. The inner journey is our formative journey, our path of becoming. It's the unfolding of our true selves in Christ as unique bearers of the divine image. There are callings and invitations that guide us forward in each. In reality, these are really one journey, but parsing them out and looking at them this way can help us navigate significant moments of discernment. You can be on a team that goes on the outer journey together, or a team that goes on the inner journey together. You can even be on a team that attempts to travel both together. But to be a team, you have to be headed in the same direction and invited by Jesus to do so together.

To discern if I'm being asked to engage the outer, missional journey with someone, I'll often use two questions. First, is Jesus explicitly, clearly asking us to team up? If so, then the conversation is basically over. It's a matter of obedience. If he is silent on the matter, or gives me room to decide, I'll ask the second question. Has Jesus asked you to do something in the world that is meaningfully similar to what he's asked me to do, and are we likely to do it better together? If so, we're in a good place to consider teaming.

Similarly, I might consider teaming up with others for the inner, formative journey. Again, the first question would be is Jesus explicitly, clearly asking us to take a leg of our inner journeys together? If so, it just remains to work out how. If he stays quiet or lets us decide, we could ask whether his present formational invitations to you (e.g., to live among the poor, to explore a particular stream of the faith, to inhabit a particular set of practices for a while) are the same kinds of things he's calling me to inhabit. If so, could we perhaps travel better together? This may be a good reason to team.

If the answer isn't a clear yes, it's probably a no, or a no-for-now. We are one in the Spirit, and this unity must be protected at all costs. But we don't all have to be working closely together on exactly the same things. In fact, that would be a wildly undifferentiated and overly simplistic strategy. We aren't better at everything together. Some animals, like oxen, pull more together. But tie two birds together, and no one flies.

Question 2: What Do We Need to Team Well?

Having been part of numerous teams across the last few decades, I'm aware that it's possible to over-describe how a particular team will function and how members will do their jobs. Usually, this situation arises when a few team members are doing an inordinate amount of the work, and they begin asking for some rules to guide the behavior of their less productive, less mature, or less circumspect teammates. But overly descriptive can feel prescriptive, rarely curbs laziness or poor behavior, and usually results in resentment and resistance. However, not being clear enough about how we will work as a team leads to its own problems of missed expectations, no shared sense of specific purpose, an inability to reliably predict what you can count on one another for, and a general sense of not going anywhere which can lead to burnout faster than almost anything else.

We've found that teams need four things to function well.[3] We call them the 4Ps: Purpose, Practices, Postures, and Priority.

A team's purpose is what Jesus has asked that group of people to give its strength and attention to right now. Some may prefer words like *mission*, or *vision*, but a mission can be accomplished, and a vision can be realized. In the places where we've worked, there are too many variables in play, and the theater is far too unpredictable to insist on reaching "mission accomplished." We may plant, another may water, and still

---

[3] Credit must be given to Tim Addington for his ideas in *Leading from the Sandbox*. He suggests kids can play freely, creatively, and collaboratively in a sandbox if they keep the sand within the four sides. He suggests teams likewise need four sides—mission, guiding principles, culture, and central ministry focus. Over time, as we have experimented, we've found the 4Ps I describe here to be a little more helpful, as our teams have had to be somewhat more flexible and dynamic, and have needed to take into account the matter of teaming for inner journey purposes.

another may harvest. But our purpose is our why statement—it reminds us of the game we're playing, and why we're playing it.

The Rivendell team in Western Europe came together to train, develop, and care for cross-cultural workers from all over the world who are working among Muslim peoples while remaining current in their own service to Muslims. Their purpose statement reads: "To mobilize, equip, care for, develop, and be workers who will magnify Jesus beautifully among Muslim people, wherever they are." They worked for weeks determining what needed to stay and what needed to go. Every word reflects something of the invitation they feel from Jesus, and no part of that shared invitation is omitted. It's important when discerning your purpose that you get as clear as you genuinely can and no clearer. You don't want to carry a burden Jesus isn't giving you.

One of the Rivendell team's practices is "We pray the Hours." This refers to the historical Christian practice of setting discrete times of day to stop the day's work for a few minutes and pray. They do this because they've seen how prayer tends to get pushed to the margins of busy work days, so in order to become prayerful people, they build their days around praying. Further, when people come to Rivendell to receive training, healing, or development, they participate in the team's rhythms of prayer. As the Muslim practice of *namaz* originated in the early church's practice of praying the Hours, workers return to their fields of service versed in a practice that creates common ground with their Muslim neighbors. This practice, like all of Rivendell's practices, was chosen for its potential to shape them and to help them effect the beneficial changes in the world they feel called together to engender.

Here's the complete list of Rivendell's practices.
We will:

- Make room
- Pray the Hours
- Pursue each other
- Pursue those in our care
- Partner with other teams wherever best
- Live the one-anothers
- Discern strategically
- Pursue 5DThrive
- Practice Sabbath

It's possible, though, to engage the practices badly. Members of Rivendell, for example, could pursue each other with a sense of expectation or entitlement. How the Hours are prayed could be over-prescribed. Those in their care could find themselves pursued by someone looking to lay on them the weight of perfectionism. As a martial artist, I know that the quality of my technique is entirely dependent on the quality of my posture. How you stand when you're doing something determines so much.

That's why clearly described preferred postures are so important. A team's postures help define team culture. It's the team's vibe—how it feels to be one of us. The combination of postures and practices will set and sustain a preferred team culture and will allow the team to become who they most want to be while preventing the weeds of accidental culture from growing in the dark.

Here are Rivendell's intentional postures:

- Submission
- Freedom
- Vulnerability
- Attentiveness
- Humility
- Grace

A brief aside here is helpful. The Rivendell Team describes *submission* a little differently for those who lead and for those who are led. They pursue a culture of mutual submission among all, and thereby they practice a concrete submission to Christ. They expect the leaders to submit to the team by seeking to serve, looking to call out the gifts and dreams within the members of the team, and never using the team to fulfill or realize the leaders' personal ambitions. Likewise, those who are led submit by making it easy for the leaders to lead, refusing passive-aggressive patterns, and looking to help the leaders guide the team to the best possible decisions without holding the team hostage to anyone's opinion. Getting explicit about how the leader/led relationships are supposed to play out is important. It may seem easier, more natural, and less threatening to keep things as informal as possible, but no one comes to leading or being led completely disentangled from the baggage of their upbringing or previous experiences. Clarity on how leading and following should be done is a gift to everyone.

Finally, the priority. The word *priority* historically was always singular. It means the thing that comes first. It's the most important thing. For our purposes here, it's the thing that, if you do it every day, is very likely to move you meaningfully toward the fulfillment of your Purpose in ways that align with who you're trying to become. Very few people can hold all the practices and postures and purpose in their minds day-to-day, but if we execute on our priority, we can go to bed pretty sure we won the day.

> Every team needs a clear purpose, clear shared practices, clearly described postures, and an absolutely vivid priority.

Now, keeping in mind Rivendell's purpose, consider their priority: "Together and alone, we attend closely to Jesus, obey reflectively, and release the outcomes." They believe that if they do those three things, together and alone, they'll effectively embody their postures and practices, and meaningfully execute against the purpose to which they are uniquely called.

Every team needs a clear purpose, clear shared practices, clearly described postures, and an absolutely vivid priority. Within the boundaries of those 4Ps, there's enormous latitude. Very little permission ever needs to be asked. As long as what you want to do serves the purpose and aligns with the practices, postures, and priority, you're free to do it. There's room to collaborate, to create, to course-correct, and to innovate. If a team has these 4Ps clarified, their chances of success multiply as does their potential impact.

But sometimes things go wrong.

Question 3: What About When It Goes Sideways?

Virology labs are dangerous places with incredible potential to shape human experience for good or ill. They're spaces where diseases are understood and cured, or they're the epicenters of cataclysmic outbreaks. They're rarely anything in the middle. The people who work in such settings know this, and they navigate the danger in order to reap the rewards. Lab leaks, though exceedingly rare, can be catastrophic, but much of the work that's done in virology labs is incredibly helpful and contributes to human flourishing. The reason behind this is simple: the people involved are explicit about how things are handled in those labs, and they're insistent that things are handled just that way all the time, every time.

Conflicts are like virology labs. Any conflict has the potential to be generative—to leave the people, directly and indirectly involved, better for having navigated it together. For the same reasons, any conflict also has the potential of causing disease, sometimes with exponential spread. Even when conflicts seem to do neither, the effects are merely being postponed and multiplied. When numerous individuals from diverse backgrounds, with significant skin in the game, work together on something immensely important to all of them, conflict is almost inevitable. Sometimes—often—things go wrong. Given the immense potential in conflict for good or for ill, and the fact that conflict is sure to happen, you'd expect teams, communities, and organizations to be explicit about how conflicts will be handled, and insistent that they're handled that way every time.

> Conflicts are like virology labs.

But if that's what you'd expect, you'd be wrong. Tremendous time and attention are given to clarifying mission and defining success, but too often parameters for handling conflict are left rather vague. Mission evolves and success is not guaranteed, but conflict is inevitable. The one thing that's sure, and which is sure to have a disproportionate and lasting effect, is improvised on the spot. Having a plan is critical, but we wing it.

We don't think we're winging it. We say something that sounds spiritual, like, "In matters of interpersonal conflict, we follow the principles in Matthew 18." Here's why saying that doesn't work.

First, saying it isn't the same as doing it. In case you're not familiar with the passage in question, here it is, from Matthew 18:15–17:

> If your brother sins against you, go and tell him his fault, between you and him alone. If he listens to you, you have gained your brother. But if he does not listen, take one or two others along with you, that every charge may be established by the evidence of two or three witnesses. If he refuses to listen to them, tell it to the church. And if he refuses to listen even to the church, let him be to you as a Gentile and a tax collector.

I have rarely seen things handled this way. Here are a few of the more common aberrations from the clear command of Jesus that I've seen just in the last few years:

- People feel offended by a brother or sister and litigate it over social media which totally skips all three prescribed steps and brings into the public square one side of a story that should have been expressed one-on-one.

- Feeling a little intimidated around the person they should confront, people may tell their stories to two or three other people under the auspices of "getting some counsel," but in reality, they're simply building a cadre of people on their side.
- Sometimes people will even ask their friends to confront a brother or sister for them which skips step one and warps step two.
- In rare cases, some people will even call up their brother or sister's boss without ever speaking directly to the offending party and catalogue their sins while hoping to enlist power to their side of things.
- Most common, however, is the quiet refusal to fight for the relationship. The perceived sin goes unmentioned and unforgiven, so the wound festers. In time, resentment, constant doubting of motives, and a passive-aggressive resistance come to replace vulnerability, trust, and cooperation. This spells the death, not only of a relationship, but also of the whole team.

The first problem with saying, "Well, we just follow Matthew 18," is that people rarely actually do it when they feel they've been sinned against. The second problem is that saying it isn't the same as insisting it's done.

I recently heard about a counselor, let's call him Mark, who was on vacation in Europe when he got an email from his friend, Jerry, back in the States. In the email, Jerry conveyed greetings, passed along a little news, inquired about his vacation, and finally asked him about some accusations that were floating around about him, coming from a former colleague. Jerry was worried about Mark and wanted him to know what was happening. Mark replied:

Dear Jerry,

We're so enjoying our vacation here. The weather is beautiful and the people are so hospitable. We wish you could be here with us, even if just for a few days!

Regarding the matter of Bob's accusations, it's unclear to me why you haven't insisted he follow Matthew 18. This is the first I've personally heard of any of this, and I'd be more than happy to hear it from Bob. Please kindly ask Bob to contact me and speak with me directly. Any other course is not only likely to be destructive to many, it's a flagrant disregard for the commands of our Teacher and King. As such, please don't communicate with me about this anymore, at least until Bob has spoken to me.

Thanks for looking in on our dog. It's a relief to have it off my mind. Say hi to Sally for us!

Love, Mark

What a masterful, if somewhat abrupt, invitation to actually obey Jesus! How many of us would have the courage to take such a stance? More importantly, why hadn't Jerry taken that stance in the first place? Mark should never have to hear secondhand about a problem Bob has with him. It also shows a lack of love and courage on Jerry's part not to hold Bob, a fellow disciple, to his obligations and commitments.

I've held several leadership positions in which there was more than one tier of authority below me in the chain of command. There have been numerous times when a worker has approached me with a serious problem concerning how their direct supervisor is treating them. In each case, I make a point to listen, to mirror back what I'm hearing to make sure I understand their perspective, and then to gently call them to obey Jesus. Sometimes I'll ask what they hope I'll do with the information they've given me, and one clever young woman said, "Well, I know this isn't the right answer, but I wish you'd just come here and straighten them out!"

If only that approach ever, ever worked.

Instead, I've learned the hard way to tell them clearly and firmly that they need to talk to their supervisor directly. When they ask if I'll sit in, I almost always decline.[4] Instead, I try to assure them that good leaders want to know how their leadership is affecting those they lead. If they go to their leader with a simple and non-accusatory description of how a specific behavior affected or is affecting them, and their leader won't listen, at that point I'm glad to sit in on a follow-up conversation. But part of trusting Jesus is believing he's smart, so let's first try what he told us to do and see what happens.

---

4 There are, of course, rare cases when a one-on-one conversation is a non-starter. But those are far rarer than we make them out to be.

The third problem with the "We just follow Matthew 18" approach, is that saying it isn't the same as knowing how to do it.

We all come from someplace. Those places we come from may not have taught us how to navigate conflict generatively. In fact, it's very likely they did not. Rather, we all approach community and team with unexamined predilections and preferences that inhibit constructive behavior and which predispose us to destructive patterns when conflict arises. Conflict is a high-anxiety, high-yield game, so we all tend to go straight to our earliest experiences with conflict and simply repeat the patterns we learned there.

> Saying it isn't the same
> as knowing how to do it.

Fortunately, you don't need a PhD in behavioral psychology or family dynamics to figure out how to move forward together in a healthy way. All you need are some rules of engagement. Here are a few I've acquired along the way.

Rule #1: Forbear personality, forgive sin.

Not everything that bothers you about someone is a sin. They chew loudly. They talk too much. They dress badly. Their leadership style is not your favorite. Just because you aren't happy doesn't mean someone needs to change. The writers of the New Testament enjoin us to forbear and tell us that love puts up with a lot.

Sin, on the other hand, isn't to be forborne. Sin is to be forgiven. If you sin, ask forgiveness. Merely saying you're sorry puts the responsibility for your feelings on the person you've harmed. Recognize the debt you've incurred and ask forgiveness. If you've been sinned against, forgive, with the same degree of readiness and willingness that God brings to forgiving you. Christ paid for that sin; you have no right to call the bill due twice.

Some sins need to be confronted as well as forgiven. Likewise, some personality quirks need to be addressed for the well-being of the team and of the quirky individual. In those cases, Rules two and three are helpful.

Rule #2: Notice and name your reaction without speculating on their motive.

Marcus Buckingham, perhaps the world's most prominent researcher on strengths and leadership at work, makes the case that people are unreliable raters of other people, but uncannily reliable raters of their own experience.[5] That means, simply, that when I do something that bothers you, you probably know exactly how you feel, but there's little to no reason to believe that you know why I did it. For this reason, once you've decided to have a conversation about what's bothering you, the best way to do it is to simply, humbly, name the behavior and offer your reaction.

As simple as this is, there are so many ways to get this wrong.

- "When you said x it was obvious that was coming from pride and fear. Your pride is causing you to hurt me, and your fear is making it impossible for you to hear me." This may be completely accurate, but it also may not. The more discerning you are, the more dangerous this one is because you can become far too confident that what you see is all there is. Leave judging hearts to God.
- "The last few weeks in the team meetings, when you keep talking, I think some people are feeling like they don't have a voice, and I really think a lot of people would feel that way if someone in their team meeting talked so much." What is someone supposed to do with this? Speak for yourself, and let others speak for themselves. Citing the faceless mob can only engender defensiveness.

Sometimes things are a little more serious, and more than a simple statement of reaction is necessary. Sometimes you have to confront someone, and some ways of doing that are far better than others.

Rule #3: Use the FBI to confront.

Simon Sinek offers a fantastic approach to confrontation. He says any successful confrontation must have three ingredients: Feelings, Behavior, Impact (FBI).[6] It doesn't matter in what order those three things appear, but all three must appear. As discussed above under rule two, you state the behavior (singular). Even if it's something they do frequently, pick one instance and focus on that. State specifically what feelings that behavior provoked and use the most vivid and precise language you can. Don't decorate, exaggerate, minimize, or deny. Finally, state the impact that concerns you should the behavior continue. Here are some examples:

---

5 Buckingham, "Lie 5: People."
6 Sinek, "Effective Confrontation."

- "In the conversation we had just now, you interrupted me six times that I counted. When you did that, I felt frustrated and disrespected, and I'm concerned if that continues, I'll find it too hard to communicate with you at all."
- "Honey, you're my husband and I love you. Tonight, at dinner with the Joneses, you made a remark that left me feeling dumb. I felt hurt, a little angry, embarrassed for me, and embarrassed for you. I'm concerned that if you talk to me like that in public, I'm going to start to wall my heart off, and I'm concerned you're going to harm your reputation."
- "Jim, I'm feeling exasperated. In the meeting on Monday, you vetoed the direction the team was moving in, and when asked what you want to do instead, you said, 'I don't know.' I'm exasperated because we have to go somewhere, and the team needs to act now. I'm concerned that if you continue to hit the brakes while offering no alternatives, the team's progress will stall out, and we'll lose engagement from everyone else."

I haven't yet faced a conflict that couldn't be approached generatively like this. Even touchy, hot-button items can be navigated calmly this way. It's key, though, to shut up right after you finish your three ingredients. Don't defend or develop them. Let the silence do the heavy lifting.[7] Sometimes, the other person will thank you or apologize. More often, they'll push back and make a case. After you listen, you simply repeat exactly what you said the first time, and shut up again. This may go on for another round or two, but eventually, they'll say, "Wow, when I said that, you really felt that way? I'm so sorry. Thanks for telling me."

> Our fruit will come from our integration with Jesus, but it will be born in and through our integration with our communities.

Conflict can be generative, but only if we walk through it with wisdom. Our fruit will come from our integration with Jesus, but it will be born in and through our integration with our communities. As we approach integrating with our host communities, we want to avoid three mistakes: confusing cultural literacy for cultural intelligence, letting

---

7 My dear friend, Matthew Rawlins, taught me this little maxim about letting silence do the work and it's been absolutely invaluable.

stress and the desire to be productive lead us to seek to be understood more than or before we seek to understand, and refusing to subject ourselves to the conditions that shape the lives of those with whom we've come to incarnate the Jesus way.

As we integrate with our teams, we should be careful to ask and to answer three questions: What is the relationship Jesus is actually giving us, and is it teaming? What does our team need in order to work well together? And what do we do when the inevitable relational storms arise? If we can avoid those three mistakes and insist on clarity with those three questions, we're likely to find ourselves enhancing and enhanced by a rich web of life-giving relationships and far less likely to go back to our passport countries lonely and burned out.

13

Leading Toward Integration

In this chapter we'll:

- Describe how to lead integrative work through coaching
- Learn how to consult when coaching is not enough
- Summarize key points from this section

The team I was on when we developed this approach supervises people all over the world. Our staff include medical professionals, educators, church planters, theologians, NGO leaders, entrepreneurs, community developers, trauma counselors, and IT specialists. In some of these disciplines that team has experience and expertise, but in many it does not. Some of our staff are free agents, while some are employed and have other bosses. Further, the cultural milieus in which our staff work are extremely diverse: Western Europe, Eurasia, North Africa, Southeast Asia, Central Asia, and Central Africa. Again, some members of my team have experience in a few of those environments but not most. In short, our staff do different kinds of work, with different expectations, in varied locations, in diverse cultural settings, and the vast majority are not where we are and doing what we're doing.

This presents a particular challenge when considering how to offer useful leadership to them in their work. The challenge, however, is not unique to us. Most leaders in Great Commission organizations are faced with exactly this situation. The people they lead don't exactly work *for* them, and often don't even work *with* them. There are things in common, of course. We share the tasks of disciple-making, teaming effectively wherever we are, language and culture acquisition, and being kingdom people in the many places we live, but almost everything else is different.

I'm on another team, as well. This team is local, focused largely on a few shared concerns. We meet in person weekly and are able to work meaningfully together. We still have diverse foci, but we are all engaged at the same table. In both cases—the local team and the dispersed international staff—I've noticed that when I'm leading best, I'm paying close attention to my colleagues' integration or disintegration in the four areas we've discussed in this section, and I'm making two key contributions.

In my monthly calls with our international staff, and in our weekly local team meetings, I'm listening for signs of integration or disintegration. Does Anne sound like she's laboring under the light, easy yoke of Jesus, or has she taken upon herself someone else's measurements of success and faithfulness? Is she mistaking productivity for fruit? How much listening to Jesus do I detect in Mike's language as he describes his encounters in his neighborhood? How vivid does his connection to Jesus seem, and how might I use just a few moments of our call to draw his attention again to that connection?

Similarly, when Jeff is describing a strategic decision he's trying to make, do I detect any signals that he's deeply engaging Jesus about it? Is he discerning or merely deciding? Does the way Martha talks about her work at the hospital sound like she is experiencing God there, or is God relegated to quiet times, and the hospital is just the grind she has to get through? I'll ask questions to help them clarify how vividly their vocation is integrated with the ministry they're called to do. I'll listen carefully for mentions of Jesus making appearances in their conversations with their colleagues at work, and I'll applaud when I hear them.

When they talk about their families, does it sound like they're stuck in that false work-family balance trap, or is the house moving together toward a shared calling? How engaged are the kids, and do they know how to engage their kids? Do they need help there? Alternatively, being single doesn't mean you don't have family. How integrated into sacred-sibling relationships do our single staff sound as they talk about the fabric of their days? How integrated are households with mission?

As our staff work to integrate with their host communities, we listen to see how much of a learning posture they're maintaining, how seriously they're taking their language acquisition, whether they're still trying to learn how their neighbors see their world, and how conscious they are of their own predilections to insulate themselves from the unfamiliar and foreign. As they live into whatever team relationships they might have, or as they explore options for teaming, we try hard to listen with them as they ask those three crucial teaming questions: *Do we team? How to team? And do we know what to do when it comes undone?*

In the regular touches we have with our people, close and dispersed, we attend carefully to these areas of integration because we know that the strength our people bring to their tasks and to their own ongoing development can either be multiplied or degraded. Further, these are the common places in their myriad kinds of work where we want to spend our time reinforcing integration and avoiding disintegration wherever we can. Our best contributions to that end are coaching and consulting.

Coach

"Have you ever been coached before?" Bob is a master coach.[1] He was leading a coaching seminar fifteen years ago at our organization's headquarters and training leaders at all levels in some rudimentary coaching skills. He'd graciously agreed to sit down with me after lunch and help me work through a twisty situation that had been stymying my team for some time.

"No, apart from just now in the seminar, I don't think so," I replied.

"Alright, well let's start with this. Coaching isn't counseling. We're not trying to get to the root causes of whatever problem your facing buried somewhere in your past. Coaching is forward-facing. We're trying to see if there are paths *ahead* you maybe haven't considered, or considered deeply enough to take meaningful action. Coaching also isn't advice. I'm not an expert in what you do. You're the expert. I'm the coach. Okay?"

"Got it."

"Good," he smiled. "So, what exactly would you like to talk about?"

I unpacked, in some detail and with much meandering, a frustrating scenario playing out in our team. He listened quietly and actively, and when I came up for air, he met me with a question. I don't remember it, but I recall feeling heard and like someone was attending to *me*. I hadn't felt that way in quite some time, and it seemed to lower my tension and open my thinking. We went back and forth like that for a while, with Bob letting his curiosity lead his questions, and me answering as honestly as possible. Sometimes the questions were as simple as, "Can you say more about that?" But always, they helped me move the conversation forward.

After maybe twenty minutes of that, Bob asked, "Do you have a pen and maybe a notebook or something?"

"Sure," I replied, reaching into my bag. I went to hand them to Bob, but he waved them off.

---

[1] Bob Hancox's book, *Coaching for Engagement: Achieving Results Through Powerful Conversations* co-authored with Russell Hunter and Kristann Boudreau, develops many of the ideas presented in this section. I'm deeply indebted to Bob for the time he's spent coaching me and helping me develop my own coaching skills.

"Nope. You're doing the work. Draw a circle. A big one. Use the whole page. Good. Now, cut the circle into 12 equal pie wedges."

"Like this?"

"Perfect. Now, I want you to come up with 12 different ideas that could possibly solve your problem. Don't censor any of them. They don't have to be radically different, but they have to be different enough that they'd require a different plan to execute. As long as they're not fantastically absurd, they're allowed. Even bad ideas are good right now. But you have to fill the whole pie."

The first three wedges took about 15 seconds. The other nine took a solid 15 minutes. When I was done, he read them to me out loud twice. Then he asked, "What commonalities do you see between many, most, or all of these?"

I wasn't expecting that question. In fact, I was expecting some answers. But when he asked it, I noticed one person's name in eight of the twelve wedges. Bob asked, "What do you think about that?"

"Well, it seems like either our problem surrounds this one individual, or our solution does. Or both." In fact, this observation opened up an entirely new line of inquiry that led to a series of experiments that helped us quite a lot.

Bob offered me no answers. But he did offer three things that, taken together, unlocked a conundrum and helped me move past a deeply frustrating roadblock.

Let's explore those three things more deeply.

1. Bob was present to me as I was present to my task.

Throughout the conversation, Bob kept his attention on me, and my attention on my conundrum. He never allowed my attention to drift to ancillary issues nor did he pull my attention toward him by telling me how he's perhaps handled something similar in the past. When Bob showed genuine interest in me, it activated something in my mind and heart that opened me to more possibilities than I'd been considering, and he did it with a curious question.

2. Bob asked curious, powerful questions.[2]

Powerful questions are curious in nature. They're driven by the coach's genuine desire to hear more about something that sparked their interest.

---

[2] A great treatment of curious and powerful questions can be found in Hancox, *Coaching for Engagement*, 72–73.

Rooted in open listening, powerful questions tend to open more pathways instead of cutting away paths that don't seem as useful to the coach. The coach isn't trying to get somewhere with curious questions; the coach is trying to see where this can go.

Powerful questions tend to be short and simple. They're open ended and often start with *who, what, how, where,* and *when*? *Why*? is better avoided, as it tends to invite defense of a decision made or an opinion taken, and defensiveness closes the process down. There is no right or wrong answer to a curious question, and this is the power. Without the pressure to get it right, the person being coached has room to discover.

Long, leading, or closed questions tend to provoke defensiveness and resistance as the person you're coaching can feel trammeled and forced in a direction they might not naturally have gone. As such, when the solutions discovered feel like the coach's, rather than their own, the solution is less likely to be truly owned and executed. Powerful questions, on the other hand, open the person being coached to a wider view while keeping the responsibility for action squarely in their court. They do all the work, so they own the solutions discovered through and through.

Which leads to the third thing Bob did.

3. Bob kept the monkey on my back.

Bob did this funny thing in the seminar earlier that day. He had a bunch of those stuffed toy gibbons with the Velcro on the hands. You can wrap their long, noodly arms around things and stick their hands together. It can look like they're hugging you if you do it right. It can also look like you've got a monkey on your back if you do it wrong.

Bob demonstrated typical management and leadership approaches to an employee with a challenge. Someone approached him with five or six monkeys on their back, and as they told Bob about them, Bob would offer advice, or offer to take part of the responsibility for solving the problem. Each time he did that, though, a monkey would come off the employee and get firmly attached to Bob's back.

Then, he ran the same scenario, but asked different questions: Which part of this is most frustrating? What have you tried so far? What resources do you need to move past this hurdle? Where could you find those resources? What are some potential solutions you've thought of so far? How about you try to think of one or two more right now, while we're standing here? What will success look like, and how will you know when you've succeeded with this?

Bob kept the monkeys on the employee's back. He did the same thing with me a few hours later. He told me plainly at the outset that he wouldn't be giving me advice. This wasn't his problem to solve. When it came time to draw the pie wedges and fill them in, he made sure I did it with my journal and my pen. Even when it came time to read the potential solutions, he read them, making sure it was me who was doing the work of assessing the potential solutions and discovering the commonalities. Bob worked hard to do none of my work for me. He kept the monkey on my back which led to me making some discoveries that he would have had neither the experience nor the context to be able to lead me to. Bob knew I was the expert on my situation, so he made sure to keep me at the wheel.

> I resist the urge to fill the space and allow the silence and absence of advice from me draw solutions forth from you.

There is, of course, a great deal more to coaching than these three tactics, and there is a rich body of literature in the discipline available, so we need not belabor it here. For now, let's notice how critical an approach like this is in a setting where your staff work in twenty different cultures, in fifteen different fields, and with any number of other supervisors telling them what to work on and how. Imagine how empowering it can be to have someone with some authority *not* use it to tell you exactly what you must do, but rather use it to help you discover what you *can* do. Even in settings where supervisor and staff are working on the same kinds of things, toward identical outcomes, a coaching approach leads to much fuller engagement from staff, and it frees the supervisor to bring out the best in her people.

Coaching is question-heavy and rooted in curiosity. Oriented toward helping staff discover their own solutions and strategies, it leverages their expertise and keeps the responsibility and agency in their hands. When I coach as a leader, I hold myself back and use my agency to make room for yours. This holding back is called negative power. I resist the urge to fill the space and allow the silence and absence of advice from me draw solutions forth from you. As such, coaching represents a positive use of negative power.

Consult

As much as I've come to love coaching, sometimes it's not enough. Or rather, it's not always what's needed.

My friend Matthew is a trained coach, but he noticed pretty quickly that sometimes coaching isn't what's called for. He'd be hired to help organizations solve real problems, and he'd attempt to apply a coaching rubric to the process, but often he'd find that they'd already mined all they could from their own mysterious inner resources, and had, in fact, hired him under the impression that he either knew something they didn't, or could do something they couldn't. These people didn't need a coach, but they still needed help.

I saw a similar dynamic in a mission agency I once consulted. They were trying to become more deliberate about how they developed leaders internally. As I interviewed young, emerging leaders, a pattern emerged in pockets throughout the organization. About a decade before, there had been something of a coaching revolution within the leadership. They had jettisoned top-down, prescriptive, the-leader-has-all-the-answers approaches for a much more engaging coaching approach to leadership. The benefits were obvious throughout the organization, but so were the costs. Emerging leaders would report:

- "I know Lou really cares about me, and he asks great questions. But sometimes I just need clarity. One more swami Yoda question isn't going to cover the distance."
- "Andrew takes a hands-off approach, and I usually like that. But when I need help, he keeps asking me what resources I can draw on. I thought he was supposed to be a resource I could draw on."
- "I know how I would do it. But when I do it like that, it goes wrong. I need to know how he would do it, and I need him to explain it to me, but I can't seem to get that out of him."

Encounters like these left cross-cultural workers, already operating under significant stress and often feeling under-resourced, neglected, or worse, feeling like what they needed was being withheld from them. This is not to say that their leaders were in any way trying to withhold necessary aid from their staff. Quite the contrary, these leaders had seen what happens when power is misused or over-used, and they were loath to make those mistakes, but when we under-lead, power can also be abdicated. Since power is for flourishing, abdicated power means aborted flourishing.

It may be helpful here to give some nuance to the notion of power, specifically in relationships like the ones described above. The relationship between a supervisor and staff is a power relationship. They are not merely colleagues in the way peers can be. Rather, the relationship is defined, at least in part, by disparities of authority and of perspective. If I'm Nick's supervisor, I have authority within our community that Nick does not. I, to a certain degree, tell him what he should do. I can also tell his colleague or team member to do something given they are also part of our organization. But Nick also has power I do not. He can affect his environment directly in ways I simply can't. We each have power, but there is a disparity in the amount—arguably, I have more than him, as I am his supervisor, and he is not mine. Likewise, there is a disparity in perspective. Nick can perceive his environment much more closely than I can, but I'm operating regularly with a much wider lens than he is. What's more, due to the nature of my role, while Nick may be well-networked there in his city, I am likely better networked at a global level and certainly within the machinery of our organization. Further, with a few exceptions, as Nick's supervisor, I'm likely to have more mileage in this line of work than he is, and hopefully I will have learned things that are useful to more than just me.

> Since power is for flourishing, abdicated power means aborted flourishing.

So, there is a disparity in power and a disparity in perspective. If I act like this isn't so, like I don't have power that I really do have, or that I don't know things I really do know, it can easily feel like neglect or withholding. But how can I bring the power and perspective I have to bear on serving my direct reports? As I was consulting for the organization I mentioned above, it occured to me that this is exactly what I was doing as I consulted for them. I was making my own capacities and competencies available to them but leaving them with the responsibility to act on what I offered.

Here's what I do now with my direct reports. I listen as they describe their lives. I ask questions about things that raise my curiosity, and I attend carefully to the four integrations I've described in this section. Before our monthly call, I will have asked them to bring anything they might need help with, and I explore that with them on the call using a coaching approach.

But about half-way through our call, I'll ask them two questions: What are your top five priorities this month (with my team it's this week)? and How can I help you? Marcus Buckingham insists that the research is clear and the data incontrovertible: effective leadership at work comes down to frequent check-ins on near-term future work.[3] I fully agree. When I ask the first question, I'm giving them the gift of scaffolded prioritization. Some things they're working on this month will be more important than other things, but tasks don't line themselves up by priority. They all scream for primacy, and unless we decide to limit our list and populate it only with the most important things, we drown.

When I ask how can I help them, the most frequent answer is, "I don't know. Nothing, I guess."

I follow immediately with, "Well, think of the 3Rs: Remove, Resource, Reveal."

- **Remove**: Maybe there's not a monkey on their back but a boulder in their way. Because of our disparity in power, I might be able to move that boulder.
- **Resource**: I may be in touch with personnel, materials, funding, or information that they don't have access to. If so, I can leverage the disparity of power and perspective to get them what they need.
- **Reveal**: Sometimes the fog is too thick to make a good decision. I don't want to make decisions for them, but because of the disparity in our perspective, it's quite likely I can clarify something that, once disambiguated, can clear the air for their own discernment processes to move forward.

In these three ways—remove, resource, reveal—I can consult for my staff, letting the disparity in our power and perspective be of benefit to them. Power is for flourishing, and work is where we are to flourish. If those who lead us happen to know a little more than we do about something, or are able to do something we can't do for ourselves, that's good news for us.

As the people we lead invest in their own thriving, we look to catalyze that pursuit and to capacitate for it. As they bring the strength that Jesus is supplying them to doing the good and beautiful work to which God has called them, we look to help them apply that force constructively

---

3 Buckingham, "Check-In Conversation."

by helping them protect four key integrations and by contributing to their work through coaching and consulting. If we do this well, we can nurture reflectiveness in those we lead, and as we reflect with them on their experiences of Christ, of their work, and of themselves, we can help them become who God first dreamed them to be. So as we learn to foster glory, it's to the branches of the tree that we now turn.

Part III
Develop | Crown

Introduction to Part III

It is not enough to help people thrive. Good leadership pursues that, but we are not only shepherds. We must also help our people work because we have work to do; they have good works foreordained for them to do, and they were made for work. However, it can't end there. Work, theirs and ours, is the main context of our apprenticeships to Jesus. He is not only allowing us to join him in his work to heal and rescue the world he loves, he's also using that work to heal us, to rescue us, and to bring us to our full glory in him. Good leaders in the Jesus way, therefore, also look with Jesus to develop the people they steward. Failure here, whether due to ignorance, incompetence, or negligence, expresses incomplete leadership, and therefore represents a failure to lead. Leading means developing.

How does development happen? In his lovely book, *Essentialism: The Disciplined Pursuit of Less*, Brian McKeown observes, "Aristotle talked about three kinds of work, whereas in our modern world we tend to emphasize only two. The first is theoretical work, for which the end goal is truth. The second is practical work, where the objective is action. But there is a third: it is *poietical* work. The philosopher Martin Heidegger described poiesis as 'a bringing forth.'"[1] Development is poiesis.

Most modern attempts at development amount to theoretical or practical work. We teach people *about* leading, or we tell them to use a particular technique or to take particular actions. If we're honest, this book by itself will only amount to that. Therefore, this book can never be more than a tool used in the third kind of work. When leaders in the way of Jesus develop their people, they aren't primarily adding knowledge or skills, though that might happen. They are bringing forth what lies deep inside them, helping the glory already inside to come to its full expression, for God's highest glory, for their deepest joy, and for the world's salvation.

What are we bringing forth? We're bringing forward and to maturity the natural gifts, strengths, and beauty God put into people at their making. We do so through reflection on their real-world experiences. What's more, we're working with the Spirit to bring forth the image of Jesus in them and give to the world something it's never had before: the

---

1 McKeown, *Essentialism*, 188. Within this quote, McKeown cites Krancberg's *A Soviet Postmortem*.

face of God made visible and knowable in the face of Christ. We are literally revealing God to the world. Finally, in seeing and appreciating who they already are, we're helping them discover and bring to the forefront who *else* they might be. There is more to God than they know, and there is more to them than they know.

Thus, along with our five dimensions of soul to thrive in, and our four integrations for good and beautiful work in the world, our task is to also attend to three key developments in ourselves, and in those we lead: poiesis by reflective experience, poiesis by Christification, and poiesis by self-discovery.

14

Poiesis by (Reflective) Experience

In this chapter we'll:

- Discuss the 70-20-10 rule and the role of experience(s) in development
- Learn how to have more and get more out of developmental experiences
- Introduce a simple tool to make meaningful work experiences a developmental win

Knowledge is not a valid or reliable indicator of competency. However, since the Enlightenment, Western societies have attempted to right social ills and elevate human experience through education, and the experiment, such as it is, has not been a total failure. Being educated—knowing more—is usually better than the alternative. But it's not sufficient, and we all know that. We've always known that. Our parents knew that, and their parents before them. It's been an adage for generations. You've probably said it yourself: experience is the best teacher.

Except for needing a plural countable noun, the adage is spot on.

Experience(s) are the best teachers.

Consider the modern resume and coverletter. While degrees and certifications are important, the most effective resumes give space for the explanation of what you actually did. Why? Because when we hire someone for a job, we know that the best predictor of what they will do is what they've done. Not what they've read or studied, or who they know or has mentored them. Those facts aren't irrelevant, but they're not the main thing. The main thing is the applicant's experience.

> Experience(s) are the best teachers.

Research has borne this out. Studies of leaders who have been successfully developed show that 70 percent of development came from on-the-job experience; 20 percent came from significant relationships (think mentors, coaches, learning cohorts), and 10 percent came from content (books, courses, lectures, etc.). Seventy percent of what *actually* developed leaders was their experience on the job. You could eliminate all the formal training they'd received and get almost exactly the same results. This picture of how development actually happens is so ubiquitous in the Human Resources field that it's earned its own catchphrase: The 70-20-10 Rule.[1] But even though this split is common knowledge, organizations on average allocate funding in exactly the opposite proportions: 70 percent to formal training and education courses, 20 percent to relationship-based development, and 10 percent to experience-driven development.

When we don't know how to leverage experience developmentally, we default to the cultural norm of educating for change even when we know it doesn't work. We want to do *something*, so we do what we know, for no other reason than we don't know how to do it another way.

Enter the plural countable noun. There's a problem with our adage. *Experience* is an uncountable noun. Like food. You can't count food, but you need it. In fact, you need enough food, of adequate variety, and digested properly to thrive. Experience isn't the best teacher: experiences are. When we say someone doesn't have enough experience for a particular role, we don't only mean that they don't have enough time on the job. We mean she doesn't have enough specific experiences of particular kinds that would allow us to see what she would do as CEO, which would give us confidence that her curriculum—the course she has run—has prepared her adequately for the role. When we think about experiences as discreet, countable nouns, we can get our hands around them, and parse them out and consider each one.

There are three questions we need to ask if we're going to do better than most companies and actually approach development—our own and that of those we lead—in a way that leverages real work experiences for all they're worth:

1. How do I get more developmental bang out of the experiences already happening at work?
2. What other experiences are needed to increase and vary the opportunities to develop?
3. How do I get those experiences?

---

[1] Lombardo and Eichinger, *Career Architect Development*.

This chapter will focus on the first question, and the other two will be addressed at length in chapter 17. There's a whole body of literature available on this topic, but for our purposes, we'll focus on a few things we can start doing right now that will radically improve the quality and quantity of development happening in and around us.

Getting the Most Out of Your Experiences

The average worker spends forty to fifty hours a week at her work, and has hundreds of largely uncatalogued and unexamined experiences each week. How do we help them to get more out of their work, and in so doing, become more than they presently are? We help them reflect on their work.

Maya teaches English in Vientiane, Laos. She also makes disciples as opportunity presents itself, though she doesn't use her time in the classroom to do so. She has a decent, but occasionally challenging relationship with her supervisor at the school, but feels she is getting along very well with her fellow teachers, some of whom are Lao and some expat. She has an encouraging relationship with her landlord, a fifty year-old Lao woman with whom Maya enjoys conversations about fairly deep matters, but the relationship is complicated somewhat by the landlord-renter arrangement.

In the past three weeks, Maya has had one such conversation with her landlord, as well as one challenging conversation with her supervisor at work. Also at work, Maya led a teacher in-service day for the rest of the department to help train the teaching staff in best practices for second language acquisition. In her words, "It went pretty well." The rest of her time at work was been spent teaching, which is enjoyable but becoming somewhat stale. Finally, one of the young women she has been discipling shared with her some disturbing information about her home life, and she's not sure she was particularly helpful in the conversation.

Imagine you are Maya's supervisor, and in a monthly check-in she has shared with you what's been going on over the past few weeks. As you consider how you might help her reflect on her experience developmentally, here are a couple common mistakes you might make:

- You might say, "Wow. That's a lot. What do you think God is teaching you in all this?" A question like this asks her to, in the few moments you're together, swallow all the significant experiences of the month at once, digest them, and present the nutrition in a few succinct lines. It seems like a good question, but it asks so much that nothing useful is likely to happen.

- Your curiosity or compassion regarding the young lady she's disciplining might be piqued, leading you to focus only on that.
- Conversely, you might unconsciously select only the things that happened at her workplace, since you're looking to use her work developmentally. But in reality, it's *experience*, not just work, that we're trying to reflect upon.

As someone looking to help Maya leverage her experience developmentally, you've just been presented with a gold mine of potential conversations. The trick is to focus on one experience and to let the others go for now. Maya can't chew one bite while trying to cram the others in her mouth. It's fine to let the others go because there will be more like them later. The conversation with her landlord, or with her supervisor, present easy opportunities for reflection. The in-service she ran is an obvious choice, but simply taking one class period of her normal teaching and reflecting upon it could be just as useful. She mentioned regular classes were getting stale which lets you know she might feel some opportunity to improve them.

How do you choose which experience to reflect upon? Normally, you wouldn't. You'd ask Maya to choose. With the exception of times when you're developing Maya for a specific role and something she mentions presents particularly fertile and opportune ground to work through, it's usually best to let the person you're developing choose which experiences to reflect upon because it's their curiosity that will lead to the best reflection, and their volition that will be needed to pursue any action steps after the reflection. So, you would ask Maya to choose and trust that enlisting her choice is the best strategy to secure her engagement in the process.

Once she has selected an experience to reflect upon, how do you do it? We've found there's a sweet spot between being thorough enough and exhausting someone's attention. You want to spend twenty to thirty minutes reflecting on one experience. Less than that usually leaves some interesting stones unturned and more than that leads quickly to diminishing returns. Attention is valuable, and we don't want to waste it.

How we use time and direct attention is important. Claudia Hill suggests moving through three kinds of questions to guide the reflection: *What?*, *So what?*, and *Now what?* The *What?* questions engage the memory, the *So what?* questions provoke critical thinking, and the *Now what?* questions activate and focus the imagination, so learning can be assimilated and improvements can be made.[2]

Alternatively, Scott DeRue outlines a four-step process that the US Army follows in its after-event reviews:[3]

1. Conduct the review as soon as possible after the event.
2. Describe the experience as thoroughly and vividly as possible.
3. Develop "counterfactuals"—alternate imaginings of how the event could have unfolded differently if different decisions had been made or different actions taken.
4. Identify and consolidate insights and lessons learned.

Steps two, three, and four map well onto Hill's three questions, while providing some additional structure, which can be crucial for those with less experience conducting these kinds of reviews.

That's where one community I served found itself a few years ago. Decades prior, the organization had moved from a field-based model which had a clear hierarchy of authority to a more agile and community-oriented team-based approach. The team-focused model had a lot to recommend it, but one thing that got lost in the transition was a clear way for personnel to be developed for increasing levels of responsibility. The field model also lacked a coherent, deliberate developmental curve, but its concrete leadership tiers at least allowed for some natural development to take place as a matter of course. Even if it was accidental, it was there.

Flash forward twenty years and senior leaders are talking about succession, but the bench is far too shallow. Without the ladder of roles the field model had provided, even accidental leader development hadn't taken place. To be fair, a few people had developed a few leaders around them, and a lot of organic growth had happened along the way. But it was not nearly deep enough or dispersed widely enough across the community to engender the kind of developmental bias and leadership competency an organization in transition would certainly need.

When I was brought in to help solve this problem, it quickly became clear that we would need a tool that leaders at all levels of the organization could train on and implement immediately. It would have to be simple

---

2 Hill, "Scaffolding Reflection."
3 DeRue, "After-Event Reviews."

enough that people could even use it on themselves, but sophisticated enough that using it would nearly ensure that adequate developmental nutrition could be extracted from any significant experience. What emerged was the After-Experience Reflection, built (with gratitude and due credit) upon the observations of Hill and Rue mentioned above.

After Experience Reflection

This conversation is designed to help you mine a recent, poignant experience for maximum developmental value. Choose an experience in which you were a major contributor, and which seems to have had some impact on you or on the others involved. Give this conversation (held either with yourself or with a trusted colleague) around 20 minutes. Don't rush it, and pay special attention to the questions in the beginning. Ask Jesus to guide your reflection, and to use it in your ongoing apprenticeship with him.

WHAT?

1. DESCRIBE

   Sensory memories?

   Who was involved?

   What was your role? What did you do?

2. NOTICE

   How did you feel? Can you name the emotions?

   How challenging was it and what made it so?

   Where, if anywhere, did you explicitly notice Jesus?

SO WHAT?

3. CONSIDER

   What was your contribution?

   How effective was it (Scale of 1-10)?

   Have you taken this approach before and (if so) how did it compare?

> 4. IMAGINE
>
> Given the same scenario, what different approach could you have taken?
>
> How might that have turned out differently (or not)?
>
> **NOW WHAT?**
>
> 5. PREPARE
>
> What did you learn about this skill? Yourself? Others? God?
>
> In what ways could you afford to change your attitudes? Your expectations? Your values? Your approach?
>
> 6. ACT
>
> Given what you've discovered, choose an action step or two and attach dates to them. Consider sharing them with a colleague, mentor, supervisor, or coach.

Figure 6 | After-Experience Reflection

If you have similar opportunity soon, make a plan of action that adjusts for what you've discovered. Be sure to ask Jesus directly if he has input he wants you to consider.

What?

The exercise opens by inviting the participant to remember what actually happened in as much detail as possible. The goal here is vividness. First, we describe what happened. Who was there? What was the space like? Help them access their sensory memories before they access their emotions about the event. It will help them remember more accurately and give them a little clinical distance from feelings that might be over-asserting themselves and biasing their reflection.

But once they've described the event in adequate detail, it's time to *notice*. Ask them to notice and name the emotions they felt. Notice how challenging this particular task was and what made it so. Noticing the challenge can help surface potential directions for development either because a needed competency is lacking or because the exhilaration of the challenge unearths a buried interest. Then have them recount exactly what they did in the order they did it. In other words, without them assessing impact, have them notice their inputs into the situation. Remember that when we notice we do so without judgement, explanation, or excuse. Measurement will come later.

But before they measure, it's important to invite them to notice where they saw Jesus in the situation, if at all. It's fine if they didn't, but if they did they need to take stock of that. Asking the question is most of the work as it attunes them to the presence of Jesus in their past work, the current reflection, and in their future endeavors.

So What?

Having remembered the event as vividly as possible, and having noticed how it affected them and the inputs they brought to the situation, they're ready to consider their role in the experience and to imagine other options. Ask them to summarize their contribution—not the discreet steps, but the overall effect. For example: "I guided the team through the entire series of exercises." Or, "I confronted my colleague by noting their behavior, describing my feelings, and articulating my concern over the potential impact to our relationship and work if that behavior continues." Then ask them to score their contribution for effectiveness. This score will, of course, be entirely subjective, but the question forces them to measure how happy they are with the outcomes of their contribution regardless of how right they feel their contribution might have been. Finally, ask them to compare the approach they took to other instances in which they took a similar tack. This allows them to connect this experience with prior experiences, and it allows for concrete comparison between events. Comparison and contrast are two of the most powerful learning mechanisms available to the human brain. The comparison with prior experience is well worth the minute or two spent here.

That comparison also prepares them nicely for the next step. Invite them to recall the situation again and to imagine taking a different approach—making a different decision, saying something different, going about things in a different order—whatever. After they imagine a different approach, have them consider whether it would have resulted in a different outcome. These questions do three things: (1) they provoke a ready contrast which increases learning; (2) they allow the participant to gain twice the value from one experience; and (3) they prepare the participant for the next step.

Now What?

Having recalled and assessed both the situation and their unique contribution to it, the participant is now ready to think forward. This step involves preparation and action. First, help the participant consolidate their learning from the reflection. What have they learned about themselves, about the skills necessary to undertake what they did, and about God? Further, what could they afford to change in their approach in the future? It's important here that we don't encourage them to find what they did wrong, so they can do it better next time. We're on a hunt for slight improvement and not a pogrom to purge all imperfection from our work. Anyone can find an error. The point of this step is to gently explore possibilities. What could they afford to change? The answer might truly be nothing.

Having assessed and consolidated, they're now ready to form a strategy for how they might approach their next opportunity of this kind. One or two concrete action steps are enough. Remember that the reflection isn't meant to lead to a product. Reflection *is* the product. They will grow and develop naturally now that the raw material has been properly digested.

There will be more experiences, so we are just after one or two insights. More development happens in these little bites of reflective experience than you might think. Certainly, more than we get from courses, books, or lectures. Content is how we learn *about* a thing. We learn the thing itself in the doing and in reflecting on what we've done.

This is not to say that there's no place for content or for developmental relationships. On the contrary, regular, focused reflection on real experiences can help us target our use of content and how we leverage those developmental relationships. Essentially, attending to the 70 percent helps us make the best use of the 20 percent and the 10 percent.

A friend and I are experimenting with a simple way to do this. Once a month we get a cohort of emerging leaders together on a video call for about two hours. The cohort has four people in it along with the two of us, and each month one of us runs an After-Experience Reflection (AER) for one of the leaders in the group while the other four people silently listen. The Reflection itself takes about twenty or thirty minutes, but then the group gets the opportunity to ask the leader receiving the AER clarifying questions for five minutes and then five more minutes to give some thoughts as to what they might have tried in the scenario presented. The leader receiving the feedback is free to take the advice or not but isn't free to respond at that moment. Two questions I'm prone to ask in this free space are: "What, if anything, was missing in your knowledge, skillset, or character that would have helped there, and that you'd like to pursue in the next few months?" And, "Is there anyone else you'd like to talk with about something you noticed during this experience or the reflection on it? (i.e., a counselor, mentor, spiritual director, coach, etc.)" Questions like these can position someone for continued learning, targeted to their presenting needs, at their own pace, and fueled by their own desires.

In a two-hour call, we'll get through two people's AERs, leaving the other two for the following month. We also typically leave ten to fifteen minutes at the end for the group to entertain the question, "What are the best resources you've encountered that speak to the issues that emerged in today's AERs?" Videos, books, lectures, podcasts, and the like populate the last few minutes of the call, leaving everyone with a small library of highly targeted resources they are then free to explore if they choose.

This approach offers numerous benefits. First, the vast majority of the energy is dedicated to reflection on real work. My friend and I get more practice running AERs, and two people receive AERs. There's the added benefit of a mastermind group working alongside them which is part of the 20 percent of learning from other people. Finally, the 10 percent to be gained from formal learning is targeted specifically to the issues that emerge in the group's real work. Since the formal learning resources meet a real, present, felt need, their benefit is likely to stick.

Becoming competent with a few simple tools for reflecting on your work, and becoming conversant in an approach that allows for that golden 70-20-10 dispersion will serve you well as you strive to mine real work experiences for maximum developmental potential in yourself and in those you lead. However, sometimes the work you're doing isn't providing enough diverse experiences to drive your development where it needs to go. We will address that challenge in chapter 17. But for now, the simple shift from merely doing our work to reflecting constructively on our work, and on what happens in us as we work, is the lion's share of development. This one step results in quantum leaps that you can start making today.

15

Poiesis by Christification

In this chapter we'll:

- Explore a biblical understanding of Christian spiritual development as Christification
- Look at Christification from the writings of Paul, Peter, and John
- Draw out practical help from Paul's accounting of his own exclusive, intense pursuit of Christification

As followers of Jesus, we know that our development isn't merely a matter of getting better at what we do or even at being people. We know there's something more afoot here, and for that reason, there's one particular kind of experience that we need to pay special attention to.

The notion that our development is a primary outcome of our lives and work isn't new. Jesus himself, as well as the Apostle Paul, seemed to think that the development of God's servants was an endeavor well worth serious effort and attention. Paul makes this case vigorously and vibrantly in his second letter to Timothy. But for Jesus and for Paul, our development isn't merely a matter of becoming more. We are, in particular, becoming more like Jesus. This is important for everyone, but especially for those who carry significant influence with others. Our development isn't Maslow's self-actualization but rather a matter of Christ-expression.

> Our development isn't Maslow's self-actualization but rather a matter of Christ-expression.

Jesus says, "everyone when he is fully trained will be like his teacher" (Luke 6:40). For Jesus, the outcome of our development will be deep resonance with and similarity to him. Paul's pursuit is the same:

> Him we proclaim, warning everyone and teaching everyone with all wisdom, that we may present everyone mature in Christ. For this I toil, struggling with all his energy that he powerfully works within me. (Col 1:28–29)

Paul's view of human transformation took as its goal humans being restored and completed not merely to one's best self, but rather to one's true self *in* Christ. To the Galatian believers he expresses it as, "until Christ is formed in you" (Gal 4:19). The picture is human beings completely formed in Christ, and Christ completely formed in people, and peoples.

Christification and Christosynthesis

If Paul's view of human transformation has as its goal this completion in fusion with Jesus, how does it happen? Paul lays out the mechanism of this poiesis in 2 Corinthians 3:17–18. Let's take a look and ask a few questions:

> Now the Lord is the Spirit, and where the Spirit of the Lord is, there is freedom. And we all, with unveiled face, beholding the glory of the Lord, are being transformed into the same image from one degree of glory to another. For this comes from the Lord who is the Spirit.

1. What is happening to us?

We are being transformed into the likeness of Jesus. The voice is passive. We are not transforming ourselves. This is not Christian self-help. This, the transformative process, is happening to us, and the arc is Christ shaped.

2. Who is doing it?

Paul says this is all the work of "the Lord, the Spirit" (v. 18). This can be a little mind-bending for people who like to keep the three Persons of the Trinity neatly separate, but just as all of God dwells in Jesus, all of Jesus, somehow, dwells in the Holy Spirit. Remember, as verse 17 asserts, this conformation, since it is being carried out by the Spirit, results not in uniformity, but in freedom.

3. What are we doing in this passage?

"And we all, with unveiled face, beholding the glory of the Lord" (2 Cor 3:18). A couple things are of note.

First, we *all* behold the glory of God. This is not relegated to a singular prophet, as it was with Moses nor is ascending the mountain the purview of a group of spiritual elites. This is the normal means of change and the calling bestowed upon *all* of us.

Second, what we do, we do unveiled. In the immediate context, this is a contrast with Moses who had to veil his face after he had encountered God, so the people of Israel could tolerate looking at him. The people God had chosen needed two degrees of separation to be comfortable. First, they sent Moses to meet God face to face as they were too scared. Then, once he had, even the afterglow of that encounter was too much for them.

But we look God square in the face when we look at Jesus. The spirit changes us as we behold Jesus—as we look at him with sustained attention. Some translations read the word *behold* as *reflect*, and there's a good reason for this. Paul is using language to build a weird image, but an image that can manage to convey how the impossibility of genuine transformation can happen. We look in a mirror, but the face staring back at us is Jesus. Slowly, our features in the mirror start to take on aspects of his, until eventually who we are looks just like us and just like Jesus.

> The Spirit transforms us into likeness with Jesus
> as we behold Christ beholding us.

The picture is a mirror though and not a portrait. This is important for at least two reasons. For one, the image on the mirror is alive and looking at us. This is an encounter with the person of Jesus and not just his memory or his teachings, and as it's a mirror, we do not encounter him without encountering ourselves. To run from self-awareness is to run from Jesus. The Spirit transforms us into likeness with Jesus as we behold Christ beholding us.

There are two processes in the natural world that help me understand this. The first is petrification. The word comes from the root *petra* which means rock. A tree falls in mineral-rich water. Over a very long time, bits of tree wash out and bits of rock—minerals—wash in. Eventually the tree is hard and heavy like stone, but it retains its shape and characteristics as a tree. It's more than just a rock or just a plant. The tree has become petrified by long exposure to the minerals. Similarly, by long exposure to Christ we become Christified without losing who we truly are. Transformation by Christification.

In another, more familiar natural process, plants open their leaves to absorb photons from the sun. They take this energy and combine it with water and carbon dioxide to create sugars which in turn become more plant or fruit. They look toward the sun, grow toward the sun, ever face the sun. They actively devote all their strength to this task and grow stronger because of it.

As we behold Jesus, we absorb who he is into who we are, and we change and deepen who we are as we do. We devote all our strength to look toward and grow toward him. We become as he is formed in us. The Light becomes life in us, and that life is still the light of humankind. Transformation of the *world* by Christosynthesis.

Transformation According to John

In the prologue to his gospel, John introduced us to the relationship between light and life that he develops in the rest of his writings. For John, the basic human problem is that we cannot, unaided, see God. We can't know what he's like, and we can't know him. Later, John will tell us that Jesus thinks the essence of eternal life is knowing God, and in the same passage, he'll assert that it's Jesus that makes that knowing possible.

But it's not just an introduction that Jesus provides. He himself solves the problem by making the invisible God visible: "No one has ever seen God; the only God, who is at the Father's side, he has made him known" (John 1:18). "And the Word became flesh and dwelt among us, and we have seen his glory, glory as of the only Son from the Father, full of grace and truth" (John 1:14).

For John as for Paul, beholding the glory of Jesus is central to how we are changed, so much so that he can assert that "we shall be like him, because we shall see him as he is" (1 John 3:2). John links seeing Jesus with transformation into his likeness. This is why the twice-offered invitation in the first chapter of John's gospel is "Come and see" (John 1:39, 46). We become because we behold.

Transformation According to Peter

In the first chapter of his first letter, Peter makes the matter of direct experience with Jesus a little more visceral. For Peter, as for Paul, salvation is an already/not yet affair. We are "born again to a living hope" (1 Pet 1:3) and to an inheritance that is "being guarded through faith for a salvation ready to be revealed in the last time" (1 Pet 1:5). Those aspects of our salvation that are waiting for "the last time" are the not-yet part. But right now, in the grind of a broken world, we can bring bits of that future into present reality even with hearts that are still, at least in part, broken. We are "obtaining [now] the outcome of your faith, the salvation of your souls" (1 Pet 1:9). That's the already part. How do we do that?

Peter says, "Though you have not seen him, you love him. Though you do not now see him, you believe in him and rejoice with joy that is inexpressible and filled with glory, obtaining the outcome of your faith, the salvation of your souls" (1 Pet 1:8–9). We love, and we rejoice, but this rejoicing isn't a cognitive exercise that we leverage to eventually drum up a little fervor. What's described here is experientially intense, and the experience outstrips our ability to express.

This language is much more emotional than what we saw with Paul or John. Both of those guys get feely and visceral in lots of other places, but here, with Peter, we learn that direct experiences of Jesus—including affection and exultations that we can't quite capture cognitively—are the means of us experiencing progressive salvation in the present.

> What's described here is experientially intense,
> and the experience outstrips
> our ability to express.

Peter takes it further. The command in 1 Peter 2:2 is to "long for the pure spiritual milk" like newborn infants. First, let's clarify what the milk is. Some translations supply "of the word" in an attempt to clarify, drawing from a mention of "the word" two verses prior. But it's better to look in the next verse, instead, where Peter clarifies his own thought for us: "if indeed you have tasted that the Lord is good" (1 Pet 2:3).

The Lord Jesus himself is the milk—the milk we have tasted, whose goodness we know, and by which we grow up into who we really are.

Why do Scripture engagement, charismata, and contemplative practice *sometimes* help, and other times hurt? Peter would say, when they are means to the milk, the Lord Jesus, they help. And when they are not, they leave you hungrier.

If you've had a nursing infant in your home, you know what Peter means by "long for." Crave, yearn for, ache for, chase, *neeeeed*. A hungry infant is reduced to one absolute, all-consuming desire. Every cell in its body screams for it, every capacity it has got is devoted utterly to satisfying that desire, and it will not be satisfied with anything but the milk.

We are in a more vulnerable state than that infant because we have become accustomed to trying to satisfy the central desire of our souls with lesser things and have in various ways deceived our own appetites away from what we really want. The work of human transformation is, in one sense, the retraining of our desire back to its source and satisfaction—Jesus.

Paul seems to understand this too.

Paul's Pursuit

The deliberate reorientation of Paul's desires becomes very apparent in Philippians 3. Paul describes his pursuit of deep, experiential encounter with Jesus—a pursuit that is exclusive, intense, normative, and communal.

Exclusive

"But one thing I do: forgetting what lies behind" (Phil 3:13). Paul has just unpacked a litany of pursuits, purposes, and props for his identity, and he has decided that they are all trash compared with the singular excellency of experientially knowing Jesus. Suffering, death, resurrection, whatever—Paul is gunning for shared experience with Jesus, and direct experience of Jesus.

He says he does one thing. The pursuit of Jesus is not first among many pursuits. Paul organizes his whole life around this one desire. To do so requires significant self-awareness and personal discipline.

Intense

"Not that I have already obtained this or am already perfect [in Christ], but I press on to make it my own, because Christ Jesus has made me his own. … straining forward to what lies ahead, I press on toward the goal" (Phil 3:12–13).

Paul borrows an athletic image and paints a picture of a sprinter in the last leg of a race going all out for the finish line. Pressing on, straining forward with absolute effort. Transformation is not something that happens by force of will or by earning, surely, but it also doesn't happen accidentally or effortlessly.

Athletic metaphor occurs again in 1 Corinthians 9 to describe how Paul orders his life:

> Do you not know that in a race all the runners run, but only one receives the prize? So run that you may obtain it. Every athlete exercises self-control in all things. They do it to receive a perishable wreath, but we an imperishable. So I do not run aimlessly; I do not box as one beating the air. But I discipline my body and keep it under control, lest after preaching to others I myself should be disqualified. (1 Cor 9:24–27)

There are approaches to life with Jesus that work, and there are approaches that don't. The Isthmian games took place in Corinth biannually. The Corinthian believers would have been familiar with the events and with how the athletes trained for them. The athletes who wanted to win, and who were most likely to do so, adhered to a strict regimen of training. Preparations for the games moved to the center of their personal worlds, and everything else moved to the periphery. Every decision would be passed through the lens of "How will this affect my training?"

Today the same can be seen with in-season athletes in almost any sport. Like them, Paul knows that there are approaches to training that work and others that don't, so he beats his body and makes it his slave so that his message and his life do not disagree.

Normative

"Let those of us who are mature think this way, and if in anything you think otherwise, God will reveal that also to you" (Phil 3:15).

Growing up in church, I was taught to see Paul as exceptional. No doubt, there have been few people in history to make so large an impact, and many things about Paul's life and words are special and respectable. His pursuit of Jesus, however, in all its intensity and exclusivity, is apparently supposed to be normal for all of us.

"Let those of us who are mature think this way" (Phil 3:15). Spiritual maturity in Paul's mind seems to have less to do with where you've arrived than it does with where you're going, how singularly you are aimed there, and what kind of chutzpah you're bringing to the endeavor. Perhaps this is why Paul tells Timothy, "Be diligent in these matters; give yourself wholly to them, so that everyone may see your progress" (1 Tim 4:15, NIV). The kind of spiritual maturity that others can follow is in motion. It's a vector with direction and magnitude and not a point.

And it's supposed to be the norm.

Communal

Paul knows that not everyone is going to see it like this. His response?

"Let those of us who are mature think this way, and if in anything you think otherwise, God will reveal that also to you. Only let us hold true to what we have attained" (Phil 3:15–16). Here, "hold true to what we have attained" is possibly better rendered, "keep the same rule." Apparently, Paul anticipates that God will eventually straighten us out if we've espoused a cultural or consumeristic approach to the Jesus way as long as we all stay together and keep the same rule. What can that mean?

Well, it doesn't mean, "Follow the rules." A *rule* isn't a set of rules. A *rule* is a description of practices and approaches that comprise a *way*. Paul insists here that even if you can't yet seem to get your head around an exclusive and intense pursuit of experiential knowledge of Jesus as normative, just stay with the community because it's a community of practice, and the practices are the places where God can best adjust your thinking.

It doesn't mean, "go along to get along," or "shut up and fall in line." As an American, I'm culturally primed to resist anything that sounds like, "Because I said so." Paul isn't telling us to fall in line. He's telling us not to turn our backs on the community. We are going somewhere together. Don't fall behind just because you can't see the path.

A return to the dojo here could help. All the good dojos I've been part of, regardless of style, had one thing in common. The senior students always showed up earlier and stayed later than everyone else. This seems counter intuitive. Compared to all the other students, these men and women needed the least extra practice and mat time. What was it that brought them early and kept them late?

I was one of these students. For me, there was this invisible force that pulled me to the dojo and held me there as I worked the heavy bag or trained a throw long after class was over. It was an invitation. I could feel deeper capacity, broader competency, and sharper skill, just beyond my reach, and it drew me in. And I wasn't alone. In both the dojos I'm thinking of—one a striking art, the other a grappling art—there were a few of us standing at the door when the instructor unlocked it and still sweating on the mat when everyone else had gone home.

If we had been comparing ourselves to the other students, it would have been a different story, but this never crossed our minds. We *knew* we weren't complete, but that didn't discourage us. Rather, it excited, invited, and drew us forward into a mastery the edges of which we could just begin to feel.

So, it shouldn't surprise us when Paul says, "Brothers, join in imitating me, and keep your eyes on those who walk according to the example you have in us" (Phil 3:17). We grow, at least in part, by imitating the behaviors, practices, and habits of more senior students just as we did in the dojo. This imitation is co-imitation. We do it together, in community, and as a community who is together practicing a way. This, perhaps, is what lies behind Paul's encouragement to Timothy to pursue virtue *with those* who call on the Lord out of a pure heart (2 Tim 2:22).

Summary

Let's review. As followers of Jesus, our development is Christomorphic—it's shaped like Christ, and it shapes us like Christ. This poiesis is the bringing forth of Christ fully formed in us and us complete in him. The mechanism of this poiesis is direct experience of Jesus. When we behold Jesus beholding us—when we have direct encounters with and experiences of the living Lord Jesus—the Spirit changes us into deeper and truer likenesses of Christ. Because the mechanism of this transformation is *experiential*, our participation needs to be *experimental*. These experiments are most fruitful when undertaken with focus and intensity, and especially when done in community with others.

So, we develop by increasing the variety of our work experiences and especially by reflecting on those work experiences well. We become more through our experiences.

> Because the mechanism of this transformation is *experiential*, our participation needs to be *experimental*.

The most portentous experience for followers of Jesus to pursue and savor is direct experience of Christ himself in the Scriptures, in his creation, in his people, in silence, and in the gifts he gives. Through these experiences, we are Christified and come to acquire a strong family resemblance to Jesus. We become genuinely, authentically like him.

But like him isn't all we are to become. A Christified you may look very different from a Christified me. As we become more like Jesus, we don't necessarily become more like one another, or less like ourselves. Rather, we become more like Christ *and* more like us. This brings us to our third poiesis, in which we discover and learn to become uniquely, truly ourselves.

16

Poiesis by Self-Discovery

In this chapter we'll:

- Consider the value of personality and strengths assessments in self-discovery
- Leverage the biblical story of Jacob to explore how transitions can be fertile moments in becoming who we really are

You are not quite who you think you are. You're more and other than you know. The bringing forth of that *more* and *other* is a matter of discovery and not decision. Becoming uniquely, truly you isn't about deciding what you want to be when you grow up and fighting to get there, but rather discovering the unique way you bear the image of God and learning to live that self out in all the different things you do.

> You are not quite who you think you are.
> You're more and other than you know.

This shouldn't surprise us, of course, given the question that lives in each of us, the question that, if we're honest, guides most of the decisions we make throughout our lives: *Who am I?* All throughout our lives, whether we know it or not, we're trying to find out who we really are and what God was making when he made us. The more conscious of this search we can become, the more intelligently we can cooperate with Jesus in the poiesis of our unique, true selves, to the glory of our Maker, for the good of the world, and to our own deep joy. Over the course of my own journey, two paths of discovery have proven particularly helpful: tests and transitions.

Tests

The other night we had a few young adults over for dinner. We'd just met, so as we sat down to dinner my ten-year-old daughter piped up with an important question. "So which Hogwarts house are you?" As funny as that question might sound, nearly everyone at the table had an answer.

We all want to know who we are, and the internet is replete with ten question quizzes to help us out. Which historical general are you? Which My Little Pony? Which Avenger? Which dog breed? Obviously not all personality assessments are created equal. Some have been validated academically, used widely, and/or stood the test of time. Let's consider a few and note what they each bring to the table.

First, perhaps the most famous of all personality assessments, the Myers-Briggs Type Indicator (MBTI). The MBTI scores you along four continua: Introversion/Extroversion, Sensing/Intuiting, Thinking/Feeling, and Perceiving/Judging. Taken together, your scores along these continua give a Type. For example, I am an INFJ (though I score very close to the center line on Introversion/Extroversion and Thinking/Feeling). My wife is an ESFP. We have only one letter in common—Feeling—so you can probably deduce how differently we see and move through the world. The great strength of this assessment is its ubiquity; nearly everyone has heard of it, and anyone can take it for free online. If none of the other tests were available, this one alone could get you a long way toward understanding yourself better.

Then, there are the strengths-based assessments. Perhaps the most well-known is Gallup's StrengthsFinder which helps you identify key personal strengths, defining those as activities or contributions where you excel *and* which leave you feeling stronger. These are to be contrasted with weaknesses, which are things you may well be good at, but which leave you drained. Marcus Buckingham, perhaps the world's foremost researcher on strengths-based leadership, originally worked on StrengthsFinder and has since created another similar assessment called Standout. Standout seems to build on what Buckingham learned at Clifton and streamlines the many diverse strengths into nine strength roles. The streamlining simplifies the task of bringing your strengths to your work.

Perhaps my favorite strengths-based assessment is the CoreStrengths (SDI). Like the others, CoreStrengths helps you identify and deploy your strengths in all your relationships, while also uncovering the unique underlying core motivations. What sets CoreStrengths apart is how it illuminates the specific ways your approach is likely to change in conflict, which, as we've noted in a previous chapter, is where the rubber really meets the road. The strengths-based assessments are very useful in that, while something like the MBTI can help you understand what you're like, these can help you see what you bring to the table—the unique contributions you're likely to be happiest and most helpful making.

The Enneagram, however, helps you understand what *else* you're bringing to the table. While not solely focused on what's wrong in you, I've gotten the most help from the Enneagram when I've used it to understand the deep, subterranean currents of sin and woundedness in my soul (and in others'), and leveraged that increased understanding, not to try to cure those ills, but to show genuine compassion to myself and others. The Enneagram can help you name *why* you might want what you want, do what you do, and fear what you fear. For that reason alone, it's invaluable.

There are, of course, others. LeadStyle, Grip-Birkman, and ProD all have good reputations and are worth a look. But really, there's no end to the assessments out there. The trick is what to do with them and what not to do.

The YouBoat

In my own leader development practice, I've found it helpful to visually map all the assessments together along with some other important data. When we see a fuller picture, we can begin to get a sense of how our strengths, weaknesses, predispositions and gifts interact in the unique ways we each live and work. One visual representation of this interplay has been particularly useful to me.

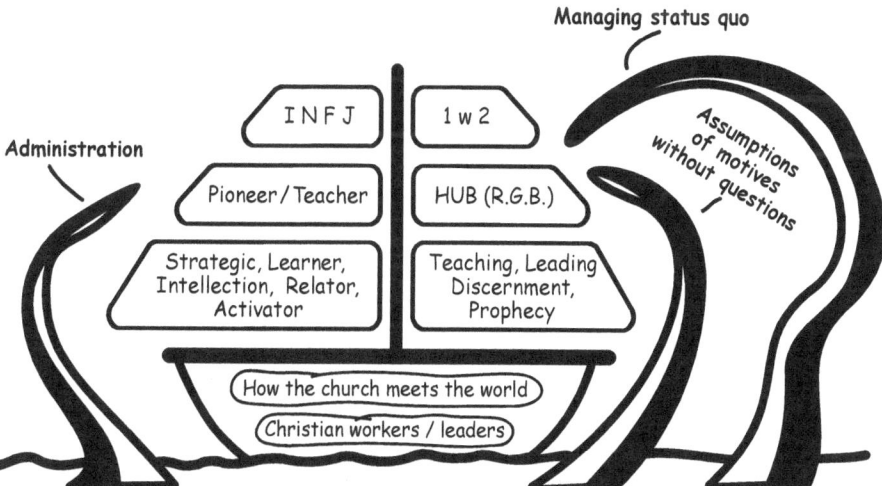

Figure 7 | *YouBoat*

This very simple drawing of a sailing ship allows us to consider several essential elements of ourselves at the same time. (The one pictured above is mine.) Before we explore the parts, a note about the whole. It's a sailboat, not a motorboat, rowboat, or steamboat. It moves under the power of the wind, and truly only under the power of the wind. In a moment we'll see why that's so important. Now, to the parts.

In the hold we place our callings, and the pieces of God's great heart that we've been asked to steward. These are the causes most important to us, the things that, no matter how wounded or tired we become, we can't stop caring about. These matters, to our best understanding at the moment, are our great work. They're what we were made for, the place where, as Buechner put it, our deep joy meets the world's deep need.[1]

The tentacles reaching up from below are those tasks or situations we've found most likely to pull us under, to swamp our hearts, or even to simply provide so much drag that we can be overcome by events. It's useful to be mindful of these things, and while they can never be eliminated or avoided completely, we can eliminate a lot of unproductive friction by mitigating against them.

Finally, the sails are the different ways to describe how we're made. Each one is a personality profile. As we map these onto our boats, we can see patterns emerging in the similarities between them as well as nuance and perspective provided by their subtle differences. These are our sails because they're how we're each uniquely designed to catch the wind of the Spirit and to cooperate with him in the world. These strengths are not our power but rather how we are powered by the Spirit who crafted us. Our burdens and callings are part of his vast heart, and he has suited us to carry and express them in ways only we can, in concert with the one who made us and who carries us along by his own breath. It's God who is at work in us through these burdens and strengths. We can trust that he who began this good work will be faithful to complete it (Phil 1:6; 2:13).

The Limits

The purpose of these tests is self-discovery. Discovery follows curiosity. These tests are useful, then, in so much as they fuel open curiosity and appreciative inquiry. As we use them to chase insights about ourselves and others, using gentle, curious questions and genuine wonder, they can help us discover more and more of the strength and beauty within, and then bring that glory to the service of the world.

---

1 Buechner, "Vocation."

More commonly, however, these tests are unintentionally used to short-circuit curiosity and to bypass appreciative inquiry. We forego getting to know someone, because we know how they tested.

- Well, you're angry because you're a One.
- You TJs are all robots.
- Your top strengths are (fill in the blank), so I can tell you right away that x is true about you.

Comments like these may be intended to help the other feel seen and known, but they can easily come across like actually getting to know them isn't worth your time.

And honestly, sometimes we have very little time, or attention to give. Overworked, overtaxed, overextended, under-rested, and socially exhausted, we can all find ourselves in the place where a simple number or string of letters is infinitely easier to deal with than the messy complexity of a real, live person.

However, we must make time and space for ourselves and for one another. We must never allow an insight gained, however scientifically, excuse us from the holy work of paying attention, even if its ourselves we're paying attention to. There is only one who can get your name quite right, and even he doesn't tell you all of who you are until the end of the story.

It seems you are a moving target.

Transitions

Growing up very evangelical, I had only taken brief forays into other streams of the Jesus way. Henri Nouwen (a Catholic priest) and Richard Foster (a Quaker) were so helpful to me through college and seminary, and Tom Wright (an Anglican) grew and nuanced my theology through my years as a pastor. Later, another Quaker (Parker Palmer), another Anglican (David Benner), and a handful of Catholic thinkers took me down the next stretch of road. They taught me about the true self and about the false self.

Your true self is the actual you—the you God intended when he first dreamt you up. It's the freest, most vibrant version of you. And it's the self that Jesus is recognizing at the end of the age when, in Revelation 2:17, he gives you a white stone with a name inscribed on it that only he and you know. It's a name utterly underived from what others think and say about you, unshaped by the lies about yourself that you've accumulated over time. It's who you were always becoming.

Your false self, however, is more complicated. You were born with a question. *Who am I?*

Figure 8 | Who am I?

But you were also born with a strong proclivity to sin and into a world where everyone else has the same proclivity. So, you sin and damage yourself, and they sin and damage you, and together the whole mess of us make systems that, like it or not, perpetuate damage. Quickly we learn which parts of ourselves receive the least censure and abuse and the most acceptance and applause. We learn young how to put those parts of us forward. We aren't necessarily trying to mislead, but we are trying very hard to keep control and avoid harm. This strategy creates the beginnings of our false self—a caricature of us that works to keep us more or less safe in a world that, frankly, terrifies us.

Figure 9 | *The false self emerges as a strategy to protect me*

Sometimes the things that happen to us are so traumatic that they have a lasting effect on our self-understanding. Sexual abuse, neglect, war, displacement, religious abuse, and a million other horrors can lead us to make vows or to deploy strategies to prevent us from ever losing control that way again. Or, conversely, they bend us into them so severely that we lose our sense of agency altogether. In either case, trauma shapes the false self profoundly.

Small things do, too. A little boy feels in his chest that he *wants* to club his brother in the head with the truck his brother just took from him, but he sees his mom watching and decides the discipline won't be worth it. His mother, rightly, applauds the self-control and tells him he's "a good boy," but the message he receives is to stuff his anger and that being loved is a function of being the good boy. Almost unavoidable, the lie enters, and it shapes his story in hidden ways from that day onward.

As these traumas, encounters, and strategies continue to repeat themselves, we begin to hold the mask closer and closer to our faces. After all, the closer we hold it, the more it protects us. But as we do so, we also begin to see more and more of the world through the eyes of the mask, and less and less around its sides. The view through the eyes is different from the view around the edges, and the cognitive dissonance can be profound. Eventually, we hold the mask of the false self so close to us that it sticks. We look in the mirror and the self we see is our false self. We have fundamentally misunderstood ourselves. It gets worse.

The view through the eyeholes of the false self is colored by our particular falseness. We begin to see the things to which we've attached ourselves all over the world, and we begin to interpret the story of the world in a way that makes sense of the character we've become. We write the story of the world around the part our mask is designed to play.

Figure 10 | *The world is perceived as a story in which the false self makes sense*

Worse still, we realize that we are made in God's image. If we look like this mask, and we're made in his image, so must he. And we consign ourselves to a false god, in a fake world, from behind a mask that tells only a sliver of the story.

Figure 11 | *If I am made in the image of God, God must look like me*

But thankfully, all hell inevitably breaks loose, and it can set us free. We encounter a crisis. We hit the wall. The strategies stop working. We burn out, or at least we lose interest. Our faith seems to start deconstructing itself. We're disillusioned, disoriented, distressed, discouraged, and sometimes even disabled. We come undone.

The dark night truly is hellish. And so, so lonely. But, like chemotherapy, while it makes our whole souls sick, it can kill the tissue that has grown between our faces and our masks. Slowly, we're able to slip a finger in between them. Soon, we can begin to pry away the mask. Here is where our courage is most needed. When we begin to see the world as it truly is, not only through the eyes of the false self, we experience the cognitive dissonance again. It's terrifying to see two worlds at once. If our courage flags, we let the mask remain, and return to the lie for the next chapter of our lives—perhaps the rest of our lives. But if our courage holds, we are strengthened to tear free of the false self and empowered to hear who we really are.

Your true self, unencumbered by accumulated coping mechanisms, is free to love, to bless, to forgive, to learn, and be loved. Your true self has full range of motion in your whole soul and is able to live wholeheartedly in the world. Your true self, in fact, is who God wants to use to save the world and to make it beautiful again.

Here's a story from the Bible that illustrates this beautifully, along with some parallels from my own story simply because it's the story I know best.

Jacob's Fight

Genesis 32:31 is a truly cinematic moment. Jacob has just endured a whole night of physically fighting with God and has somehow emerged with a blessing and a limp. It reads, "The sun rose upon him as he passed Penuel, limping because of his hip." Incredible. I can see it in my mind. Scrappy, middle-aged man, climbing up out of the creek bed, his limping frame silhouetted by the rising sun.

But the writer doesn't stop there. "Therefore to this day the people of Israel do not eat the sinew of the thigh that is on the hip socket, because he touched the socket of Jacob's hip on the sinew of the thigh" (Gen 32:32).

Sigh.

It was beautiful, right up until, "And that's why Jews don't eat hip meat." As a writer, it bothers me. It seems like such a writing fail. One day, though, it occurred to me that rules about diet are really important to the people of Israel. What they do and do not eat is a matter of identity. It's a way they understand, remember, and preserve who they are. Genesis is a book of origin stories, and this story, in particular, is Israel's origin story. What happens at Penuel is so important to Israel's identity that they codified and protected it in a dietary rule, so they would never forget who they truly are. They love the way that reads.

The story of Jacob being renamed Israel at Penuel is a story about receiving one's true self. To understand this story, however, we need to see the false self as well. Take a few minutes now and read Genesis 25–33. In what follows, I'll be unpacking key scenes from this story but will not include the passages themselves in the text. It will help immensely to read that portion of Scripture now so the words and images are readily available to you.

Early Childhood and the Lie

Jacob's birth story is peculiar. The second of twins, he is born hand-first, clutching his older brother's heel. Such a peculiarity is not to be passed by, so from his very first breath, he is named *Heel Grabber* (the meaning of *Jacob*). The word itself can literally refer to grabbing someone's heel, but when someone grabs your heel, it's usually to knock you down and take your place. So, it also can mean *supplanter*. In common parlance, though, it means *liar* or *manipulator*.

The very next scene in the story has him living up to expectations. His brother, Esau, comes back from an extended hunt at the brink of collapse with hunger. Instead of just sharing some of the hearty stew he was making, Jacob leverages Esau's hunger and diminished capacity and barters food now for Esau's eventual birthright as the eldest son. Esau agrees, and the die is cast.

I was a weird kid. I learned to read at two years old. Math came easy. Everything cognitive came easy, actually. I had double vision, a lazy eye, and was really small for my age. Taken together, that's a recipe for social isolation. My brain worked faster than my mouth or my hands could go, and I had little grasp of social cues. I'd interrupt my teachers, argue with them when I was sure they were wrong, and almost never finished writing one sentence before starting the next. My second-grade teacher,

I can see now, was having her own personal problems, and one day I was apparently too much for her. "That's it," she spat. "I'm having you tested. You're retarded and I'm going to prove it!"

The school psychologist came in that week and administered a few tests. A couple weeks later I was in a different school, participating in the gifted and talented program, while spending half of each school day in the second-grade classroom, and half in the fourth-grade classroom. This, together with my wacky eyes, consequent inability to excel at ball sports, small frame, and social incompetence profoundly isolated me.

I belonged in neither class totally and, therefore, I had no real peer group. I heard every day from my mom that I was different. Due to a family tragedy when she was fourteen, she was forced to quit school and take care of her siblings. My success in school became, unintentionally, her way to live what she never got. So, at school and at home, I learned that I was different. Special. A freak. A population of one. Alone. By the third-grade, the die was cast.

Reinforcement by Family

In his defense, lying and scheming were kind of a tradition in Jacob's family. Abraham and Isaac had both done it, to avoid being killed by powerful men after their wives and riches. But Jacob would elevate it to an art, using the skill not only to survive but to get ahead.

Isaac, Jacob and Esau's father, is at the end of his life, and the time comes for him to pass on the blessing to his eldest son. Rebekah, Jacob's mother, initiates a conspiracy with Jacob to swindle away Esau's blessing. In the Ancient Near East, the end-of-life blessing was a big deal. It was legally binding like a will. At the behest of his mother, Jacob dresses up, changes his scent, gathers his props, and goes to deceive his dying father.

Isaac asks, "Who are you?" (Gen 27:18).

To which Jacob responds, "I am Esau your firstborn" (Gen 27:19).

Remember that conversation. It's important later.

After a few more rounds of confirming his identity, Isaac blesses Jacob and makes his brother subservient to him. When Esau later hears of this, he cries out, "Is he not rightly named Jacob? For he has cheated me these two times. He took away my birthright, and behold, now he has taken away my blessing" (Gen 27:36). The disappointment quickly becomes rage as Esau plans and vows to kill Jacob as soon as the mourning period for Isaac is passed.

Rebekah hears of this plan and sends Jacob running far away to her brother, Laban. In this whole, appalling misadventure Jacob becomes more fully his false self. He cements his identity as a liar. He charts a life course of reacting to Esau. He had always been in Esau's shadow, and from now on the fear of Esau would haunt every shadow. His mother teaches him that he's not the only one who lies and games the system. She does too, so perhaps it's just what people do. And he learns to run away.

Jacob tricks, and Jacob runs. This misunderstanding of who he is will shape the entire first half of his life.

I was a nervous kid. My mom was well-acquainted with anxiety. Even at nine and ten years old, if I had that anxious look on my face before school, she'd sit with me in her rocker, and sing the lullaby she'd invented for me when I was very small. Wordless, with just a series of *la-la's*, it would calm my little heart. Then, she'd carefully put the whole armor of God on me from Ephesians 6, and say, "Now, remember the parable of the talents. Jesus said to whom much is given much will be required. The tests say you're smarter than 99 percent of everyone in that school, so you can count on it; you'll be judged on the last day for how you use that. Have a good day!"

She thought it was a pep talk. She had no idea she was cementing my view of myself and of God.

Since my mom didn't get to go to school and because she dreamt big dreams for me, grades were really important. Except in handwriting. I always got *C*'s in handwriting, but no one cared. But every grading period, when we got our report cards, as subtly as I could, I'd get around to every kid in the class to see how they did. It made me look like a total jerk, and it further isolated me. They didn't know why I was doing it, but I knew that when I got home, I'd face two questions: *Did you get all A's?* Yes, mom. *Did anyone do better than you?* No. I checked. I'm the best.

She also taught me many other wonderful, beautiful lessons. She was trying so hard to make sure I got access to all the opportunities she missed. But the lessons I learned were less helpful than that—I learned I had to be perfect, and that perfect wasn't enough. I had to be the best. Some boys grow up wondering if they have what it takes. I grew up knowing for sure that I did and terrified that I wouldn't live up to it. Judgement was coming, and there were only two grades: flawless victory or rejection. This misunderstanding would shape the entire first half of my life.

Reinforcement (Apparently) by God

Jacob runs for it and makes camp in the middle of nowhere. He sleeps on a rock and has a dream. He sees what's most likely the enormous staircase of a ziggurat—a Mesopotamian temple. Angels of God are ascending and descending the stair. Yahweh himself appears and blesses Jacob with the Abrahamic blessing—the same blessing that had been given to his father and his father's father.

Jacob awakes, sets up the rock he slept on as a pillar, makes an offering, names the place Beth-El (House of God), and concludes that he had stumbled upon God's house and the very door to the heavens.

Consider the impact this encounter could have had. Hearing God himself tell you that he would be henceforth protecting you wherever you went might make you less afraid of Esau. But not Jacob. Remember, that was already set. Hearing God tell you he would give you the very spot you were sleeping on and prosper you there might make you stop running. Not Jacob, though; that was set as well. But what might have happened is what I often see happen with young men and women. We do something, and utterly unrelated to our actions, God kindly blesses us. The blessing is concurrent but not consequent. He isn't blessing us because of what we've done, but we think he is. We misinterpret God's kindness as his confirmation of our internal narrative.

My own distortion of God, which began with the parable of the talents, was more subtle. Put simply, God blessed my attempts to do ministry. My efforts to teach, to lead, to inspire, to drive change, and to unlock situations others thought immovable and impossible. I'm sure he subtly offered counter-narratives to the horrible burden I was living—the responsibility to change the world enough to justify whatever giftedness I felt I had been charged with. But I don't recall ever being brought up short or him withholding his blessing on my work simply because I was using my work to answer the question *Who am I, and is it enough to justify what I've been given?*

Looking back now, I can see that the blessing of God on my work, read through the lens of my false self, led to a second, even more destructive lie. I began to view myself as a conduit of grace but not as the recipient. God blessed me *only* to be a blessing. He would get out of me a return on his investment, but I never could quite feel like I was the end user of grace. While at the time I was totally unaware I was doing it, I took God's blessing on my work with his people as confirmation that I was just an asset, and that Yahweh was the god of leveraged assets.

Reinforcement by the World

Jacob makes it to Laban and stops running for a while. He asks for Rachel to marry, and gets the cockeyed daughter instead. Laban swindles Jacob into fourteen years of indentured servitude for a wife he wants, a wife he doesn't, and (assumedly) protection from Esau. This further confirms to Jacob that deception and manipulation are how the whole world works. This is simply how it's done.

I went to college and did well. I went to seminary and did even better. Students and faculty alike affirmed my giftedness. They may have affirmed other things, too, but I could only hear through the filter of what made me different. Men I deeply respected would put their hand on my shoulder and say, "Son"—(At that word my *Who am I? Who am I? Whoamiwhoamiwhoami?* would fall silent for just a moment to hear the answer to my always-question.)—"Son, God's going to do great things with you."

But I always heard, "Son, God expects great things from you."

So, great things I set out to do. I did some. Some impossible things. I also made some embarrassing, hurtful mistakes. I was easy to approach but hard to correct. I wanted correction, but deep inside I knew that correction meant I wasn't flawless, and this meant rejection. I needed to do wonders and to do them without error. But who can do that? Not me, it turned out.

Crisis and Blessing

Through some animal husbandry mischief that I don't quite understand, or through God's kind blessing of Jacob's selfish pursuit, Jacob manages to turn Laban's attempt at gaming him back on itself. Jacob wins the manipulation game, but the prize is the hot resentment of Laban's sons. God appears to Jacob again, and tells him to go back to his homeland. Jacob doesn't just go. He absconds with all his winnings, with his wives, and without a word to Laban. He runs. Again.

But for Jacob, the world is the domain of Esau. It's as if the whole world—not the house—is haunted by his brother. Jacob runs, and angels of God meet him on the way. Perhaps, to his eyes at least, the same angels from the stair at Beth-El. There's no stair this time, so he names the place Two-Camps, thinking he was hiding his camp within God's camp.

He sends servants and gifts to Esau, but the servants return with news that Esau himself is coming to find him, and Jacob is terrified. The thing he most fears, the thing he's been running from his whole life, the outcome he'd been gaming the system to avoid, is coming for him.

He sends more servants and more gifts. All the while, it doesn't seem to occur to him that he's in the camp of the God who promised to protect him. He doesn't know that God. He only knows the god of liars and cheats. Finally, he gathers up his own wives and children in a group, and crosses a creek by himself. Everything he has, plus the only natural boundary he can find, is between him and the one he most fears. He has made his last, best play. He's run as far as he can.

"And Jacob was left alone. And a man wrestled with him until the breaking of the day" (Gen 32:24).

Imagine this. You're terrified. You've done everything you can to avoid a violent encounter with someone you're convinced is out to hurt you. You're alone, in the dark, and out of nowhere someone tackles you, and you find yourself in a fight for your life. What is going through Jacob's mind?

I've been in fights. I've taught fighting. Many street fights are over in less than ten seconds. The average fight lasts no more than a minute. A minute of maximum, terrified effort, and one of the fighters is gassed out with nothing left. A minute into this fight, and Jacob is likely spent. But for seven hours and fifty-nine more minutes, give or take, God keeps fighting Jacob.

Have you ever felt like that? Like a terrible, terrifying thing is happening to you? Or in you? And it feels like it might be God's fault. You wait for it to pass, then ask for strength to endure, then beg for it to stop. But it doesn't, and you wonder if it ever will.

We sometimes refer to this scene as Jacob wrestling with God. I'm sure he fought back, but that's not how the text reads. God wrestles Jacob. Jacob is the victim of a severe mercy.

At some point Jacob recognizes that this is the same person who appeared to him at Beth-El and who later told him to leave Laban. Maybe as the sun rose, Jacob began to catch on. But somewhere between sunset and sunrise, God has managed to beat the false self just about out of Jacob. God never does all the work for us in this aggressive treatment. But his ruthless, painful, relentless, loving work on us in the dark night makes it possible for us to choose to let the false self go and receive from him who we truly are.

For Jacob, it went like this. By the time the sun rose, Jacob was done running. You can see it because when God goes to leave, it's Jacob that holds his ground and refuses to let go without a blessing. God himself has, with a touch, dislocated his hip, and still he holds on. He's traded in flight for fight and manipulation for main force.

God asks him, "What is your name?" Recall the last time he was asked that—Isaac asked him who he was, and lied claiming to be Esau.

This time, he says, "Jacob." I'm me. I'm the Liar. Cheat. Trickster.

To which God says, Not anymore. Now, your name is Fighter. Grappler. Wrestler-with-God.

It seems like a totally new name, but it was there all along. The heel-hook is one of my favorite takedowns. It's a staple of wrestling systems the world over. He was always *Grappler*. But it was hidden under layers of coping mechanisms, survival strategies, and misunderstandings.

Jacob asks, "Tell me your name" (Gen 32:29).

To which God replies, "'Why is it that you ask my name?' And there he blessed him" (Gen 32:29).

It seems an odd exchange, until we remember that Jacob wasn't only wrong about himself. He was wrong about God, too. God was setting him free from that misunderstanding, as well. God was saying, "You know why I asked your name. You lie, sometimes. But I don't. You don't have to make sure about me. I am who I said I am. You are not who you thought you were, and neither am I. I am more and other than you thought, and so are you."

And what a grace it was to cripple Jacob's hip. The false self is ever at hand, ready to be taken up when we forget who we truly are. Jacob always had a proclivity to run, and that running had become part of his false identity. It's hard to run with a limp. But it's easy to remember how you got it.

My terrifying night happened largely in the shed in my back yard in Central Asia. To understand that we'll need two points of context.

First, I'm part of a rag-tag little group that throws a conference every couple of years for emerging leaders in church and mission. I started as a delegate, became an occasional devotional contributor, and now frequently serve as a keynote speaker. It's where I realized that my heart is made to be the friend of leaders and workers. This conference factors into my dark night.

Second, about halfway through our eight years in Central Asia, I began leading nearly all the mission workers in the country (about fifty people from twelve cultures and seventeen different organizations) through a process of collective discernment and strategy over dinner in our home once a month. Every month God seemed visibly, palpably with me, and my deep joy met others' deep need in a way that gave them life and took them off the chain so they could run free and do good in the world. In this experience, Jesus taught me that sometimes someone having authority and using it benevolently means everyone can live more joyfully and in deeper freedom.

But between those Saturdays, I was in the dark. It was like he could use me for those people, but there was nothing left for me. Worse than that, he just seemed gone. The young woman that lived with us was experiencing continual night terrors as well as assault on the Metro several times a week. We prayed but little happened. My friends' children had cancer; our local friends just couldn't seem to believe Jesus. Persecution continued. We prayed, and God didn't seem able or willing to do anything about any of it.

I would go to my shed in the backyard where I held my morning prayers, and it was all I could do to sit with my hands in fists on the desk asking God if he was real or not, and in the absence of an answer, I began to suspect deeply and frighteningly that we had made him up. In fact, at times I hoped that we had. In those times I would say to him, "You're either a figment of my imagination, or you're real, and you're a monster, and I might hate you. And in either case I don't know what to do." The disciples' words to Jesus *to whom shall we go?* (John 6:68) lost their devotional flavor for me and sounded more like middle aged men aware that they had gambled on a fraud, but since they had gambled all they had, they were in it to the end.

What I didn't know at the time was that I was really facing the fear that *I* was the fraud. If I was who I was supposed to be, the results would have been different. I had moved to Central Asia to save the world, but I wasn't enough. It hadn't happened, so I must not have been flawless. But in the moment, it seemed like if God was as flawless as he claimed, he would have made up the difference. Since he hadn't, I was growing to hate him. Because of the role I held with all of the workers in the country, I couldn't share this with anyone. So, that year was the loneliest of my life. I was called upon to help strategize and inspire for all the workers in the country while harboring a real suspicion that the faith was fiction.

This state persisted more or less until we got kicked out of the country. A few weeks after our ejection, I was supposed to speak at that leaders' conference again. As the plane took off to carry me from Nashville to Miami, I grappled with God, "If you're even there, I don't know what to tell them. These people are so important to me. What am I supposed to do? Fake it? Be honest and trash their faith?"

In my heart I heard, "Stop striving," and almost without choosing to, I did. I sat back, went to sleep, and woke up when the plane landed.

I was slated to be the first speaker, but before I got up to speak, the conference organizer asked everyone in the room to briefly share what they were carrying in with them. One by one, everyone shared their burdens, and every item on my list of reasons why God might be a fraud had been mentioned. These were my people, and I had been prepared to hear their grief and fear and feel it with them. The very things I was doubting God for were making me into a person who could do what I most wanted to do—love with force and skill. I was able to do that now because of the questions that lived unanswered in my heart. The silence God had offered had been generative all along, cultivating spaces within me where others' despair and God's own hope could meet.

When that light went on it was very much like Psalm 73. I felt like a beast before him until I went to the temple, and then I understood. If I had said what I was feeling before I would've destroyed the faith of many, so my feelings had isolated me. But just like the Levite in Psalm 73 who felt that he had washed his hands for no reason and that he had lived his Levitical life meaninglessly, I realized then that my worries that God might be a fraud were really worries that I might be. It was this realization that led to the cracking of my false self away from my true self, the first peeling back of a misunderstanding of myself, of the world, and of God that hadn't really served me well. It had protected me somewhat for a while, but now it was preventing my emergence into the second half of my life. The year in the dark had been like chemotherapy for my soul, sickening all of me but killing the cancer enough that I could finally see around the mask again.

This emergence of my true self wasn't totally discontinuous with who I had so far been. I was made for action, not an ivory tower academia, but my character was more sage than soldier. I was made for finding the way and not just following orders and doing it right. I was still a martial artist, but I was suddenly less concerned with how legit the fighting style was, and more concerned with how beautiful it could be. I was still a leader to my core, but now I could see I was more abbot than executive and more sensei than school teacher. I was still an Enneatype One, but instead of being concerned with making right what was wrong, I became fascinated by making what is beautiful more beautiful. I was still who I was, but more precisely, vibrantly, freely, genuinely so. I was less driven by expectations of who I should be (by myself or by others), and more an expression of the person I had been given to become.

Like Jacob, I am still learning to receive myself from my Maker, and when pressed or when triggered by old traumas, I'm able to drift back into the patterns my false self taught me. But God changed my gait—crippled the bits of me that might prefer the mask. It makes it hard to stay in those old motor patterns for long and easier to remember who I really am. It also makes it easier to be grateful for the dark nights, and for the limp.

Who Am I Becoming?

Transitions—puberty, marriage, midlife (*especially* midlife), empty nest, retirement—are moments when the clay is softest. Our self-understanding is in flux, and since it's in flux, we are far more able to entertain doubt about our narratives and open ourselves up to other, truer possibilities. Transitions between careers, cities, social groups, etc., though a little less powerful, are still moments ripe with possibility. In the stretches between changes, we have to put so much weight on what we know about ourselves that there isn't as much room for new discovery.

But be warned: you can double down. Jacob could have lied to God. I could have clung to my delusions of terrible purpose. You can live your whole life replaying the first act over, and over again, and never move to the much more fruitful second act.

Remember, God is more and other than you know, and so are you. The world waits with baited breath for you to discover more of the beautiful wonder you really are. Be brave, and fight for the blessing.

Self-discovery can be a very fruitful path for development. And while tests and assessments can help us discover more of the truth of us, they can pose a danger when we use them to avoid the slow work of attending. Transitions can be full of possibilities—remember Jacob's story and my own—especially when we allow God to use them to unencumber us from our false selves and gift us with our true selves.

Next, we'll consider how to help those we lead steward their own developmental potential to the glory of God and for the good of the world.

17

Leading Toward Development

In this chapter we'll:

- Learn how attention, affirmation, and affection are developmental rocket fuel
- Think practically about how to more carefully consider those we lead

Before we consider how to lead ourselves and others toward development, let's take a moment to review.

You are a soul, an integrated, embodied self. You have five primary systems in which to cultivate antifragility and vibrancy. You want to thrive physically, spiritually, cognitively, emotionally, and relationally. What's more, you want to use your influence and position as a leader to help those you lead to thrive, and you view this as central to your work. Your role in their thriving is two-fold: you catalyze and capacitate.

In order to bring your increasing vigor and vibrancy to work it becomes crucial that you learn to integrate. Weaving the diverse strands of your life together allows you to coordinate your new-found strength and helps avoid injury. When helping those you lead to do integrated and integrating work, your task is to coach and consult.

Drawing vitality from Jesus through all the dimensions of your soul and bringing it all to your apprenticeship with him in the many paths of your life will always potentiate real, powerful change, not only in your environment, but also in you. Perhaps especially in you. I am increasingly convinced that we change the world less by trying to change it than by simply being changed in the world. This salvific change is neither additive nor automatic. It's poietic—a bringing forth—and it requires identification and stewardship. As you attend to your development and that of your colleagues, your part will be to *consider* and *cultivate*.

Consider

Twentieth-century mystic and philosopher Simone Weil famously said, "Attention is the rarest and purest form of generosity."[1] I couldn't agree more. To be seen, and more, to be looked at, considered, and beheld is a fundamental human need. Our attention is the one thing we have direct control over, and to offer that freely to another is among one of the most validating things we can do.

Social researcher and strengths expert Marcus Buckingham says every employee is asking two things of those that lead them: *know me*, and *focus me*.[2] Know what makes me tick, what makes me strong, and what I uniquely bring to the task we are trying to accomplish, and then help me focus my efforts there. To do this for those we lead requires us to pay attention, not only to the task and the scoreboard, but also to the individual. This is perhaps especially true when there isn't a problem that demands that attention. Because then the attention can come with genuine affirmation. Attention and affirmation together can instigate and aim development.

> Attention is the rarest and purest
> form of generosity.

The Apostle Paul knew this and took it a step further. His letter to the church at Philippi is addressed, "To all the saints in Christ Jesus who are at Philippi, with the overseers and deacons" (Phil 1:1). This is the only letter of Paul's that includes a specific reference to leaders in the greeting. We should take that to mean that whatever Paul says in this letter is either to the leaders of the Philippian church, or it's being said to the saints themselves in the express hearing of the leaders. In either case, what Paul offers here is purposeful coaching for how to lead people on mission.

What he says next is particularly helpful:

> I thank my God in all my remembrance of you, always in every prayer of mine for you all making my prayer with joy, because of your partnership in the gospel from the first day until now. And I am sure of this, that he who began a good work in you will bring it to completion at the day of

---

1 Weil, "Letter to Joë."
2 Duff, "Unleash Your Strengths."

Jesus Christ. It is right for me to feel this way about you all, because I hold you in my heart, for you are all partakers with me of grace, both in my imprisonment and in the defense and confirmation of the gospel. For God is my witness, how I yearn for you all with the affection of Christ Jesus. (Phil 1:3–8)

Paul makes it clear that he thinks often of them, and prays often for them. Prayer is, of course, the hidden curriculum of development. But notice also that Paul is drawing to the Philippians' attention that they are often on his mind. Further, when he thinks of them, he does so joyfully. This joy is, in part, due to his confidence that God will continue the work he began in them, but it's also connected to Paul's deep pleasure in their faithfulness and partnership. We can see Paul's attention and affirmation at work.

> Attention, affirmation, and affection
> are developmental rocket fuel.

Taking it a step further, Paul says he holds them in his heart and that he yearns for them with the affection of Jesus. Holding someone in your heart is a tender, intentional, emotional kind of commitment. He says his connection with them is through an affection for them that he shares with Jesus. Literally, his guts (*splanchnois* in Koine Greek) reach for them through the guts of Jesus. This is a physical, bodily experience of intense emotion—both his and Christ's.

Finally, note that Paul doesn't say that his posture is somehow emotionally compromised. On the contrary, he says, "It is right for me to feel this way about you all." Despite theories of leadership that demand emotional distance from those we lead or who find affection incidental to leading well, Paul asserts that his compassionate attachment to those he has led is the right way to lead.

Attention, affirmation, and affection are developmental rocket fuel. In fact, they appear to be the very fuel God uses to complete the good work he has begun in those we lead. This is the kind of consideration they need from us. This allocation of attention and affection is easy to skip but impossible to replace. And that posture sets the tone for what comes next. But before we get to that, having noted *how* to consider those we lead, let's focus for a moment on *what*, exactly, to consider.

You could start with their YouBoats. Of particular interest are the ways their strengths allow them to act on their unique spiritual gifts. Places where their skills or experience don't quite measure up to their natural or supernatural gifts or aptitudes are also great places to spot developmental potential. While it should be obvious by now given the enormous volume of research supporting strengths-based leadership and development, it's critical that you spend most of your time thinking about what they're doing right and why it's working, while sparing only a little time for what they're doing wrong. Buckingham notes, "Most of the people joining the work force right now have much more fascination with who they aren't and how to fix it, than who they are and how to leverage it."[3] We all have weaknesses, and we all need correction from time to time, but we need the people leading us to be thinking about what makes us good, so they can help us become great. We aren't likely to do it on our own.

Depending on the cadence of the contact you have with those you lead, you likely hear a lot about their lives and have a good sense of *when* they are in their lives. Are they in one of those long stretches of relative sameness? Or are they in one of those violent punctuations in the equilibrium, a time between times—a transition? An essential thing to consider as we pay attention to those we lead, is the moment, the life-stage, or the transition they're in. We need to know *when* they are.

Finally, you could consider what kinds of developmental opportunities their work provides. If they work closely with you, this will be easier than if you're supervising someone who actually does their day-to-day work with another team or in another country. But in any case, they can help you build enough of a picture of their work to know what kinds of opportunities their work readily provides and what it doesn't.

Considering our people—their make-up, their life stage, and the unique shape of their work—positions them, and us, to cultivate what God has specifically given them to steward to their deep joy and his highest glory. Seeing them, and helping them see themselves, readies them for what's next.

Cultivate

The word educate comes from the word *educe* which means, literally, *to draw out*. That is just about the opposite of *to drive in*, which is how development is usually approached. We have some content, a competency,

---

[3] Buckingham, "Why Do We."

a compelling vision, and we use all our wiles, charm, charisma, wit, multimedia presentations, and maybe even a smoke machine to drive it as deep into our audiences as we can. When we've done our best, we wonder, *did they get it?*

However, educing, educating, developing people isn't a matter of what we can get into them. It's a matter of what we, in concert with them, can draw up out of them. It is more a matter of discovery than delivery, and our best lens for that discovery is reflecting with them on recent experiences. Recall that, experiences, when reflected upon, are the authentic units of change. As we look with them at what they've done, and how they and others experienced their contributions, we begin to see more clearly the ways they are developing, and further potential to develop.

The first step is regular deployment of the After-Experience Reflection (AER), which we discussed at length in chapter 14. If you have a decent rhythm of reflecting with your people on significant experiences, scaffolded by the compassionate, affirming attention of someone they respect, you're miles ahead of where most leaders live.

There is one caveat. Sometimes the work we do in the life we have doesn't offer us the specific experiences we need to grow in the particular ways we need to. When that's the case, it's our leaders' job to help us to find those experiences and reflect with us developmentally on those. There are two ways to approach this: role-specific and person-specific. Let's consider each.

Identifying the Role-Specific Experiences You Need

Alice is a Canadian nurse working in Sudan. Her team staffs an orphanage that operates at or above capacity most of the time. She is very good at her job and consistently provides excellent medical care with apparently endless compassion and indefatigable endurance. She has been working in Sudan longer than any of her teammates except Liam, the director of the project, and she's been on the African continent longer than he has.

In eighteen months, the director and his family will move back to their home country. Alice is the heir apparent to take over as director at the orphanage. Most likely, Liam will increasingly disengage from his work, and consciously or not, Liam will make the very common assumption that because Alice is good at what she does, she will be just as good at something else. Probably, Liam and the rest of the team will assume that Alice will take over. Only minimal orientation will be offered to Alice on the unnoticed assumption that being a great nurse translates to being a great leader. However, competency in a particular role is not a reliable predictor of aptitude for another.

Here is what should happen instead. First, what's assumed should become explicit. A decision should be made as to whether Alice will replace Liam soon, and even if it's a tentative or probationary decision, Alice and Liam both need to recognize that a major task facing them both is to get Alice ready for her new role.

By far the most common approach is to compare Alice to what's called a *competency model*. Basically, this is a list of competencies that have been deemed necessary for an individual to be able to fill a particular role. Alice will be compared (subjectively, if we're honest) with this list of competencies, and where her competencies don't measure up, that's where effort will be allocated to rectify her present incompetence. If no competency model exists for Liam's role, the go-to solution is to make one up.

The problems with this approach are numerous, but the biggest issue is that it's absurd. While it's far and away the most common approach to role-specific personnel development, there is a sea of research[4] that clearly demonstrates it doesn't work, and what's more, it can't.

Instead, what if we make a list of experiences Alice would need to have in order to be considered adequately experienced for the role? Remember, when we say someone has or doesn't have adequate experience, we don't mean time on the job. We mean they've had the requisite experiences to have seen and done what they'll likely have to see and do in the specific role. We know she's done the nursing work. But as a leader? We're not sure. Fortunately, we can be.

The Experiences List

Liam can track his activities for one week. Then, at the end of the week, he adds a little detail to each entry and fleshes it out enough that someone else reading the record would know what each item basically entails. What we as leaders do often, repeatedly, and over a long period of time is the better part of leadership. But it's not all we do.

Liam needs to repeat the exercise, now but for one month. He doesn't need to write everything down again. Rather, he should note and briefly describe everything he does related to his role as team leader that he didn't already note in the weekly list.

---

[4] Marcus Buckingham, https://youtu.be/d0WV90kgyQc?si=aD--76XDHL-mKSQV.

Leadership isn't comprised only of the *always* and *often* kind of tasks, but also the *sometimes* and *rarely* sorts of things. For example, we hope that as team leader, Liam is not always or usually having to mediate significant conflict on his team, but conflict mediation is probably part of his job, *sometimes*. To find those sometimes and rarely kinds of items, it can be useful for Liam to ask himself:

- What's the hardest thing I've ever had to do as a team leader?
- What's the best thing I've ever done as a team leader?
- What have I done as a team leader that went astoundingly well? What accounts for that?
- What have I done as a team leader that went disappointingly poorly? What accounts for that?
- What part of my job do I most dread every year?
- What part of my job do I look forward to every year?

Liam is now ready to clean the list up a bit and should run it by a supervisor or a peer to see if he's missing anything. Once he's done that, he's ready to sit down with Alice. They'll want to talk through each item on the list and give Alice time and opportunity to reflect on her own experiences to see when and if she has had similar experiences in her life and work. Alice should story these experiences aloud. In some cases, her experiences will have prepared her well. In others, her experiences will not have been quite enough—either intense enough, frequent enough, or similar enough—to have prepared her well. And in still other cases, Alice's life and work will not have presented her with opportunities to have some of the requisite experiences at all or at least not in ways that resulted in the necessary development.

Once we know what kinds of experiences Alice needs to have in order to be ready for Liam's role, we can help her find those experiences and reflect fruitfully on them. Sometimes there isn't a ready role to prepare someone for, but we can sense they are ready for development, so let's consider how to find developmental experiences when there is not a specific role in mind.

Identifying the Person-Specific Experiences You Need

A great deal has been said about T-shaped people and T-shaped development elsewhere, so we don't need to belabor it now. Here are the basics.

Imagine a letter *T*. The wide cross-bar represents breadth of experience and skill, and the vertical bar represents depth of experience and expertise. If someone I am leading is looking to increase the variety of their experiences, but not angling for a particular role, this is how I approach selecting experiences.

We'll work to identify what they're already very good at, comfortable with, or known for being competent in. That's the vertical bar. Then, we'll look at other skills or experiences that someone with their particular job is likely to have or need, and we'll make that the horizontal bar. Alternatively, we'll consider an imaginary role, either a role with more responsibility within the community they currently serve, or something more like their dream job. Then we'll list the kinds of tasks and skills that job is likely to entail and make that the horizontal bar.

I'll be on the look-out for projects, side-jobs, or task forces that involve experiences on the horizontal bar that require significantly more skill or sophistication than they're accustomed to. Then, I'll talk with relevant parties and assign them to those tasks. We'll only do this once or twice a quarter, and we'll make room in their normal responsibilities to allow for this split of attention. This may involve off-loading some of their regular work to someone else. Then, once the project is done or the task force adjourns, we'll debrief the experience with one or more AERs and milk the experience for maximal developmental potential.

If the person leading you isn't doing this kind of thing for you, ask for it. If they won't, or feel they can't, do it for yourself. But certainly, do it for at least some of the people you lead. Since you're the boss, you have some authority to change what's on their plate. You'll never again find yourself at a succession with a bench too shallow to support the hand-off.

Summary

The people we lead need to know we see them, not just what they're doing, and not just the hill we're trying together to take. They also need to know *how* we see them, especially when we see them in a good light. Attention, affirmation, and affection constitute a recipe for development that is really hard to beat. Our people long for us to consider them in this way.

They also need us to cultivate them—to educe and bring forth the unique greatness and glory God has put inside them. We are to draw it out, not drive it in, and we help bring it forth to God's praise, and their deep gladness, which meets the world's deep need.

There are hundreds of tools at our disposal for this. We've listed a few:
- The After-Experience Reflection
- Experiences Lists
- T-shaped developmental assignments

> Your leadership will come to not only feel like sunshine and rain feels to the grass, but it will be sunshine and rain.

This may seem like a lot, so let's simplify further. You want those you're developing to have real experiences and to reflect on them, and you have to do something to ensure that happens. If you can only do one thing, make AERs standard for your field of influence. Make them frequent and make them mandatory. If you can do two things, form cohorts and either have them do AERs together (which amounts to real time case-studies) or have them work through case studies together. Just doing those two things (AERs and case studies) will cover 60–70 percent of your developmental need.

If you can do three things, then simply add developmental assignments. Give the people you're developing one or two of these per year. These three interventions will create within your community so much developmental bias that simply being part of that community will change people. That's how your leadership will come to not only feel like sunshine and rain feels to the grass, but it will *be* sunshine and rain. You will be helping those you lead become authentically *more* as you consider and cultivate them with Jesus.

Afterword

On Leading and Following

This book has been about leading. I've contended, along with King David and the Holy Spirit, that it's possible to lead in a way that feels to those we lead like sunshine and rain feel to the grass. I've argued that this kind of generative, developmental leadership amounts to fostering glory in those we lead, and that it's the surest way to see the image of Christ formed in the many places our people serve. Finally, I've laid out a way to lead like that in hopes that it helps leaders steward the people and the gifts with which they've been charged.

But ultimately, because this has been a book about leading, it takes into account that someone is following. This relationship that is at the heart of everything that happens in the world. I'm convinced that the space between the leader and the led contains everything true about a community, organization, church, or mission agency. It's the fulcrum upon which everything moves. So, getting this relationship right amounts to getting it all right.

Because this relationship is, by definition, an inequality, it is fraught with possibilities for catastrophe and pregnant with the potential for greatness. It's no small thing, and it behooves us to attend to it carefully. What follows is a litany of four axioms offered to help leaders and followers steward this most essential relationship well. They are:

1. People want to help, and they need help
2. Power distance isn't bad
3. People fail
4. Self-awareness goes a long way

People Want to Help, and They Need Help

When it comes to church leadership, mission leadership, and ministry leadership in general, the rewards really never outweigh the sacrifices. At least not in this life. Especially in the present milieu as fewer and fewer people are willing to lead simply because the likelihood of being pilloried or canceled is just too high. Certainly, we can have broken motives hidden in our hearts, but for the most part, leaders lead because they want to help. They see something worth going after together, and they rally us to the endeavor and show us a way to win.

But leaders also need help. My background in the martial arts shapes how I think about this. Remember that no fighter starts off complete. They have to be shown what they don't know and carefully trained in a balanced and coordinated way, so they can bring a complete fight to the ring.

No leader starts out a complete leader. Some of us are naturally attuned to people's thriving. Some are great at integrating life and helping people do excellent work, and a few of us are gifted at developing the people around us. Any of us can become more complete with a little intentional coaching, and our people really need us to get better at the whole thing. This is why I've made this as straightforward and simple as I can. You can hold what I call the OneTree approach in one hand. Count it down with me:

- 5 dimensions of soul to thrive in,
- 4 integrations to attend to in our work,
- 3 poieses to pursue for development,
- 2 cues to help us engage make
- 1 tree, because the whole process works when it all works together as one.

The people we lead want to help as well. None of them got into this work just for the rewards. The life they've chosen is hard, and over time it can degrade their ability to do good, beautiful work, until eventually they fracture, burn out, or lose their way. The people we lead also need help.

In my own leadership, most of my direct reports live in countries different from me, so my cadence of intentional contact is monthly. Each month, each of my direct reports fills out this simple form and sends it back to me. (See figure 12 on the next page.)

Then, we schedule a video call, and we talk through what they've told me on their check-in.

The *thrive* questions draw their attention to how God has been active in the different dimensions of their lives as well as to their own desire for more. The questions allow them to guide what we discuss which keeps responsibility and agency squarely with them and allows them to let me know what kind of help they're most likely to accept from me. This prevents me from swooping in and rescuing them, and it prevents them from trying to hide from me by inviting them to reveal what they most want seen. This is the only place they'll accept help from a supervisor, anyway, so most of the time, there's no point insisting on more.

The *work* questions, like the *thrive* set, draw their attention to God's activity before they consider their own. Over time, this practice trains them to work like Jesus and do only what they see the Father doing. The second question invites them to notice that some things they do are more important than other things. Having their supervisor ask them that helps them slip free of the tyranny of the urgent, so they can work more vigorously on what's most important.

The *develop* questions begin with their desire, not mine. We will work on the development goals they set for themselves, instead of, or at least before, the ones I might have for them. Desire is the fire in the furnace of change, so accessing and activating their desire for development is primary. The second question allows me to direct their attention to the developmental potential in their upcoming work. At the very least, this predisposes them to approach that work with a developmental mindset, so they'll learn more. Even better, they may identify something we can use for an AER, ensuring ongoing development.

Each question set ends with me asking them how I can help. For me, this is servant leadership. Three times during every monthly meeting, I'm asking in a focused and comprehensible way how I can bring my strength and skill to bear for their best interests, and I'm allowing them to call the shots. Servant leadership is much more than being the boss though. It's also being willing to take the trash out and clean up after meetings. Servant leaders acts like servants, and invite those they lead to treat them as such from time to time.

There's another layer of cadence with these calls. We get a call every month, but each quarter we go through a cycle of sorts. Every month they give the same attention to the questions on the check-in form. This is consistent, but we use the calls to focus on different things each month.

The first month in a quarter we'll spend most of our time talking about their thriving and exploring their Thrive Plan which they will have just refreshed and updated for the quarter. Five minutes of an hour will be given to their work, and five or ten to identifying upcoming developmental opportunities. The rest of the call will look deeply at their wellness.

The second month's call will focus more on work. We'll spend maybe five minutes on a vector check, and we'll remind ourselves of the developmental task we identified earlier. But the vast majority of the call will be spent with them describing in some detail their real life and their real work. I'll be listening actively and seeking to identify the four integrations in their life narrative. If a particular integration pops out, I'll ask some follow-up questions designed to reinforce and strengthen that integration. If I see significant fraying around an integration, I'll bring that forward and ask if we can talk about it some before asking them how I can help.

The third month's call will touch on work and will include a quick vector check, but the majority of the call will be spent doing an AER either on the developmental opportunity they identified earlier in the quarter or on a particularly interesting experience that has come up in the interim. It doesn't matter much to me what the experience is as long as we reflect on it thoroughly.

In this way, the OneTree approach helps me lead holistically from roots to fruit. This focused and consistent attention, then, helps those I lead to flourish where they are, to do beautiful work without fraying at the edges and to become all they were created to be.

We all want to help, and we all need help. This is a way we can all get what we want.

Power Distance Isn't Bad

Cultures tend to feel differently about disparities of power. A culture's Power Distance Index is a measure of how the people within that culture with the least amount of power feel about the inequality of that power. In low power distance cultures, people with less influence tend to feel that things should be more equal, that people with power should act like they don't have it and that decisions should be dispersed throughout the community. People from high power distance cultures, believe it or not, find that absurd. They tend to feel that the people who have power *should* have power, and that threatening that power would threaten the whole community. In these cultures, decisions lie with a few people near the top of a clear hierarchy. For reference, Ireland and Australia are some of the lowest power distance cultures in the world, whereas Malaysia and Mexico are some of the highest. The United States falls in the lower part of the middle.

Thrive-Work-Develop *Monthly check-in*

Name: Date:

THRIVE

S — Spiritual
P — Physical
C — Cognitive
E — Emotional
R — Relational

SICK   WELL   FIT

1. Which of these would you like to discuss?

2. How have you seen God active in you this month?
   In what area do you find you most want revival?

3. How can I help?

WORK

1. Are there ways you would like to grow this month or competencies you'd like to acquire or sharpen?

2. What upcoming work could present a developmental opportunity for you?

3. How can I help?

DEVELOP

1. Where are you seeing God most active in your relationships/work?

2. What priority or priorities will you be focused on in the coming month? (maximum of 5)

3. How can I help?

Figure 12 | Thrive-Work-Develop

Low power distance people love Matthew 23:8–12, where Jesus says:

> But you are not to be called rabbi, for you have one teacher, and you are all brothers. And call no man your father on earth, for you have one Father, who is in heaven. Neither be called instructors, for you have one instructor, the Christ. The greatest among you shall be your servant. Whoever exalts himself will be humbled, and whoever humbles himself will be exalted.

In their imagination, there's little room for someone to think of herself as a leader, or to think it's in any way appropriate for them to submit to someone other than Jesus Christ himself. I once heard an American spiritual formation teacher say, "I have no authority but Jesus." He was proud of himself when he said it, too.

High power distance people are shocked by this and wonder what those people do with passages like Hebrews 13:17: "Obey your leaders and submit to them, for they are keeping watch over your souls, as those who will have to give an account. Let them do this with joy and not with groaning, for that would be of no advantage to you."

Obey? Submit? Lower power distance Americans would call you spiritually abusive if you let those words slip past your lips. But they're in inspired Scripture. As are Jesus's words about not being called teacher or father but all being brothers on an even footing. So in real life, which is it to be?

I think we can get some help from Jesus's command in John 13 spoken just after he had assumed the role of lowest and least and washed his students' feet. "You call me Teacher and Lord, and you are right, for so I am" (John 13:13). This is a very high power distance statement. A low power distance alternative would be, *You call me Teacher and Lord, but I wish you guys would cut that out. We're friends, bros!* But he doesn't. He says that the disparity of power between them is real, and that they are right to recognize it.

But then, he goes on, "If I then, your Lord and Teacher, have washed your feet, you also ought to wash one another's feet" (John 13:14). In other words, *I'm not denying that a disparity of power and authority exists between us. I'm demonstrating how to use that disparity. Take all that power and bring it to the service of those you lead. Don't deny the power. That doesn't help anyone. Make the disparity of power good news by leading with a towel over your shoulder.*

Jesus-style leadership is high power, low distance. It accepts that some have more power than others, and then turns it upside down by insisting that the power be used *not* to secure the outcomes of the powerful but to dignify, empower, and ennoble everyone else.

It's hard to imagine a power dynamic more beautiful, compelling, and healing than that. Who would ever want to sully it by misusing or fumbling that power? Who would ever want to extinguish that potential by insisting that any power distance at all is evil or by simply being unwilling to be led?

Well, we would.

People Fail

I've seen a lot of failures. I've over-led. More often, in a bid for consensus or an attempt to avoid exerting too much influence, I've under-led. In my twenties and early thirties, largely unaware of the childhood trauma haunting my sense of self, I was often defensive and sometimes insecure. I followed social customs at times that I really should have broken. Other times I stepped right across arbitrary lines, like Jesus, and brought healing to people and broke cycles of isolation and shame. But occasionally, I stepped over lines—usually unaware I was doing so—and did more harm than good. Unlike Jesus, in those moments I could draw no comfort from being sure my motives were pure. One thing I know for sure: even when your motives are good, they're never perfectly pure.

> The only way to do no harm at all
> is to never risk loving people with your flawed heart,
> and that's not an option.

I'm willing to bet you've failed too. Probably spectacularly, and your heart probably wasn't perfectly clean when you did it either. Perhaps you've had a significant moral failure. There is forgiveness, restoration, and a hard journey to go with it. But even if you haven't had an affair, stolen money, or been involved in some other legitimate scandal, you've done harm. There is a wide field between a perfectly blameless leader and an abusive leader, and we all spend some time walking that field. The only way to do no harm at all is to never risk loving people with your flawed heart, and that's not an option.

Further complicating matters is the fact that those we lead are also flawed. Following comes with its own risks. There are the obvious mistakes followers can make, but there are less overt problems that emerge specifically because your team leader is also your friend and probably wears a few other hats in your lives.

Jack was leading a team in Southeast Asia. His good friend Eric was on his team. Eric was always wanting Jack to hang out, to go get coffee, to go out after work, or just to see a movie. But Eric also rarely ever came through on action steps he was given by his team in their weekly meetings. It frustrated Jack to no end that Eric seemed to have all the time in the world to watch *Monty Python* but never could bring himself to meet a deadline. While Eric talked at length about being a friend to Jack, wanting Jack to not feel isolated, and wanting Jack to know that he had someone he could talk to, what Jack needed was for his friend to do his job. Jack may have wanted to be Eric's friend, but as long as Eric didn't do his job, he wasn't really behaving like Jack's friend.

Jesus said it best in John 15:14–15, "You are my friends if you do what I command you. No longer do I call you servants, for the servant does not know what his master is doing; but I have called you friends, for all that I have heard from my Father I have made known to you." When one friend is the leader and the other friend is being led, in matters of work friendship means doing what the leader asks. Jesus even says that he had given his friends full disclosure—everything he heard from his Father he had given to them, holding nothing back. That's what he needed from them, now.

The leadership relationship is always complex, and this is particularly true in ministry relationships. This book is written with all kinds of ministry leaders in mind. When you move overseas to plant churches, make disciples, identify with the poor, etc., you're often on a team. This team, though, is also your friend group. Your kids start calling your team mates Uncle Mark, or Aunt Amy. The same living room will house team meetings, language learning for several couples, game night, birthday parties, and house church. It is absolutely impossible to know when someone is speaking as an adoptive sister, a language classmate, a friend, coworker, or team leader. Everyone is every one of those things all the time, and everything is happening in the same spaces. The people don't change. The context remains the same. But the rules of engagement for each of those relationships is different, and there's no way to know which hat you're wearing when. An off-handed remark or an emotional outburst that would be bad form over board games could be an HR issue if it happened in the board room. When those people, and those spaces are exactly the same, things will at times go bad. This is especially true in your first few years overseas, when you're categorically the worst and most intolerable version of yourself. You are going to make very unfortunate mistakes in that setting, and you're going to hurt people.

Not every leadership role has that degree or kind of relational complexity to it, but all ministry leadership roles are complex. Because ours is an endeavor rooted in love and relationship, we almost always have more than one relationship with many of the people we lead. Further, as we said before, the remuneration for our work is rarely commensurate to the blood, sweat, and tears we put in. And that's okay, because we got into this to help people. The inverse of this is also true—we tend to be the kind of people who absolutely loathe hurting people. There are exceptions, of course, wolves in shepherds' clothes, and those situations can break really badly. But most of us abhor the idea of doing harm.

> Be brave. Be humble, and move toward love.

So, when we do harm, it crushes us. Most of us aren't frightened off by the idea of others hurting us. We would never have volunteered to raise our own money to go work in war-torn, limited access countries if getting hurt were a prohibitive possibility. Hurting others, though, can be a show stopper. But know this. If you never get close enough to accidentally do harm, you'll never be close enough to really help. I know the idea that you might make a mistake, inadvertently or not, is terrifying sometimes. Especially once you've made a real mistake or two. Be brave. Be humble, and move toward love. There's no way to avoid bruising or being bruised, and no perfectly sterile approach to loving your neighbor. Again, I'm not talking about affairs, abuse, or the like. Avoid that like the plague. However, there's a lot of territory between making no mistakes and wrecking your life, and if you walk in love, you're going to walk close enough to cut people with your unformed edges. Sometimes they'll hate you for it, but in most cases, love covers a multitude of sins even when you lead.

It's important to note, here, that some people do abuse power. Probably, all people do at some point, but some people do it persistently. This is bad, and should be dealt with firmly and humbly. However, it's worth noting that failures made while being a leader are not necessarily leadership mistakes. Therapists and counselors will often avoid having more than one kind of relationship with their clients because switching hats is difficult, and both people have to do it at the same time for it to work. When it doesn't work, things can get messy. Leaders typically don't have that option available, so considerable grace is called for on the part of the leader and of the led. All leaders fail, but not every mistake made while being a leader is itself a leadership failure. This nuance will prove important.

The solution to failure, for leaders and followers, is threefold.

First, suspend judgement. You don't know their motives. You don't even know your own. You barely know the edges of your deep inner urges, so you certainly don't have any real idea of all the reasons that could be operating in the person leading you or in the person you lead. Leave motives to God. He alone knows the human heart.

Second, communicate. Follow the rules we covered in the chapter on integrating with your team. Say things like, "Bob, when you said x, I felt y. I just thought you should know." Don't say things like, "Bob, I worry that when you do x, people will get the wrong idea," or, "Bob, you always do x, and that's because in your heart you really want z."

A few times people I led or led with have approached me with one of those, and it hasn't helped. I don't care much what imaginary people might one day maybe misunderstand about some action I took in a particular moment. But if they had said to me, "Listen, when you did x the other day, I felt y. I believe you have my best interests at heart, so I just wanted you to know how I reacted to that," they would have received an immediate apology. I'd likely never have done that thing again, and I'd have taken the encounter to my wife or a trusted friend to help me learn all I could from it. I don't care about imaginary people. I care about the people in front of me. If the person in front of me communicates honestly, I'm positioned to make things right and to lead better.

Third, forgive. You've been forgiven. God let you move on. Let them move on, too. Who are you to hold anything against anyone? Remember the axiom: people fail. It's the one thing you can count on everyone to do. Leave motive-hunting to God, communicate clearly and honestly, then forgive. Forgive those who lead you, and forgive those you lead. Don't let the mistakes accrue to the point that they shape the whole story. Ours is a story of grace. If you're going to tell that story, you'd better live it too.

If you lead, you'll fail. Just don't be unapproachable about it. The Apostle James says:

> Who is wise and understanding among you? By his good conduct let him show his works in the meekness of wisdom. But if you have bitter jealousy and selfish ambition in your hearts, do not boast and be false to the truth. This is not the wisdom that comes down from above, but is earthly, unspiritual, demonic. For where jealousy and selfish ambition exist, there will be disorder and every vile practice. But the wisdom from above is first pure, then peaceable, gentle, open to reason, full of mercy and good fruits, impartial and sincere. And a harvest of righteousness is sown in peace by those who make peace. (Jas 3:13–18)

If you're comparing yourself to others, or needing to win, it isn't coming from God. Godly leadership is defined by its meekness and approachability. Don't be hard to confront.

When you follow, you're going to fail. Just don't be hard to lead. Psalm 32 is all about failure, sin, and compulsive inner twistings toward the wrong. But it's even more about open, honest confession, and abundant forgiveness. At the end of the Psalm, the writer turns to us and says:

> I will instruct you and teach you in the way you should go;
>   I will counsel you with my eye upon you.
> Be not like a horse or a mule, without understanding,
>   which must be curbed with bit and bridle,
>   or it will not stay near you. (Ps 32:8–9)

Look, he says, *you're going to sin, sometimes abominably. It's going to hurt you, and it's going to hurt others. Don't hide it. Confess it; receive forgiveness, and move on. No one is expecting more from you. You'll be taught how to do it better. Just don't be hard to lead. Don't be the stubborn, willful mule who won't come when you are called. Don't be the bucking horse that won't cooperate. Don't use your will to reinforce your sinful insistence on being king. It's okay that you're a sinner. We all live there. Just don't be hard to lead.*

People fail. Suspend judgement, communicate gently and clearly, and forgive. There is absolutely no other way to steward the disparity of power between leader and led when someone fails. When we don't do this, the outcomes are always tragic. Satan wins. But when we do, when we actually take Jesus at his word and do what he commands, somehow the beauty and love that ensue are even greater than was possible before the offense. That's how powerful grace really is. It doesn't return us to Eden; it takes us somewhere better.

Self-Awareness Goes a Long Way

Many offenses can be avoided through some simple self-awareness. The emotions and cognitive malware running in your head, to the degree you're not aware of them, are controlling every decision you make. Becoming aware of the narratives, triggers, and predispositions inside you allows you to uncouple your decisions and your reactions from them and actually engage the real situations you're in.

When my friend Rhine became a team leader, his mentor said to him, "Congratulations! Now everyone on your team is going to work out their daddy issues on you." Sometimes your leader is going to do something either very much like one of your parents or very much unlike one of your parents. In either case, you're probably going to react. Knowing what's going on inside you will allow you to engage your leader as they are. Not knowing what's going on inside you will doom you to replaying your family of origin trauma and to take it out on your leader.

Self-awareness is even more important for leaders. Alex Draper observes, "A lack of self-awareness generally explains overconfidence, poor judgment and the inability to learn from mistakes, build teams or relate to others."[1] In her book *Insight*, Tasha Eurich argues that self-awareness is the "meta-skill of the 21st Century." However, she found that *only 10 to 15 percent of people are self-aware*. Overconfidence, poor judgement, and inability to learn are like the unholy trinity of leadership failure. Who could trust a leader like that? Conversely, a leader who knows her own values, knows the names of the attachments that most often pull her off-course, and knows how to bring her strengths forward and mitigate for her weaknesses is able to inspire confidence. She can lead others because she can lead herself.

---

1 Draper, "Bad Leadership."

We don't have to have all of our family of origin issues worked out. We don't have to have our values perfectly clarified. We are all works in progress. Perfection isn't even a goal, but self-awareness goes a long way.

As They Walk Through the Valley of Weeping

Every organization has an organizational chart. Most of us hate them, but imagine one for a moment. Every single down line on that chart represents a disparity of power, and that's a good thing. Marxists want to topple those disparities, but engineers know better. You need lots of water above the dam and less below because all that potential energy becomes motion with which you can power factories, homes, hospitals, and universities. Wonders are possible when power flows properly.

> The weeping world waits for the revelation
> of the glory of the children of God,
> and we'd be giving them a teaser.

Imagine, now, if in every single one of those downlines lived a story that went something like, "When one rules justly, in the fear of the LORD, they are like the rain and sun on the mown grass" (see 2 Sam 23:3–4). Imagine what might happen if every one, or at least almost every one, of those downlines represented a relationship in which the leader and the led were capable and committed to securing vibrancy in all five dimensions of the soul and stewarded all four key integrations as they leveraged the newfound strength and vigor in meaningful work, and discovered through that work the wonders unfolding through the three main poieses of human development in Jesus. Imagine if every one of those relationships amounted to making each individual down the line into what George MacDonald called "a living glory of gladness."[2]

What would happen is this: that whole community would become a pilgrim people. They'd find themselves swept along on a journey of becoming. As they moved through the world, they would leak light and beauty and strength. As they were progressively, slowly, but inexorably transformed in the world, the world would be transformed with them. The weeping world waits for the revelation of the glory of the children of God, and we'd be giving them a teaser.

---

2 MacDonald, "Meditation Day 4."

God would meet us in this endeavor. Filling up our efforts, correcting for our errors, and making up the difference. He'd rain blessings to fill in the gaps, and we'd heal the land we walk through.

> Blessed are those whose strength is in you,
>   whose hearts are set on pilgrimage.
>
> As they pass through the Valley of Baka [Weeping],
>   they make it a place of springs;
>   the autumn rains also cover it with pools.
>   (Ps 84:5-6, NIV)

Five dimensions, four integrations, three poieses, two cues each, make for OneTree to foster glory in the people you lead. You have what you need. Go make the desert verdant, and know that I'm praying for you, "that our God may make you worthy of his calling and may fulfill every resolve for good and every work of faith by his power, so that the name of our Lord Jesus may be glorified in you, and you in him, according to the grace of our God and the Lord Jesus Christ" (2 Thess 1:11-12).

Amen.

Appendix

The following are some sample Thrive Plans from some of my colleagues in various stages of life.

Thrive Plan: Married Female, 60s

- Spiritual: Withdraw, Gather, Obey
    - Abide, Sabbath, Bible study and prayer alone
    - Pray morning, midday, and evening prayer with husband and those I'm with (alongside team)
    - Bible study with ladies
    - Local Sunday School and church weekly
    - Memorize a verse per month
    - Fast one day a month
- Physical: Eat, Move, Recover
    - Limit sugar and flour
    - Exercise six days a week:
        - Walk 45 minutes four to five days a week
        - Hand weights three days a week
    - Sabbath rest
- Cognitive: Learn, Focus, Play
    - Continuing medical education > one hour per month
    - Books: read (work and non-work related) one to two per month
    - No email for one hour before bed
    - Sabbath rest
- Emotional: Notice, Interview, Manage
    - Walk four to five times a week, if possible with husband, once or twice a week
    - Tell Jesus how I am feeling; ask why
    - Sabbath rest
- Relational: Discern, Invest, Grow
    - Walk and talk with husband; work on being a cheerleader
    - Intentional investment in team, family
    - Walk with friend weekly
    - Selective investment locally

Thrive Plan: Married Male, 70s

- Spiritual: Withdraw, Gather, Obey
    - Morning devotions: Scripture, prayer, missional focused reading
    - Morning, midday, and evening prayer with wife, sometimes with team
    - Weekly Sabbath, Saturday evening to Sunday evening, no phone or computer
    - Local church: Bible study and worship service weekly
    - Process questions, thoughts, plans with wife
- Physical: Eat, Move, Recover
    - Eat: Low carbs, lots of fruit and vegetables, limit processed foods
    - Move: Hand weights three times a week, daily walk—aim for three or four 45-minute walks a week
    - Recover: Aim for eight hours sleep a night, Sabbath afternoon nap
- Cognitive: Learn, Focus, Play
    - Learn: Read books and articles that interest me
    - Focus: Plan on no computer or phone until after morning devotions
    - Knock off work at least one hour before bedtime
    - Play: Walk and talks with wife; watch mutually enjoyable shows with wife
    - Video calls with family (especially new granddaughter)
- Emotional: Notice, Interview, Manage
    - Pay attention to the things that delight, frustrate, or confuse
    - Process my emotions with wife to get perspective
    - Ask if what I am feeling is in line with a biblical response
    - Strive not to give free reign to expressing my emotions before examining them
    - Pray for grace to bring my emotions into a biblical response
- Relational: Discern, Invest, Grow
    - Maintain high bar for starting new relationships
    - Co-discern with wife which current relationships to go deeper with
    - Spend time with closest friends. Free ranging conversations. Iron sharpening iron. Laugh.
    - Building trust that supports transparency
    - Continue work with coach on peace pursuit process

Thrive Plan: Pregnant Mom of Four, 40s

- Spiritual:
  - Withdraw: Journal twice weekly, quiet morning
  - Gather: three daily prayers, Sabbath, prayer with friend weekly
  - Obey: Steps toward forgiveness
- Physical:
  - Eat: drink more than three liters of water, watch weight, eat healthy
  - Move: squats, walk daily
  - Recover: stretch and rest even during the day
- Cognitive:
  - Learn: Read *When the Church Was Family*
  - Focus: Journal on *When the Church Was Family*; limit FB to once a day
  - Play: Fiction book, games twice per week
- Emotional:
  - Notice: My body tightness
  - Interview: Journaling
  - Manage: Seek help when needed—don't avoid
- Relational:
  - Discern: How to pray and hold—be willing today
  - Invest: Calendar/Pattern for supporters
  - Grow: Ask questions of wise people specifically "2s" on caring for people

Single Female, 30s

- Spiritual
  - Withdraw
    - Thirty minutes with mentor before bed
    - Morning office
    - Pray the Hours
  - Gather
    - Weekly Sabbath dinner/home church
    - Team meeting
    - Group Spiritual Direction once monthly
  - Obey
    - Practice a weekly Sabbath
    - Power: Learn, incorporate, reflect
- Physical
  - Eat
    - Incorporate fish once or twice per week (but first learn how to cook fish!)
    - Drink adequate water and take vitamins
  - Move
    - Continue with kettlebells four times each week
  - Recover
    - In bed from 11pm–7am
    - Practice stretching/yoga as needed
- Emotional
  - Notice
    - Pay attention to body cues
    - Practice identifying broad emotions from Dodd's "Voice of the Heart"
  - Interview
    - Be quick to journal in the moment of high emotion, review later

- Manage
  - Breath prayers at night to clear
  - Daily run-throughs of the third movement of Kennan in E♭
  - Continue re-read of *The Body Keeps the Score* by Bessel van der Kolk
- Relational
  - Discern
    - Be Covid-wise
  - Invest
    - Focus on Hajar's family/household
    - Continue regular contact and conversation with specific affinity group members
    - Remain a sounding board/motivator/brainstormer for refugee ministry partners in Barcelona, Vienna, and Athens (and be a networker for them)
- Grow
  - Invest in my own leadership development
  - Daily podcasts in Spanish

Bibliography

Addington, Tim. *Leading from the Sandbox: How to Develop, Empower, and Release High Impact Ministry Teams*. NavPress, 2010.

Army Publishing Directorate. "Army Leadership." Army Doctrine Reference Publication, 2012: 1–2. https://armypubs.us.army.mil.

Bahl, Rajiv. "No, Sitting Isn't as Bad as Smoking a Cigarette." *Healthline*, 2018. www.healthline.com/health-news/no-sitting-isnt-smoking?c=1002760948418.

Barton, Ruth Haley. *Strengthening the Soul of Your Leadership: Seeking God in the Crucible of Ministry*. InterVarsity Press, 2018.

Buckingham, Marcus. "Lie 5: People Need Feedback." Jan 8, 2019. YouTube, 6:00. www.youtube.com/watchsaweq3?v=Dmw8rOzMgS0.

Buckingham, Marcus. "Unleash Your Strengths with Marcus Buckingham." Interview by Charlie Duff. *HRZone*, September 16, 2020. https://hrzone.com/unleash-your-strengths-with-marcus-buckingham/.

Buechner, Frederick. "Vocation." *Frederick Buechner* (blog). July 18, 2021. https://www.frederickbuechner.com/quote-of-the-day/2021/7/18/vocation.

Crouch, Andy. *Playing God: Redeeming the Gift of Power*. IVP Books, 2013.

Cultural Intelligence Center. "Cultural Competency & Awareness Trainings." Cultural Intelligence Center (CQ), Mar 3, 2021. culturalq.com.

Czeisler, Charles A. "Sleep Deficit: The Performance Killer." Interview by Browyn Fryer. *Harvard Business Review*, October 2006. Audio. http://hbr.org/2006/10/sleep-deficit-the-performance-killer.

DeRue, D. Scott "After-Event Reviews: How to Structure Reflection Conversations." In *Experience-Driven Leader Development: Models, Tools, Best Practices, and Advice for On-The-Job Development*, by Cynthia McCauley, D. Scott DeRue, Paul Yost, and Sylvester Taylor. Wiley, 2014.

Draper, Alex. "Bad Leadership Stems From A Lack Of Self-Awareness—Here's How To Improve." *Forbes*, January 14, 2022. https://www.forbes.com/sites/forbescoachescouncil/2022/01/14/bad-leadership-stems-from-a-lack-of-self-awareness---heres-how-to-improve/?sh=3dc4ccc51007.

"Ep 8 Dan John - Being Reasonable, Humour for Coaching and Simple Habits." Uploaded by Adam McCubbin. January 27, 2018. YouTube, 1:05.36. www.youtube.com/watch?v=oYdUPzwlqyY&t=835s.

"Family Plus," Spirit of Revival. March 15, 2018. https://www.familyplus.org/our-mission/.

Glassman, Greg. "Fitness, Luck, and Health." *Crossfit, the Journal*, October 14, 2016. https://journal.crossfit.com/article/fitness-luck-health.

Grenny, Joseph, Kerry Patterson, Ron McMillian, Al Switzler, and Emily Gregory. *Crucial Conversations: Tools for Talking when Stakes are High*. 3rd ed. McGraw Hill, 2021.

Hancox, Bob. *Coaching for Engagement: Achieving Results Through Powerful Conversations*. Tekara, 2010.

Hill, Claudia. "Scaffolding Reflection: What, So What, Now What?" in *Experience-Driven Leader Development: Models, Tools, Best Practices, and Advice for On-The-Job Development*, by Cynthia McCauley, D. Scott DeRue, Paul Yost, and Sylvester Taylor. Wiley, 2014.

Horsfall, Tony, and Joyce Huggett. *Rhythms of Grace: Finding Intimacy with God in a Busy Life*. Bible Reading Fellowship, 2012.

Janzen, David. *The Intentional Christian Community Handbook: For Idealists, Hypocrites, and Wannabe Disciples of Jesus*. Paraclete Press, 2017.

John, Dan. "Dan John: 5 Basic Human Movements." On Target Publications. January 22, 2017. https://www.otpbooks.com/dan-john-5-basic-human-movements/.

Kelly, Matthew. *The Rhythm of Life: Living Every Day with Passion and Purpose*. Simon and Schuster, 2005.

Khatri, Minesh. "How to Measure Your Waist." WebMD, July 19, 2024, www.webmd.com/diet/guide/calculating-your-waist-circumference.

Lim, David S. "God's Kingdom as Oikos Church Networks: A Biblical Theology." *International Journal of Frontier Missiology*, 34 (2017): 25–35. https://www.ijfm.org/PDFs_IJFM/34_1-4_PDFs/IJFM_34_1-4-Lim.pdf.

Lombardo, M. M., and R. W. Eichinger. *Career Architect Development Planner*. Lominger, 1996. Cited in Cynthia McCauley, D. Scott DeRue, Paul Yost, and Sylvester Taylor. *Experience-Driven Leader Development: Models, Tools, Best Practices, and Advice for On-the-Job Development*. Wiley, 2014.

MacDonald, George. "Meditation Day 4." The Northumbria Community, 2015. https://www.northumbriacommunity.org/meditations/meditation-day-4/.

Martin, George. *A Song of Ice and Fire*. Bantam Books, 2011.

McKeown, Greg. *Essentialism: The Disciplined Pursuit of Less*. Crown, 2020.

Member Care Europe. "What Is Member Care?" January 15, 2015, www.membercare.eu/articles/what-is-member-care.

Peterson, Eugene H. "The Good-for-Nothing Sabbath." *Christianity Today*, 38 (1994): www.christianitytoday.com/ct/1994/april-4/good-for-nothing-sabbath.html.

Peterson, Jordan. "Why Would A Dragon Hoard Gold." *With A Green Scarf* (blog). June 6, 2016. https://withagreenscarf.wordpress.com/2016/06/06/why-would-a-dragon-hoard-gold-jordan-peterson/.

Pryor, Jeremy. "How the Biblical Family and Western Family Collide." August 22, 2011. YouTube, 47:13, https://www.youtube.com/watch?v=iBiim2klim4.

Sinek, Simon. "Effective Confrontation." January 24, 2020, YouTube, 5:00. www.youtube.com/watch?v=2M_kCCcNDts.

Taleb, Nassim Nicholas. *Antifragile: Things That Gain from Disorder (Incerto)*. Random House Trade Paperbacks, 2014.

Tilley, Terrence W. *The Disciples' Jesus: Christology as Reconciling Practice*. Orbis, 2008.

Van Der Kolk, Bessel. *The Body Keeps the Score: Brain, Mind, and Body in the Healing of Trauma*. Viking, 2014.

Weil, Simone. "Letter to Joë Bousquet." Translated by Raymond Rosenthal. April 13, 1942.

visit us at missionbooks.org

*Leading from Below:
Lessons from the Crucible of Global Mission*

William D. Taylor

This narrative theology combines elements of autobiography, theological insight, and practical guidance where leadership lessons emerge more from the crucible of life rather than books, podcasts, or seminars. Bill's honest stories reflect vulnerability but also the strength to live into the sometimes painful, often inscrutable promises of God. He concludes with a series of reflections on leadership and finishing well. *Leading from Below* is both inspirational and instructive.

*Learning to Lead at the Feet of Jesus:
Encounters with Grace and Truth*

Todd Poulter

Despite our best intentions, many of us struggle to consistently reflect Jesus in our leadership. *Learning to Lead at the Feet of Jesus* highlights the rich relational setting in which Jesus exercised leadership and developed his followers into leaders. In the context of his intentional "with-ness," Jesus generously shared his life and authority with the Twelve. Poulter draws on a wide variety of cross-cultural experiences and invites leaders to a refreshing journey of discovery, intimacy, and transformation.

*Multiplying Leaders in Intercultural Contexts:
Recognizing and Developing Grassroots Potential*

Evelyn and Richard Hibbert

This book focuses on how to develop grassroots Christian leaders across cultures. These often-unrecognized leaders mostly lead small groups at the growing edges of the church. Another focus of the book is shaping the character of developers as they humbly walk beside leaders in the leaders' community. The authors use the four Cs of Christian leadership—Community, Character, Clarity, and Care—to weave together research, experience, and practical application.

www.ingramcontent.com/pod-product-compliance
Lightning Source LLC
Chambersburg PA
CBHW052134070526
44585CB00017B/1826